# MYSTERY WRITER'S MARKET PLACE

## AND SOURCEBOOK

# MYSTERY WRITER'S MARKET PLACE
## AND SOURCEBOOK

Edited by Donna Collingwood

Assisted by Robin Gee

**WRITER'S DIGEST BOOKS**
Cincinnati, Ohio

This hardcover edition of *Mystery Writer's Marketplace and Sourcebook* features a "self-jacket" that eliminates the need for a separate dust jacket. It provides sturdy protection for your book while it saves paper, trees and energy.

97  96  95  94  93    5  4  3  2  1

International Standard Serial Number
ISSN 1068-8528
International Standard Book Number
ISBN 0-89879-612-1

Edited by Donna Collingwood
Designed by Brian Roeth
Cover illustrated by John Hart

The following page constitutes an extension of this copyright page.

# Table of Contents

## *From the Editors*

You have purchased a book that is a synthesis of what we at Writer's Digest Books have been doing for years: teaching people how to write and helping them to sell what they write.

*Mystery Writer's Marketplace and Sourcebook* is a hybrid of our two lines: It has some aspects of a market book and some features of a "how to write" book. We've melded the two specific types of information to make a specialized book for a specialized audience.

The marketplace aspect of the book is, of course, the listings. The listings that appear in *Mystery Writer's Marketplace and Sourcebook* represent the publishers, magazines and agents that either (1) handle a large volume of mysteries, (2) are most open to new mystery writers, or (3) are a combination of the two. These listings are hand-picked for mystery writers. A more comprehensive treatment of fiction publishing can be found in *Novel and Short Story Writer's Market*.

Besides including listings that are of particular interest to mystery writers, we've made special efforts to include the strongest publishers in mystery. These markets are explored through interviews with the editors. We are thankful to these people and proud to be able to bring you the opinions, expectations and predictions of the top mystery editors. These are the people you must sell your ideas to, the first link between you as writer and the readers you wish to entertain.

The sourcebook highlights the book clubs, stores, magazines, reference books and organizations that are of particular interest to mystery writers. There is a wealth of material out there: books and articles you'll want to read purely for enjoyment, those that will help you improve your writing, and others to familiarize you with a particular market or trend. This book will help point you to some of the best sources for all of these.

There is a culture of mystery lovers—a culture that is changing now perhaps more than at any time in its long history. The traditional and the contemporary, the classic and the unusual, all have an audience. This book is your tool for reaching them.

We at Writer's Digest Books hope this book will help you reach your goal, whether that be breaking into the field of mystery writing, selling a series idea, or making it to the best-seller list!

*D. Collingwood*

*Editor*

For mystery writers, the *Mystery Writer's Marketplace and Sourcebook* picks up where *Novel and Short Story Writer's Market* and *Writer's Market* leave off. The other market directories present a broad range of markets and marketing information, but this book goes beyond, focusing exclusively on mystery writing and publishing. Whether you write about hard-boiled private eyes, overworked police detectives or nosey archaeology professors, you will find valuable information on who's buying mystery, what's happening in the current mystery market, and how you can become more involved (and better informed) about the mystery field. In other words, this book contains valuable clues to solving the mystery of publication.

*Robin Gee*

*Assistant Editor*

# *How to Use This Book*

Mystery writers are almost always mystery lovers. As one mystery editor put it, "I couldn't do my job well if I didn't (love mysteries)." This book addresses both the writer and the reader and, as is often the case, the writer/reader. Mystery writers not only read mysteries because they love them, but because they learn so much from them. So in this book you'll find information on (1) how to write mysteries; (2) how and where to market mysteries; and (3) how to find mysteries, mystery lovers and mystery "events."

## I. Trends in Crime Fiction

This first section serves as a general survey of what's happening in mystery and suspense today and what may be happening tomorrow.

## II. Writing the Mystery

Instruction on how to write mysteries is presented by experts on that subject: Michael Seidman, John Lutz and Stephanie Kay Bendel. These writers offer tips on creating mystery protagonists, clues and plots—all essential ingredients of a mystery. On the nonfiction side of things, we have an article on true crime because of that category's popularity, as well as an interview with Marcia Muller for some additional firsthand advice.

## III. The Markets

What do you do after you've written your mystery? Robin Gee, an expert on markets as editor of *Novel and Short Story Writer's Market*, shares overall tips and advice on marketing. This is followed by the markets themselves, broken into short story markets, novel markets, foreign markets and markets for reviews and nonfiction articles. The market listings were created from questionnaires we sent to publishers, who were selected for the volume of mystery books they publish, for their accessibility to new writers, or for a combination of the two. Personal interviews with editors at the top markets provide invaluable advice.

*Short story markets* are divided into two categories. "Primary" markets are publishers that publish mystery, publish some mystery and are open to new writers, publish mystery and have a large circulation, or satisfy a combination of these requirements. "Secondary" markets are markets that are open to mystery or are seeking mystery, but don't pay or have small circulations. Some secondary markets have a limited

interest in mystery but are open to new writers of all stripes.
Short story market listings appear like this:

---

# Dagger of the Mind, Beyond the Realms of Imagination

► **Considers:** short shorts
short stories
novelettes
novellas
► **Categories:** private eye
hard-boiled detective
police procedural
amateur sleuth
malice domestic

**Address:** K'yi-Lih Productions, 1317 Hookridge Dr., El
Paso TX 79925, (915) 591-0541
**Contact:** Arthur William Lloyd Breach
**Profile:** *"Dagger of the Mind,* from the onset, was a publication dedicated to the intellectual reader. As both a
reader and writer I concern myself predominantly with
the moral of the story rather than its trappings. I want
*good* fiction that moves and makes you think. Don't retell
old trite themes (the butler did it, ghosts, vampires and
werewolves), *you* lead the way. Be a leader—not a follower. *That's* what gets my attention." Established 1990.
Magazine: 8½ × 11; 62-86 pages. Published quarterly. Circulation: 5,000.
**How to Contact:** Send complete ms with cover letter.
SASE required for query and ms response. Electronic
submissions OK. Receives 250 unsolicited mss/month.
Accepts 8-15 mss/issue. Reports on queries in 2 weeks;
on mss in 3-4 months. Comments on mss. Guidelines
available for 1 first-class stamp. Sample copy available for
$3.50 and 5 first-class stamps.
**Terms:** Pays ½-1 cent/word plus 1 contributor's copy on

publication. Buys all first rights. Publishes ms 1 year after acceptance.

**Tips:** "Familiarize yourself with the market. I receive so many manuscripts per month that I don't have the time to read material that doesn't fit into my guidelines. Send in *only* your very best and make sure you send a good, clean copy. If you have a manuscript, be it fiction or nonfiction, and you're uncertain if what you've got will fit in with what I have, query with the idea."

The first section of the listing is the Profile, which covers the editorial slant of the magazine, as well as the size, format, circulation and establishment date. How to Contact explains what to send and what to expect in terms of response time. A general note: Always send a SASE (self addressed stamped envelope) with submissions. Under Terms the information varies. Some publishers feel that payment and rights are something to work out with authors on an individual basis. Basically the information includes: payment rates and schedules, rights purchased and lead time. Tips are just that — specific bits of advice from the market. Considers tells you what formats the editor will consider, and Mystery Categories lists the specific subgenres that are of interest.

Novel markets follow the same format but these listings are not divided into primary and secondary categories. They are listed alphabetically, and to help you distinguish the submission interests of the markets, we've devised a system of symbols. The ⇔ indicates a publisher that is a big market for mysteries or that is entirely devoted to mystery publication. The ✎ indicates a mystery market that is most open to established or agented authors. The ✍ indicates a market that is open to unagented or unpublished authors.

Phone numbers in the listings are *not* invitations to call in your query. Phone queries are almost never desirable. Numbers are included mostly for follow-up purposes: If you've sent a manuscript and the response time has passed, you may want to call to ask the status of your submission.

Many of the novel markets are accompanied by a personal interview with the mystery editor of the house, offering further insight into that particular market.

*Agents* are of special interest to many published writers. Gary Provost discusses working with an agent on page 193. This article is followed by names and addresses of agents interested in mystery and suspense. If you need to know more about an individual agency, consult

*Literary Agents and Art/Photo Reps* (Writer's Digest Books).

We queried both foreign publishers and bookstores and can offer you some insight into what chance a writer has of being published in Canada and the United Kingdom as well as what types of mysteries are being published there. And, considering Bouchercon will be held in Nottingham, England, in 1995 attendees might want to find a good bookstore in the area.

## IV. The Sources

The first item in *The Sources*, "Magazines About Mysteries" by Michael Seidman, gives an insightful view into some of the industry's top publications and what they feature.

*Writer's Organizations* includes listings for groups devoted to the interests of mystery and crime writers. More general writers' organizations can be found in *Writer's Market* and *Novel and Short Story Writer's Market* (both from Writer's Digest Books).

*Conventions* are discussed by Michael Seidman, who has been to many of them and can offer firsthand insight. We've also included addresses and contact people so you can make plans to attend.

The *Book Clubs* section focuses on those book clubs that specialize in mystery or crime fiction and we've investigated them for you.

*Bookstores* includes sources that will help you market your own work and stay familiar with the mystery field. We mailed questionnaires to a variety of bookstores. Listings take this format:

---

## Almark & Co. — Booksellers
**Address:** P.O. Box 7, Thornhill, Ontario L3T 3N1 Canada, (416) 764-BOOK
**Owner/Contact person:** Al Navis
**Established:** 1974
**Profile:** "We have a mail/phone order service. We're a 'by appointment only' store of almost 6,500 square feet and more than 30,000 titles. We specialize in modern first-edition fiction: literature and general fiction; crime, mystery and detective fiction; science fiction and fantasy; dark fantasy and horror; historical and military fiction; Kennedy assassinations; true crime and espionage; Churchilliana; and United States Civil War history."

**Services:** Buys, trades and sells used books. 90-95% of books are old or rare. Catalog available by request. Conducts author book signings.

Listings with an * indicate a catalog only service. The Profile tells you something about the store's specialty or focus. The Services covers whether a store buys, trades or sells books, the availability of old and rare stock, catalog availability, the number of mystery magazines featured, and whether author signings or readings are sponsored. Not only are these stores a great place to find good mysteries, many also hold events or publish newsletters.

*Awards*, the last item in The Sources, includes the addresses, guidelines, frequency, and a brief description of awards open to writers of mystery and suspense.

## V. For Your Reference

The final section of this book is for general mystery reference. In it you'll find a "bookshelf" of mysteries recommended by several known authors, who also detail why the books were important to their writing, and a list of nonfiction books you can refer to again and again for advice and information.

"Real-Life Private Eyes" reads like a story, but is an actual account of a day in the life of a real P.I. and how that life differs from fictional depictions. "Real-Life Homicide Investigations" is written by an investigations professional with more than twenty years of experience.

The glossary includes general writing and publishing terms in addition to words used by mystery writers and readers.

## Using This Book

We've explored the sections and features of this book. Now let's look at some common uses thereof:

• You've read a wonderful book and think it must appeal to the same audience as a manuscript you're trying to place. Look up the publisher in *Mystery Writer's Marketplace and Sourcebook*, see if they're looking for any particular genre and if they accept manuscripts only through agents.

• You've discovered that the publisher you're interested in does require that you have an agent, so you look one up in the Agents section. Next, you want to make sure the manuscript is in shape, so you refer to the Marketing the Mystery section to see if there's anything you've forgotten.

• You've read every traditional British cozy at your local bookstore and library, and you're looking for a new book. Flip to the Bookstores section and see if there's another store in town or another city in your area. If not, contact one of the mail-order book catalogs listed among the stores (indicated with a *). Or, go one step further and contact a British publisher listed in the Foreign Markets section and request a catalog.

• You can't make it to Bouchercon, but you would love to get out and mingle with fellow mystery enthusiasts, so turn to the Conventions section for contact information about other conventions.

• You're writing a story in which there's a dead body. You want to reveal that the death happened earlier than your investigator first thought, but how long can a body be around before it starts to decompose? Turn to "Real Life Homicide Investigations" for the answer.

• To accomplish a fictional murder you need to include a rare poison with very specific characteristics, and you would like to consult a book on the subject. In Bookshelf you discover a book called *Deadly Doses* and run to the bookstore to pick it up.

There are many more instances in which you'll refer to *Mystery Writer's Marketplace and Sourcebook*, but the best instance may be an editor's request to see your manuscript—when you've misplaced her address!

# Trends in Crime Fiction

## Whither Thou Goest . . .

*by Michael Seidman*

Okay, we're going to talk about trends, about what some of us perceive as what is going to be happening in crime fiction. If the thought of sitting down in front of a blank screen causes anxiety, that nervousness increases tenfold when I consider the topic of this piece. After all, by the time I'm done writing this, the trends may have changed. By the time you read these words, the possibility that everything I've said is outdated grows stronger. And by the time you've researched the subject area and written your book according to all the guidelines herein, odds are someone else will be writing an article on new trends in mystery—discussing how everything herein has gone by the boards.

Fine, so there's some hyperbole in the preceding paragraph; the fact is that trends— fads really—are usually short-lived. Some maintain a tenacious grasp, but writers—and wise publishers—are always looking for, or *should* be looking for, that something new and exciting that breathes new life into a category and brings new readers to the racks. We need new customers in order to have a writing future, and those new customers are coming from the MTV generation. Sound bytes, quick action, splashy color and powerful visuals compete with the printed word for ever-decreasing attention spans.

So, we have to give the customers—that's what Mickey Spillane calls the readers—what they want, while simultaneously finding a way to entice new flies into our parlors.

This is being written very early in 1993; for the past several years, the most highly touted and visible trend in crime fiction has been books by and about women. Publishers have known for decades that women represent the largest part of the book-buying market. In the mid- to late eighties, with the founding of an organization called Sisters in Crime, the women writing crime fiction took a stand, demanding more equitable review attention and more respect from the publishers. Through some brilliantly coordinated publicity and promotional efforts, they've managed to have the kind of impact Washington lobbyists dream about. Their influence has been so great that when agents call me to check on my current needs, one of the first questions they ask is, "Are you looking for books by men?"

The answer, for me, is yes. The problem with trends in writing, as I see it, is that they speak to the needs of a vocal group—often a majority—but result in the neglect of another segment of the market. If those disenfranchised readers can't get their fix, they're going to turn to something else. The better editors and publishers, then, while paying very real attention to the *vox populi*, make certain that they maintain a balance on their lists, seeing to it that there's at least a little something for everyone. Every trend, every fad, eventually dies down (perhaps—like the cicada—to reappear several years later), and a top-heavy, trend-oriented list is going to topple.

With that as background, let's take a look at some of what is very strong today and see where we may find ourselves in the near future . . . and let's examine how you can keep track of what's goin' on.

*Publishers Weekly*, one of the most important publications for people in the book industry, including writers, does features on the various categories of fiction, interviews editors about what they're looking for, and publishes early reviews of upcoming books. These reviews appear about three months before publication date and if read regularly, can give you a sense of what may be developing in the industry. If, over a period of three or four months, for instance, you see reviews of five or six mystery novels that seem related in some way, that indicates a trend, and you'll be aware of it. It's going to require some thought and insight on your part, but the patterns are there. The problem is that the reviews appear so close to release date that by the time you notice a trend, you may be too late; there are probably too many books already in the pipeline—from author to publisher to bookstore—and the competition becomes stiffer.

The specialty magazines (*Mystery Scene, The Armchair Detective* and *The Drood Review of Mystery* are the foremost; see the article on page 205 for more information about them as a source, and page 188 for information about them as markets) and the mystery conventions (see page 214) are both valuable information mines. Consider, too, membership in the Mystery Writers of America, Private Eye Writers of America or Sisters in Crime; the insights gained through peer group discussions and newsletters are priceless.

*Writer's Market* and *Writer's Digest* provide solid marketing information. All publications suffer from a gap caused by lead time, however. The information you see in January typically was submitted in October of the previous year. Editorial wants and needs may not have changed dramatically, but new phenomena affecting buying decisions are not necessarily present.

To my mind, the best way to spot a mystery fiction trend when it is building is to become friendly with a bookseller, especially one who runs a mystery specialty bookstore. These folks can tell you what they see their customers buying, what the customers are asking for, or not asking for anymore, and they can give you a peek at the publishers' catalogs. With catalogs, you can see what has been scheduled for publication anywhere from six months to a year down the road. This gives you two bits of information: exactly what kinds of books publishers are doing and if, because eight of the twelve books on the list are about vampire-iguanas acting as police dogs, there is a new trend in mystery publishing. (That might be a clue.)

I suppose I've stalled enough. I'll have to confront the question now and try to tell you what I see coming – or going or staying – as of January 1993.

Two of the hottest commodities in the genre have been female private investigators and cats. Not together in the same book – although at least one author has named her character Kat – but as central figures in their own adventures.

The female P.I., as a contemporary phenomenon, was created by Marcia Muller in her Sharon McCone series (see the interview with Muller on page 43). A couple of years later Sue Grafton and Sara Paretsky brought bestsellerdom to this subgenre. And with the attention, the floodgates were opened: Virtually every mystery list – paperback and hardcover – has at least one female shamus, and their personalities are as varied as their authors.

Reports from the bookstores tell us that the books are still selling, although some stores have remarked on a falloff. That's not only understandable, it's expected. The question for you is whether it makes sense to try to break in here. The answer, from my perspective, is no — unless you have a completely new take on the subject, some angle that hasn't been explored. Sally Chapman, a writer in California, is working on the second in a series about a male/female team (the woman is the narrator) that specializes in computer crimes. That's different enough that there might be some interest in the marketplace.

I wasn't kidding about cats. Lillian Jackson Braun has a best-selling series featuring a feline, and Carole Nelson Douglas has begun to make inroads with her novels from the same litter. I'm told that dogs are beginning to appear. Each season seems to bring at least one anthology featuring cats, and the joke among one group of writers is that they're going to put together a collection of stories in which animals never appear at all. I don't think it will sell, at least not if it's presented that way. (I guess you had to be there, but you get the point.)

As with any publishing trend, past or present, if something catches the public *interest*, it will last. The cream rises to the top (avoid clichés at all costs), the rest sinks thankfully out of sight. There will probably always be an interest in the female P.I. as a character; the real task is to write well enough that some editor will see *your* potential and risk putting you into competition with authors who've carved out comfortable niches.

This doesn't mean that you should avoid writing about a male P.I.; it does mean that your work will be more difficult to sell. As I said, the better publishers try to maintain a balance. But, again, your writing has to shine. Something in the manuscript has to make us willing to take a chance on you in a shaky market.

Not so much a trend as a standard, is the so-called traditional mystery. These are fair-play puzzles, contests between the reader and the author. (If a novel is called a *mystery* it should always have that element. It is one of the major differences between mystery and suspense — both of which are crime novels.) The traditional mystery will never go away, and there will always be a very strong market for the amateur detective, male or female (again, guess which sells better). If there is an evolution here, it is in the search for new professions: lawyers have been done to death (no pun intended), the neighborhood busybody appears regularly, and there have been bookstore owners, antique dealers, jockeys, wine merchants, actors and academics galore. (Academics form their own subgenre.)

If you can create a character whose profession hasn't been overdone and give it a logical positioning, you should be able to get notice. The character's background will be integral to the solving of the puzzle, and you should know everything there is to know about your hero's day job; you can count on someone out there calling you on any errors or mistakes.

As political correctness insinuates itself into our national consciousness—and as younger editors who have received their educations with that slant move in to replace us older folks—there is a movement toward including minority groups in crime fiction. This is fine, but sometimes it gets out of hand. One writer with whom I work has added an Arab character to her already polyglot cast because "it has come to my attention that Arabs do not get good press in the United States, and I felt an obligation to do something about that." I disagreed, strongly: The character's sole function in the story was as a mouthpiece for a point of view that may be valid but that did nothing to advance any given story line. The character was created simply to fulfill a perceived sociological guilt.

It certainly makes sense that all kinds of people be portrayed in our fiction. Joseph Hansen, Sandra Scoppettone and Tony Fennally have developed mainstream homosexual characters, and other writers have been following their lead, most often in what is termed the "gay press." Walter Mosley and James Sallis have black detectives, as did Chester Himes. George Chesbro's Mongo is a former circus star—a dwarf— with a Ph.D. in criminology. I think we'll see a lot more of this in the years to come, and generally the more successful writers will be those who not only know the people they're writing about, but who can feature different types of people without hitting the reader over the head with a cause. At my desk, I much prefer discovering the character through the reading, rather than receiving a cover letter explaining why this senior citizen, physically challenged, non-Western cultural minority is going to be popular, important or whatever else the author thinks. When all is said and done, it is—or should be—the writing, the story, that is going to sell the book to a publisher and to the readers. The important thing for you to recognize is that there's no reason to avoid a specific character because of an alleged bias against its "type."

Right now, the historical mystery seems to be the form that is creating the most excitement. These range from Ellis Peters's medieval mysteries to Elizabeth Peters's Victorian Egypt. Max Allan Collins has developed a private investigator whose cases range from the 1930s to the 1950s, and Marian Jackson sets her Miss Abigail Danforth mysteries at the turn of the century. In the early 1980s I worked with a writer attempting to create a series in which a character based on Leonardo da Vinci was the detective; we were too early. Today I think that series might have a chance.

Each editor is going to define "historical" differently; for my taste, the further back you go, the better. (I'm editing one that's set in Pharaonic Egypt.) Research is a blatant necessity, and the avoidance of anachronisms that will jar the reader back to the present is a cardinal rule. This doesn't mean that you have to use convoluted, archaic language; it does mean that you can't use contemporary slang, nor can your detective make use of knowledge that wasn't extant.

Finally, and at least for right now, the serial murderer has gained popularity, and I don't see that slowing down. David Lindsey, John Sanford and, of course, Thomas Harris are the leaders in the field; the more successful novels are longer than the category mystery, with a richer tapestry of character and event. (The debate as to whether these are mysteries or suspense will continue in another time and place . . . and without me.)

While acknowledging the reasons people are interested in trends, in what's happening, in what's hot (and in trying to find the easiest way to break in by jumping on a bandwagon), as a writer and editor I've always believed that it was more important to create the surge, not ride the wave, and that the writer who forces his or her work into a category because of a misguided thought that that's the way to the top, is not going to be a good writer. If there's any trend I'd like to see, it's writers writing what they want to write and what they can write because that is what they should write.

# Writing the Mystery

## Plotting the Suspense Story
*by Stephanie Kay Bendel*

I couldn't put it down." "My heart was pounding as I read the last chapter." "I stayed up late last night to finish that book—I had to find out how it ended!"

All authors would like to hear remarks like these about their works. Reality, however, reminds us that relatively few books provide truly memorable levels of suspense. On the other hand, those that do usually sell well and often stay in print for years. While the life span of most short stories is less than a year, unusually suspenseful ones are reprinted regularly in anthologies and are often adapted as screenplays. Well aware of these facts, my students frequently ask me how one goes about creating a suspenseful plot. After several years trying to help them analyze their plots for suspense, I've come up with a few guidelines.

### Suspense Defined

The word "suspense" can be used several ways, at least three of which can be applied to suspenseful writing: (1) to define a state of anxiety; (2) to define a state of uncertainty or indecision; and (3) to define a state of interest and excitement experienced during a period of waiting.

It is worthwhile to keep all three definitions in mind when writing suspense fiction, since almost all stories can be reduced to a simple formula: The protagonist has a problem. How suspenseful the story will be depends upon how much the readers care whether the problem is resolved—in other words, how anxious we can make them. In turn, how much the readers care about the resolution of the problem depends in large part upon how much they care about the people the problem affects. Therefore, suspenseful writing demands that the author emotionally involve the readers both in the events taking place in the story and in the character(s) who stands to suffer if things don't turn out right.

Thus, the author must initially give the readers someone to root for and to identify with. The aim here is to get the readers so involved that they imagine they are the protagonist and experience the anxiety of being in the protagonist's dilemma. Remember to make the main problem big enough so that the person(s) the readers are rooting for will suffer a good deal if it isn't solved.

Once the initial problem is created and the readers are emotionally involved with one or more characters, the author can increase suspense in several ways, all of which produce either more anxiety, uncertainty or excitement:

- By creating more obstacles for the protagonist to deal with. The obstacles may be part of the problem at hand, or they may be unrelated; for example, personal problems may be intruding, making resolution of the main problem more difficult.
- By making sure that obvious solutions to the problem don't work. This increases the protagonist's—and therefore the readers'— frustration.
- By raising the stakes. What happens if the main problem is not resolved? Can the situation be made worse than it already is?
- By isolating the protagonist. Make sure that he or she can't simply turn to someone else for help or emotional support. Make your character solve the problem alone.
- By cultivating uncertainty. Suspense is increased when we don't know whom to trust or whether or not a plan will work even if we manage to carry it off.
- By keeping up the action. As soon as the readers begin to feel that the protagonist has a problem in hand, suspense levels will fall. We can raise them again by making sure the protagonist always has an immediate problem to deal with.

• By creating a deadline. As the time allowed for solving the problem grows shorter, tension automatically increases.

To illustrate, let's consider a sample plot: A young woman — we'll call her Rachel — is brutally murdered, and the detective assigned to take charge of the investigation will be our protagonist — we'll call him Jake. At this point, so far as the reader is concerned, the murder is just another case for Jake — the motivation to solve it is his desire to do his job well. On the other hand, if he doesn't catch the murderer, it won't be the end of the world — merely another unsolved case, a fact of life for policemen. How do we take a run-of-the-mill case and turn it into a suspenseful story?

## Involve the Reader's Emotions

The first order of business is to emotionally involve the readers by showing them that Rachel was a likeable person. We'll make her a reporter whose friends and co-workers describe her to Jake as an honest, hardworking, caring woman who believed in what she did — and she did a lot of good, perhaps exposing corruption and deceit. It will be even better if we can show that those affected by the corruption and deceit were particularly vulnerable — for instance, children, the elderly or the handicapped. Perhaps Jake even has firsthand knowledge of her accomplishments.

Now Rachel is not just another corpse. Jake — and the readers — will think of her as a real person — a likeable person who did not deserve to die.

We'll further involve the readers by showing them that Jake is a decent fellow — someone they can identify with. We'll give him some good qualities and some faults. It is important that we make Jake a real human being — neither a superman nor a saint. The readers cannot be anxious about a superman who can take care of himself in any situation, nor can they identify with a saint. None of us has ever met anyone who was perfect — and we are all too aware of our own shortcomings to identify with someone who has none.

So what will Jake be like? To be a policeman, dealing constantly with the seamy side of life, he has to be pretty tough. He must witness death, suffering and injustice without going to pieces. We want our readers to admire that strength. On the other hand, Jake can't be insensitive or completely cynical, or the readers will emotionally distance themselves from him.

Remember it's important to show — not tell — the readers what kind of man Jake is. How can we do that? Let's show Jake at the murder scene. He'll see the brutality Rachel suffered before her death, and he'll clinically interpret the meaning of each piece of evidence: the blow to the right side of her head may mean her attacker was left-handed; her broken fingernails will show that she fought desperately for her life; the blood on the carpet, the walls, the tablecloth and the chair will tell him that she didn't die quickly or without pain.

Though Jake is being very professional, we'll simultaneously make it clear that he suffers because of the trauma his work entails. Perhaps he has ulcers or nightmares or insomnia, or maybe he drinks more than he should. And again, we won't just tell the readers he is suffering; we'll show him popping antacid tablets as he works or waking in a cold sweat in the middle of the night after dreaming about Rachel's death or needing a drink to fall asleep.

Jake must impress the readers as a real human being. He'll have some faults, but they won't be failings that the readers have no patience with, because they'll understand why he behaves the way he does. For example, if somewhere in the story Jake forgets his son's birthday, we'll show that his absentmindedness is not a by-product of insensitivity—he feels terrible when he realizes what has happened. But he's been so overwhelmed by the complexity of his case and the pressures put upon him that the readers will honestly feel as though they too might forget their child's birthday under the same circumstances. When Jake loses his temper with the amiable young officer who is trying to help him, we'll already have shown that Jake has a pounding headache, he hasn't slept for two days, and he's beginning to believe that whoever murdered Rachel has a good chance of getting away with it.

If we do these things well, the readers will certainly be emotionally involved with Jake. At the same time, we've already enlarged the original problem to some extent. No longer are we watching a detective solve a routine murder—there is something special about this case. We've made the problem more important—but have we made it important enough? Could we do even more?

## Enlarge the Problem

One of the ways to make the protagonist's dilemma worse is to make the villain(s) more powerful. Remember, we said Rachel was an investigative reporter. Suppose she told one of her co-workers that she was onto a big story. As Jake tracks down information, he begins to suspect that Rachel had discovered something damaging about an influential person—someone of great wealth or political power, someone

who has a good deal of control over many other people. Now Jake is
not up against an ordinary killer. He's trying to catch someone who has
the ability to thwart the investigation, to buy off policemen, destroy
evidence and silence witnesses.

## Provide Additional Obstacles

Once we are satisfied we've made the main problem big enough,
we need to look at what other obstacles Jake is encountering. Some of
them may arise directly from the case itself. Because Rachel was a
reporter, the media focuses more than usual attention on the murder,
demanding daily to know that progress is being made, putting Jake on
the spot. We'll further complicate matters by having Jake make some
progress that he must keep secret to avoid tipping off the suspect(s) in
the investigation. Now even though Jake is doing a good job and getting
closer to solving the case, he is perceived as failing. His superiors,
worried about the negative image the department is projecting, disassociate themselves from him as much as possible, and put even more
pressure on him. Most of the other detectives don't want to be connected to a case that may be political trouble. The only person Jake can
depend on is his long-time partner and friend, detective Walt Hanson.

Other obstacles may arise from personal aspects of Jake's life. Let's
give Jake a wife — we'll call her Myrna. She's a fine woman — a good
policeman's wife — so our readers will like her and want Jake to have a
good relationship with her. It is important to remember that if we want
to cause problems between Jake and Myrna, we need to do it in such
a way that the readers are not alienated from either of them. If, for
example, we made Myrna a shrew who made unreasonable demands
on Jake, our readers wouldn't feel much conflict — they wouldn't understand why Jake would feel a need to accommodate her. Considering the
problems he has at work, they'd feel he'd be justified in ignoring Myrna
for the time being.

Thus, we have to show that Myrna is a decent person. She under-
stands the strain of Jake's job and tries to be supportive of him. She
puts up with the long and irregular hours he must work and usually
handles most of the day-to-day problems at home by herself so Jake
won't be further pressured when he returns from work. We need to
know that she and Jake love each other very much, and that conflict
between them is truly distressing.

Accordingly, we won't let Myrna become upset over relatively small
problems. We must give her an important reason for needing Jake's
attention at this particular time. For example, suppose her mother has

just been diagnosed as terminally ill. Now Jake's wife is understandably upset and is looking to him for emotional support. Our readers will sympathize with Myrna and will hope that Jake can comfort her. But they'll also see that he is being pulled in two directions at once, and every time Myrna needs him, a serious development at work will be taking him away. And whatever he's doing to solve Rachel's murder, part of him feels he should be with Myrna. No matter what he does, Jake will feel bad.

### Eliminate Obvious Solutions

It is important to remember that every time we pose a problem for Jake, the readers are going to say to themselves, "If I were Jake, what would I do?" and they will try to come up with possible solutions to his problems. What we must do is stay one step ahead of the readers and show them that their solutions won't work.

At this point in the story, what might the readers think Jake should do? Take some time off to be with his wife? We'll show there's no way he can do that. Even when he tries to spend some time with her, the phone rings—he's urgently needed elsewhere. Should he get more manpower on the case so it will be solved more quickly? We've already partially blocked that possibility by having his superiors and fellow detectives wanting to disassociate themselves from the investigation of Rachel's murder, so Jake and Walt have to carry on alone.

What will the readers expect them to do now? One obvious course is to talk further with Rachel's co-workers who said she'd been working on a big story. Perhaps more information will lead to the killer. But let's show that talking with them won't help Jake and Walt anymore— why not? Suppose everyone is now reluctant to give our heroes any information. Some of them even deny what they've said earlier. Perhaps one of the informants is murdered. Thus, Jake and Walt not only have been reminded how powerful their opponent is, but they've had some of their options destroyed. The murdered informant cannot ever testify, and the others are less likely to come forward.

In this way, the first three or four methods that come to mind for reducing the stress Jake is under must be shown to be unworkable. Each time the reader realizes that a course of action is not possible, or that it won't work, tension levels in the story are elevated.

### Raise the Stakes

To further increase suspense, we'll raise the stakes for Jake. When we first began, failing to solve Rachel's murder would have been a personal frustration for him, but not the end of the world; all policemen have to live with unsolved cases. So far we have changed the situation so that if Jake doesn't solve the case, he'll look bad professionally, and the police department's image will suffer. His superiors will be angry with him and possibly his job will be in jeopardy. Can we make things worse? Well, let's suppose that as Jake continues to investigate, he begins to uncover evidence that points to himself! Now he's in a terrible dilemma: If he suppresses the evidence and is caught doing so, he will look very guilty, will be taken off the case, won't be able to find the real killer, will probably lose his job, and very likely will be tried for a murder he didn't commit. If he doesn't suppress the evidence, the same things will still happen. His only chance is to suppress the evidence and hope he doesn't get caught before he solves the case. To make matters worse, Jake can no longer confide in Walt without involving him in an illegal activity.

Notice how neatly we've boxed Jake in. Undoubtedly it will have occurred to some readers that Jake might simply quit his job if things become too bad. After all, a policeman can always find work as a private detective or a security consultant, and if Jake did that, he would also be emotionally available for Myrna. But now that evidence has turned up pointing to him, we've cut off the possibility of Jake just walking away from the problem. If he leaves, someone else will certainly turn up the evidence against him, and he'll look guiltier than ever.

## Isolate the Protagonist

Another device for raising suspense levels in a story is to isolate the protagonist—prevent anyone else from helping him solve the problem. To a certain extent we've already done this: Jake's co-workers are avoiding involvement in the case, and his superiors are putting pressure on him. His informants won't help him any longer, and his wife can't comfort him because she's got her own serious problem to deal with.

How can we isolate Jake even more? Well, let's suppose Myrna's mother lives a couple of thousand miles away, and of course, now that she's so ill, Myrna wants to be with her. Now Jake will be physically alone. We can even arrange to give him another problem to deal with— he has to borrow money to pay for Myrna's trip. Furthermore, he'll feel bad that he can't accompany Myrna, but the way the murder case is going, he cannot possible leave town.

Now there's no one at home to give Jake the emotional support that he needs more than ever, and there's only one person who can help him solve Rachel's murder: his trusted partner. To some extent, we've put distance between the two men by forcing Jake to keep an important secret from Walt. However, most readers want to feel that if push comes to shove, Walt would come through for Jake, even risking his job in the process. Can we isolate Jake even more by removing even that hope? Yes, but we must proceed very carefully, and we'll do it by means of yet another helpful trick: promoting uncertainty.

## Promote Uncertainty

Until now, we've worked hard to convince the readers that Jake can trust Walt. If we change the situation too quickly, our story will lose credibility and won't be at all suspenseful. What we need to do is to plant little seeds of distrust.

Suppose Jake realizes that Walt has lied to him. We'll make it a small lie, something almost trivial, and there might be a good reason why Walt tells it, but Jake can't be sure. All he knows is that he's beginning to distrust his partner.

As the story goes on, Jake will realize that the false evidence pointing to him must have been planted with the aid or knowledge of someone within the police department. As much as he doesn't want to, he — and the readers — will have to begin suspecting Walt.

Uncertainty can also be used to produce suspense in other ways. Suppose Jake comes to suspect that Rachel had some hard evidence against the villain(s) and that she may have hidden it. Can Jake figure out where it is? Will he recognize it when he sees it? Will it be enough to exonerate him and indict the real culprit(s)? Does anyone else know or suspect that Rachel hid some evidence? Will someone else find it and destroy it before Jake gets there?

Of course, we could go on all day piling problems up for poor Jake, but we must exercise good judgment in deciding when enough is enough. I once wrote a story about a family in which six of seven siblings had heart attacks. I took the situation from real life — that is exactly what happened in my father's family — and I hoped to convey the sense of helplessness and horror the family lived with. Instead I found I had created an emotional overload. I read the story to a small group of writers and discovered that they were giggling uncontrollably by the third or fourth heart attack.

The point to remember is that in real life the six heart attacks occurred over a period of twenty-five years, giving the family time to adjust and accept the emotional strain of one illness before facing another. I was asking my audience to absorb the total impact in one evening! As a result, my story had no credibility even though I was describing actual events.

If, for example, Jake's mother-in-law dies, and Myrna threatens to divorce him if he doesn't drop everything and travel a couple of thousand miles for the funeral, and then it becomes apparent that not only is his friend Walt somehow involved in Rachel's murder, but he is trying to frame Jake for it, and then his sister calls and informs Jake that her son has been kidnapped, a ransom note has arrived and Jake must come right away — well, our story will be in shambles. The readers will surely throw the book down in disgust and disbelief.

There are no firm guidelines as to how much your protagonist can believably endure. A truly skillful writer can make an audience accept almost any premise, but you need to be acutely aware of your own limitations.

### Create a Deadline

The final thing that a suspense story needs is a clock ticking in the background. The greatest problem in the world won't create any anxiety if there's an infinite amount of time available to resolve it. On the other hand, if the reader is aware that dire consequences will follow if the problem is not solved by a certain time, suspense will continue to mount as that time draws near.

Let's suppose that the villain of our story is a prominent industrialist who has curried favor with local politicians for years. He is donating a large tract of forested land to the state to be used as a park and recreation area, thus affording him a large tax write-off. What Rachel discovered and Jake finds out is that the forest was used for many years as a testing ground for various pesticides and herbicides that the industrialist manufactured. The land and water are contaminated with long-lasting toxins, and the park is scheduled to be opened tomorrow. Jake must gather enough evidence to force state officials to prevent thousands of people from camping and picnicking there, and he has only a few hours left to do it!

Now, when we've made things just as bad as we feel we can while maintaining credibility and time is running out, we'll have reached the climax of our story — suspense is as high as we can make it. The time has come to start solving our protagonist's problems in a satisfying way — but that's another topic!

### Planting Clues in the Mystery
*by John Lutz*

I tell lies for a living. So I have to be good at it.

When my fiction is read to the final word, everything must click into place for the readers. *I should have known!* they must think. *Could have known!* That sense of revelation, satisfaction and admiration that the reader feels when the penny drops and the solution is apparent is what the mystery writer is striving for, and its achievement depends largely on the skills and techniques of planting clues.

But what is a clue? The answer isn't quite as simple as it seems, because beginning writers often confuse planting clues with foreshadowing. Knowing the difference between these two techniques is essential, bearing in mind that while they are by definition different elements of fiction, the distinction isn't always clear.

Foreshadowing is hinting: It is setting up situations that will occur later in the story in such a way that they will be plausible. Planting clues is the introduction of facts that will, later in the work, support the logic of the solution.

The trick here, usually, is to present clues in ways that aren't obvious; they must not appear to be what they are. There are various techniques for hiding clues. They can be buried in a deluge of other information that is irrelevant to the solution. They can be presented forthrightly but disguised as something else, perhaps a tidbit that is ostensibly about character, a snatch of vivid description, an exchange of dialogue that is apparently about something more important. The following is an example of both foreshadowing and the planting of clues.

Here's the situation: Colonel Jarvis has been found dead in his study, a knife wound in his chest but no weapon in the room. All doors and windows have been locked from the inside, and there are no hiding places or hidden passages. All of the house's occupants have ironclad alibis.

Now, we can later explain that the room was prefabricated and the last wall was put into place after the murder. All the occupants of the house have ironclad alibis because all of them stand to gain financially if the murder is officially ruled a suicide, so they are lying to protect the killer.

A mention that the suspects and victim were in the construction business would foreshadow the explanation, make it more plausible. So would the knowledge that the victim was wealthy and despised by all the suspects. Perhaps he'd recently and unscrupulously outfoxed them in a business deal. The emphasis here is on laying groundwork for plausibility. Foreshadowing.

On the other hand, a shiny new nail discovered outside the room is a fact that indicates concretely what occurred. It isn't a simply normal condition; within the rules of the game, the parameters of good fiction, it must mean something. A clue.

But we still need to explain how and who dunit. The missing knife, as many of you no doubt guessed, was fashioned from a blade of ice which, after being wielded as the murder weapon, melted. Now, if you were to mention a blood-tinted puddle near the body, which your detective will later determine is the melted weapon, you would be creating a clue. The reader, as well as your detective, would know about this puddle and have a chance — a slim one, if you've written this correctly — to figure out what it means. At tale's end, the detective could point out the presence of this puddle to some of the other characters, as well as to the reader, as evidence leading to his or her conclusion about the method of murder. And, of course, method often leads to opportunity, motive and suspect.

If you were to make the colonel's study uncommonly warm, mention that the eventually-to-be-revealed murderer was seen getting a midnight snack from the freezer, drop the fact that one of the suspects was earlier working in the garden and wearing gloves (possibly used to wield the icy dagger removed from the freezer at snack time), you have foreshadowed.

The puddle next to the corpse, a clue, was certainly made by something, is tangible and remarkable, and must be explained, even if the explanation isn't relevant to the murder. It must be dealt with if the writer is to keep faith with the reader. After all, a tinted puddle isn't something one would normally find in a gentleman's study. But the other above-mentioned circumstances don't necessarily mean anything other than what they appear to mean. It might well be that the murder simply occurred on a warm day, that the suspect raiding the refrigerator merely had an attack of the munchies, and certainly there's nothing unusual about wearing gloves to work in a garden; the writer might well be remiss in not mentioning gloves in a description of the suspect viciously ridding the garden of weeds (a scene vaguely analogous to murder and in itself a sort of foreshadowing). While all of this adds plausibility, it is only that mysterious puddle as clue that needs to be explained, that lends the impression that if the reader had been a bit sharper, more logical, he or she might have figured out this nasty business a few steps ahead of your detective. And it will all fit neatly and create a sudden and complete picture because of the foreshadowing.

Remember, clues are about possibility, foreshadowing about plausibility. The explanation for the puddle falls within the realm of possibility.

The weather, snack and gardening gloves don't necessarily mean anything unusual and require no explanation.

But we don't want the puddle to be too obviously the key to how the crime was committed. So let's also have in the study an open ledger book on the desk, an unusual hat on a hook, a fishbowl containing a piranha (a possible, even if unlikely, source of the puddle). We can later explain these away. In fact, we must explain them, as they are unusual even for the unusual circumstances and might be clues. Let's reveal that the victim was a ruthless slumlord who kept his own books and collected hats and vicious fish. But at the time the ledger, hat and fish are brought into the story, the reader might be more intrigued by them than the puddle near the victim. Just as a solitary duck in a flock being shot at by a hunter has a good chance of individual survival, your clue will probably fly by unnoticed only to touch down dramatically at the end of the story.

How about a little misdirection? The gardening gloves might be mentioned in such a way that emphasis is placed on them rather than on the puddle or the shiny new nail. This is an acceptable bit of distraction, as when a magician does something with one hand to draw your attention while his other hand is busy setting up the illusion.

It's been said that the reader must be led by a slender thread of exactly the correct tautness. While that's true, it's also true that you will be much more aware of the clues you're planting than the readers will when they encounter them while reading hundreds of words per minute. So don't be too subtle. You must learn to become a split personality, be the readers peering over your shoulder even as you write. Remember that you'll know where the story is going, and exactly how the illusion is created, so you won't be nearly as impressed as the readers, who'll be encountering the clues for the first time.

One of your most important advantages as a writer is that you can spend a great deal of time on a passage or a page that the readers will absorb within minutes. It's a good idea to let your first draft sit for at least a few days so you can reread it with a fresh perspective. Situations where additional clues are needed, or where existing ones are too obvious, will then be much more apparent to you.

Remember: Disguise your clues as some other element of your story. Hide them in an array of similar but irrelevant information. Slip them past the reader barely noticed while you provide pyrotechnics to distract and mislead, perhaps some sizzling dialogue or action. Or present them quite blatantly as clues, if you're sure they won't enable the reader to discern their meaning without additional information. This can be effective if you're misleading the reader in other respects, and is ultimately satisfying to both writer and readers.

The idea is to be fair with your readers, yet deceptive. Readers expect this sort of duplicity from you. After all, this is fiction, not real life. From the time they pick up your book or story, they know they're dealing with someone who tell lies for a living.

They ask only that you be good at it.

## Creating the Mystery Hero
*by Michael Seidman*

If you're sitting down to write fiction, you've already got some plots in mind. The next step is to create the people for your story: the protagonist and the antagonist — the hero and the villain — the two players in the game your readers will be watching. The novel is sometimes a contest of wits between the author (represented by his characters) and the audience. Your hero and villain must be worthy of that challenge . . . and just as important, they must be worthy of each other. You don't use an elephant gun to go varmint hunting and you don't send Superman to police parking violations.

If you're writing series-oriented genre fiction, the characters — especially the hero but sometimes the villain — reappear in book after book. Your first challenge, then, is to create a hero readers are going to like, respect, and want to spend time with again and again. The history of genre fiction echoes with the names of protagonists who have become part of our heritage: "Sherlock" has become virtually synonymous with "detective," and "Scarlett" is known to most everyone, including those who don't read genre fiction. Sometimes it takes just one appearance to earn that kind of renown: Consider Sam Spade, whose first outing in *The Maltese Falcon* earned him a place in our consciousness.

If protagonists are at the heart of fiction, they're even more ingrained in the core of genre writing, and deepest of all in mystery fiction. What, then, are the attributes of a good mystery hero?

Traditionally, the detective is a loner. (There may be a sidekick or assistant, but we'll save that character for later.) The reason is simple, though to my mind, distasteful: There has long been a feeling (supported by sales) that all the reader wants is the puzzle and that love interests (as opposed to occasional couplings), back story (unless applicable directly to the crime under investigation), and other involvements a person might be expected to have in a normal life slow—or stop—the story and are, therefore, to be avoided.

There are writers who seem to get away with fiddling with this rule: Robert B. Parker's Spenser has an ongoing romantic relationship, but that is an exception. The easiest route for the new writer is to keep things simple when it comes to the detective's personal life. Any friends or lovers you want to create are best used as sounding boards for the hero's ideas. Conversations serve to update the reader on what has been discovered, to recap the investigator's thinking so far; in short, to ensure that the author continues to play fair with the fan and not keep anything germane to a solution hidden. All other characterization, unfortunately, must evolve from the hero's action relative to getting to "the end."

This lone wolf principle serves another purpose: The reader of a series likes to identify with the hero. The simpler his or her life, the simpler the task of identification.

What is your hero's function in society? How does this character earn a living? That's a crucial question, one you must answer early on, because it is going to dictate the tone, style, approach and form of your novel. The three foundation subgenres of criminous fiction are the amateur detective, the private investigator and the police procedural (which can be expanded to cover intelligence agencies and other official law enforcement operations). Each has traditional guidelines, advantages and disadvantages, and each shapes its detective's character.

## The Amateur

The amateur detective is you and me. Lacking any real investigative background or training, this character relies on instinct, native ability and wits to solve the crime. The amateur is completely on her own, usually unarmed, with no legal support for any of her actions. Role models range from Jane Marple to Jessica Fletcher and include Ralph McInerny's Father Dowling, Harry Kemelman's Rabbi David Small, Jonathan Kellerman's Dr. Alex Delaware, and Elizabeth Peters's Amelia Peabody.

While Sherlock Holmes continues to be the model of investigative ability, today's readers do not readily accept that kind of know-it-all sensibility in contemporary detectives, and while the general-purpose busybody does occasionally appear, most amateurs have a specific expertise that gives you the heart of the story line. If you choose wisely, it also allows you to limit the amount of research you have to do. Barbara Mertz, who writes the Amelia Peabody mysteries as Elizabeth Peters, is an Egyptologist. By creating a heroine who spends a large part of her time exploring the ruins in Egypt during the Victorian era, the author makes excellent use of the knowledge she already possesses. Her settings, the crimes she creates for Amelia, the knowledge Amelia needs to deal with them, and the local color, not only of place but of time, are already vivid in the author's mind, so she can spend her time on the creative process, rather than research.

Many professions and hobbies, from antiques to zoology, lend themselves to the development of amateur detectives. Being able to tell a Ming vase from a T'ang, knowing the nocturnal habits of the gorilla, or recognizing that the Arapaho generally buried their dead while the Lakota left the bodies on scaffolds all might serve your detective. Whatever bit of arcane knowledge your character possesses must, remember, be shared with the reader early; your detective cannot spring that kind of information as part of the solution if the average reader cannot be expected to know it.

One of your character's most important attributes is the power of observation (and it should go without saying that all detectives share that). Because the mystery novel, when well done, is also a social commentary; your hero's sense of what is going on is something not only shared with the reader but, more often than not, a clue. The idiosyncrasies of the suspects, the vase out of place, the slip of the tongue — everything that happens — must be observed. What makes the busybody protagonist so effective is the fact that he or she knows everything about the neighbors and doesn't have to go door to door, as the police do, to gather background.

The expert shares that ability to a degree: An art dealer/detective knows all the gossip in his little world; that knowledge helps him eliminate some suspects and pinpoint others. It also gives the police a reason to call on him.

Forget about citizen arrests. The amateur, having brought all the information together, has to get it to the attention of a law enforcement agency. If a series is set in a small town, it is more than likely that one particular police office is going to become the detective's foil. As you create that secondary character, use discretion: All too often the police are depicted as being bumbling at best and corrupt and incompetent at worst. The police, however, are bound by rules of evidence, Miranda warnings, and a ton of procedural directives, most of which preclude their doing things an amateur relies on. (I don't doubt that 75 percent of the evidence an amateur gathers would be unusable at an actual trial.

Fortunately for the writer, reality sometimes takes a backseat to the puzzle.)

The classic amateur, then, is intelligent, knowledgeable, perhaps witty (though rarely a stand-up comic), sometimes reckless (doing things that a "normal" person would think twice about), and possesses the kind of charm that makes others — both readers and characters — comfortable to be with him.

In the course of the investigation, the amateur will teach the reader something, be it a sociological insight or why wine has "legs," but he isn't (in today's mysteries, at any rate) pedantic. These lessons often have something to do with solving the crime, so be certain they appear early on, giving the reader an opportunity equal to that of the detective.

Because most of the novels in this category do not depict a lot of violence, your detective need not be preternaturally strong; it is a battle of wits rather than fisticuffs and flying lead that makes up the action. More than in any other form of mystery, the amateur hero allows for character/reader identification. And that brings the reader back for more.

## The Private Investigator

In both real and philosophical terms, the private investigator fulfills the definition of the word "hero." The P.I. is often likened to a knight on the Grail hunt; rather than a chalice, the detective is looking for Justice.

Your investigator, therefore, is first and foremost a moral person with a very strong sense of right and wrong. Once right of center politically, that attitude seems to be shifting today as younger writers with a different sociopolitical background begin to emerge (bringing a different sense of political correctness, and thus justice, with them). While the police characters in your P.I. novel will often be disparaging in their comments about, and descriptions of, your hero (sleazy seems to be a popular adjective), the private detective has a firm sense of right and wrong, and adheres to it unwaveringly.

In the real world, P.I.'s generally do not get involved in active murder cases; they do look for missing persons, investigate errant spouses and, increasingly, offer security services — fighting employee theft and industrial espionage — and sometimes even work for the police. A common hook in fiction is the murder that's uncovered during the course of another investigation.

Most of the private detectives being created today owe much of their character to the works of Raymond Chandler, Dashiell Hammett and Ross Macdonald. A loner, the P.I. tends toward cynicism and world weariness. (John Lutz's Alo Nudger lives on antacid tablets.) While that form of characterization can still be successful, there's something to be said for pushing the boundaries.

Marcia Muller, Sue Grafton and Sara Paretsky have all created very successful series featuring female detectives. Joseph Hansen's David Brandstetter is a gay insurance investigator, and other writers are taking the definition of "detective" and turning it on its side as they explore the world of crime.

There's been a debate among the members of the Private Eye Writers of America as to what constitutes a private detective. He or she does not work for an official law enforcement agency—that's first. But whether or not the detective is licensed by the state is open to question. In a formal sense, the character should be, and the license comes as a result of previous law enforcement training, either as a police officer or as an employee of a security agency such as Pinkerton. In order to obtain a license, the detective usually has to post a bond. The laws vary from state to state, so you'll want to check on the background your character needs.

Because the P.I. walks the infamous "mean streets," and is likely to be coming into contact with hardened criminals (the difference between the "cozy"—which features amateurs—and hard-boiled fiction, as Chandler pointed out in his essay "The Simple Art of Murder," is that in the latter novels crimes are committed by the kinds of people who really commit them, for the reasons they really commit them, and in the way they are really committed), the P.I. will be as likely to be armed as not and have some physical abilities that allow for self-defense. (There have been, however, some handicapped detectives: deaf, blind, in a wheelchair. Obviously, things work a bit differently for them.) Given the necessary background to obtain a license, the skills and training can be quickly put in place without upsetting the willing suspension of disbelief. Without a license, even if the tale is noir or hard-boiled, the detective is an amateur.

The investigator is, traditionally, a social commentator, someone seeing the world through a jaundiced, often bloodshot eye. The nature of the work means the hero is dealing with people whose lives are not quite in order: runaways, cheating husbands or wives, abusers and hardened criminal elements; it is not difficult to understand why they go home feeling all is lost. While you want to have these emotions— and the insights they lead to—expressed, you will also want to achieve a certain balance, one of the reasons so many P.I.'s are given to one-liners. This wit, even if it is bitter, serves to offset the darkness that is part of the genre.

Unlike the amateur, a private detective has a deep network of sources, as well as investigative and surveillance skills, learned and honed in the back story. A skill in photography is more than reasonable, and knowledge of the proper use of electronic eavesdropping equipment wouldn't be unlikely for someone entering the business today, while computer abilities — including hacking — can almost be assumed.

The relationship between the police and the P.I. has become cliché: There always seems to be a sergeant or lieutenant threatening to pull the investigator's ticket or telling him to keep out of a case. The nature of the P.I.'s job makes it plausible to assume some conflict: Families will hire investigators to help clear the accused in some criminal action — they might, for instance, be called in to help find a missing witness who can substantiate an alibi. (In fiction, the witness often shows up dead and the games begin.) Clichés have their place, but it is also reasonable to assume that your hero will have friends in the department, know someone at the Department of Motor Vehicles, the phone company or other agencies. And somewhere along the line, the detective is going to have to pay in similar coin for the help received from those sources.

Other interpersonal relationships have already been discussed. Significant others (past or present) can be around, but the interaction should not stop the action of the story, though events experienced in one adventure should allow the hero to grow through the series. The detective's role is to set things right, to find justice. And justice, as we know all too well, is not necessarily what is found in a court of law.

Like the amateur then, the P.I., while perhaps more aware of legal protocol, is likely to bend the rules. The end very much justifies the means.

## The Police Procedural

Not ten feet from where I sit in Riverside Park penning these lines on a notepad, members of the New York City Police Department's Emergency Services Unit (NYPD ESU) are hip deep in the murky waters of the Hudson River, attempting to retrieve a body (floater). At the scene are sixteen patrolmen (uniforms), four blue-and-white patrol cars (radio mobile patrols, or RMPs), an emergency medical service ambulance (EMS bus). I have to wonder how many calls to 911 for an ambulance are going unanswered: The floater is beyond any service the paramedics might perform. Is their presence now legally required at the scene?

An older officer (hairbag), looking about ready to retire (pull the pin), is making jokes — "Don't tug too hard, fella, you might rip his head off" — while the rubbernecking civilians (vultures) turn several shades of pale. The body's been in the water for about two months; not a pretty sight. Indeed, it's been floating for longer than one of the patrolmen, as pale as the vultures, has been with the department (in the job). The hairbag tells the rookie he's lucky. His first DOA might have been a crispie (burn victim).

The police procedural is a relatively new form in the mystery, first gaining recognition in the 1940s. It has a lingo all its own, and an ever-changing set of rules, since police departments are always updating and amending their procedures. The form is particularly challenging because you, as a writer, must keep up with the regs in the town you've chosen to depict. That's one of the reasons Ed McBain's popular 87th Precinct novels are set in fictional Isola. If you are using a real city, the people who live there and, certainly, the local policemen are going to know if you make a mistake.

Investigations are carried out by detectives assigned to various squads and units. They've risen through the ranks and are hardened, usually, to the things they see and deal with on a daily basis. Their lives are in a constant state of risk, and they are never really off duty. Very few people understand the pressures — that's why most cops only have cops as friends. It is why the divorce rate is so high among officers, and why most departments have a bow-and-arrow or rubber gun squad: assignments that keep an officer out of the line of fire and out of the public's eye as well. Those are the forces shaping your character. He or she might know that justice isn't being served, but will be bound by law to perform in a certain way. The conflicts those forces cause, coupled with the lack of manpower and hours in the day, multiplied by the policeman's drive to bust the perp all have to be part of the detective you create.

Another reality is that a caseload might have as many active files as the imagination allows. While your detective is going to focus on one particularly heinous crime, other elements and story lines will weave through the tapestry of your procedural. That means your hero is something of a juggler.

Cops come in all shapes and sizes and a variety of physical conditions; their training makes them capable of dealing with just about any situation you will create — at least to some degree. Most of them never actually draw their weapons in anger, never fire except on the range. Of course, fiction is rarely served by that reality; make certain, though, that the weapons they use in your story are the ones that might be available to them.

Among the peripheral characters you will have to create are other officers (most police detectives work in groups; the lone wolf principle doesn't always apply in this category), the various support personnel provided by city agencies, and stoolies. A cop's job is gathering information that leads to the apprehension of a criminal; in addition to the neighborhood canvasing at a crime scene, then, your officer is going to have to turn to a variety of street people to gather the information he needs. Most informants are criminals themselves—petty thieves, drug addicts, minor mobsters. The relationship is symbiotic. The cop gives a little to get a lot. The cops are also very protective of their sources: They rarely reveal names or turn the stoolie over to another cop, and when something happens to a source, the cop takes it personally.

Department brass may become involved—there's always pressure from the mayor, isn't there?—and municipal politics will, therefore, probably become a subplot element. If this begins to take over the story, though, shift gears and get back to the case at hand.

While procedurals are, almost by definition, the most realistic mysteries, your detective must still be slightly larger than life. The vogue today allows for cops who have very wealthy backgrounds, who have law degrees, who have the same kind of special expertise one might expect to find in an amateur. This gives you a lot of latitude in the development of your hero; used judiciously, you can create very engaging characters, men and women who are believable, acceptable and can get the job done.

Like P.I.'s, the police use a mordant wit to protect themselves from the brutality that surrounds them. As in any organization devoted to life-and-death issues—from the coroner's office to the army—there is a lot of razzing, good-natured and often purposeful banter, and a sense of camaraderie that borders on urgency. That psychology will have to be part of the characters you create if you want your particular homicide squad to have not only a successful arrest-to-conviction rate, but also a successful reorder rate at the bookstore as well.

## A Classic Combination

Having developed your detective, no matter which genre you choose (and the list of possible sleuths goes on: lawyers, forensics specialists, doctors; your detective will, ultimately, fall into one of the three basic foundation categories of criminous fiction), you have to come up with a worthy opponent, a criminal, a villain, that your reader will want caught. (No one cheers the Sheriff of Nottingham on in his pursuit of Robin Hood, after all.)

In the amateur ranks, the criminal is not, usually, a sociopathic personality. The crimes tend to be of passion, the result of overpowering love, lust or greed, and not the work of someone who makes illegal doings a way of life. These amateurs are also far more clever than most real criminals; they seem, even in what appears to be a spontaneous crime, to have the time to take steps to hide the fact and then are tripped up by their own brilliance when they are faced down by the hero. Yours will probably have a surface charm, but will reveal an underlying nastiness as the pressure mounts, especially in stories that turn on greed.

They also must be acceptable company. Because these villains are often part of the amateur detective's social set, the reader has to see them as part and parcel of the hero's daily life. At the same time, as we know, there are poseurs at every level. By mixing well, having the "pro-life" lady professor dine beside the killer, you fulfill the need for social commentary and the appetite for the red herring that is a mystery reader's culinary delight.

In the police procedural and P.I. story, however, the bad guys really are bad. Some villains have been almost as popular as the detectives stalking them: Moriarty, Sherlock Holmes's nemesis comes to mind, as do SMERSH and SPECTRE from the James Bond saga, and, more recently, Hannibal Lecter of *Red Dragon* and *The Silence of the Lambs*, by Thomas Harris. Again, the character portrayed is painfully clever, a master criminal, plotting carefully, having knowledge and resources that leave most of us in the dust. (While this isn't realistic, your readers will expect it.) Because a successful criminal must be a bit of a con artist, your villain can be charming, almost dazzling. And, depending on the direction in which you wish to go with your crime writing, having someone escape to kill again (or at least threaten to) is fine. Generally speaking, however, if you are creating a master criminal, it's best not to make him a murderer.

It cannot be emphasized enough that the villain and the hero have to be matched; the congruence, however, does not have to be strength for strength. The detective may not be as "brilliant" as the criminal, but she knows how to use the resources available to her; the investigator may not be as physically strong, but he knows a psychological trick or two and can exploit a perceived chink in the perp's armor.

The villain must also suit the crime. A murderous personality might commit a robbery in the course of committing another crime, but breaking-and-entering is not his thing; a safecracker might have to kill someone, but he doesn't leave a trail of bodies.

Spend as much time creating your villain as you do the detective; they are co-leads in the drama you're producing, and maintaining that kind of balance makes your book a more entertaining read.

The mystery, as it currently sells, is not a novel of especially complex character; when characterization becomes a strong point, the book is suddenly elevated to the ranks of mainstream fiction. Following the basic guidelines will allow you to create the kinds of mysterious people you need for the creation of successful criminous tales. Anything you want to add beyond that is to the good of the genre. After all, if it doesn't change and grow, no matter how slowly and subtly, it will become moribund.

The development of the mysterious people you need for your crime fiction follows the pattern of all character portrayal, of course. It is in the functions they perform, in the style of the story, that the crucial differences lie. There are private detectives whose creators have chosen to tell their stories in the cozy form more often used to tell the tales of the amateur sleuth. And there have been some amateurs who are as hard-boiled as any private dick on the streets. Language and action will be dictated by those choices. The drive of the detective, however, will not. There is a crime to be solved, and your detective can do it . . . with charm, style, intelligence, an occasional outburst of temper, and in no more than a page less than it takes the reader.

## Creating the Sidekick

There is, of course a third character type that adds to the charm of many mysteries: the sidekick, the buddy, the assistant. There have been several famous ones in literature: Holmes's Watson, Nero Wolfe's Archie Goodwin, and Travis McGee's Meyer are among the more memorable.

The way a sidekick is to be used pretty much dictates what kind of character you are going to create. Watson relates the tale, serves as a foil to emphasize Holmes's brilliance, acts as a gofer, but rarely does anything concrete in terms of solving the case at hand.

Goodwin is Nero Wolf's legman; he's the one on the streets, the one getting into fights, and the one who brings the information to Wolfe, who can then present the solution. Other "buddies" may share the action more directly with the detective, but in the end it is the hero who gets the credit.

There's no hard-and-fast rule saying you need a sidekick, but you might have a character in mind who's just too good to pass up. As we've seen, the most important function of this person is to allow the author, through the hero, to present information to the reader: "This is what I've discovered so far, this is what I'm thinking and why." If you are having trouble getting the facts to the reader as your story is structured, adding the sidekick will help.

As a character, the sidekick is typically not an equal to the detective, not as smart, not as "good" at the job. He cannot be incompetent, however, because the sidekick does share in the action of the story, an essential function, advancing the plot actively by being part of it.

## Introduction to True Crime
*by Gary Provost*

### The Father of the Modern True Crime

November 16, 1959, Truman Capote, then a well-established and much-celebrated fiction writer who had turned increasingly to journalism, was intrigued by a small story on page thirty-nine of the *New York Times*. It was a story about a wealthy Kansas farmer, Herb Clutter, who had been murdered in his home along with his wife and two kids. The family members had been tied up and shotgunned in the middle of the night. Capote was inspired to drive to Kansas where he intended only to write a magazine article for *The New Yorker* about how such a brutal murder affects a community. But this story swept into his life as suddenly as any tornado surging across those midwestern plains, and he was caught up in it, almost, it seemed, against his will. For the next several years Capote could think of little else.

In 1966 Random House published the fruits of Capote's obsession, the book called *In Cold Blood*. It became the most discussed book of our time. Capote's 384-page story about the murder of the Clutter family in Kansas, the investigation that followed, and the arrest, trial, imprisonment and execution of the killers, Dick Hickock and Perry Smith, brought attention to the publishing industry that has never been equalled, unless you count the *Satanic Verses* controversy of 1989, which was really about censorship, not about a book.

Gerald Clarke in his impressive biography, *Capote* (Simon & Schuster, 1988), writes,

> *When the book was published in January 1966, the modern*
> *media machine—magazines, newspapers, television and radio—*
> *became a giant band that played only one tune: Truman Capote.*
> *He was the subject of twelve articles in national magazines, two*
> *half-hour television programs, and an unparalleled number of ra-*
> *dio shows and newspaper stories. His face looked out from the*
> *covers of* Newsweek, Saturday Review, Book Week *and the* New
> York Times Book Review, *which gave him the longest interview*
> *in its history.* Life *ran eighteen pages, the most space it had ever*
> *given a professional writer, and advertised its huge spread by con-*
> *tinuously flashing the words "In Cold Blood" on the electronic*
> *billboard in Times Square. "Such a deluge of words and pictures*
> *has never before been poured out over a book," observed a some-*
> *what dazed-sounding reporter for the* New York Times.

When *In Cold Blood* came out I was twenty-two years old. I inhab-
ited a one-room apartment in Manhattan, and I earned my living—forty-
five dollars a week—by running errands for a watch company. I was a
struggling writer who had not published a word. Though it had not
occurred to me to write a true crime book and would not for another
sixteen years, I was thrilled by the attention Capote got for his book. I
saw myself as a writer and he was one of "us." I remember staring
dreamily at the tall stacks of *In Cold Blood* piled in the windows of
bookstores along Fifth Avenue. My heart beat faster just because an
author was finally getting as much attention as a movie star or an all-
star third baseman. And when I saw that one national magazine had
Capote's picture on the cover along with the bold headline, "Death
Spurs a Masterpiece," I was beside myself, not with envy, but with
hope. It seemed to me that I had witnessed the ultimate dream of an
author coming true. What could be better than to have a national magazine put you on the cover and say that your book is a masterpiece?
Capote's success strengthened my resolve to become a writer.

During this publicity blitz a good deal was written about the form
of the book. Capote was a master of self-promotion, and he insisted
that he had done something entirely unique. He brought a new term,
"nonfiction novel," into the literary lexicon, and he was fond of telling
the press that he had invented a new art form. In fact, he hadn't. The
telling of true stories in fictional form is certainly as old as storytelling
itself. While the term "nonfiction novel" is sometimes useful, it is never
really correct. Capote's biographer, Clarke, writes:

*In Cold Blood was a remarkable book, but it is not a new art form. Indeed, the term he coined, nonfiction novel, makes no sense. A novel, according to the dictionary definition, is a fictitious prose narrative of considerable length: If a narrative is nonfiction, it is not a novel; if it is a novel, it is not nonfiction.*

Clarke's criticism nonetheless, Capote had written an excellent book, arguably the best true crime ever written. If he hadn't invented the technique of writing a true story as if it were a novel, he was at least its best-known practitioner and most enthusiastic promoter. His book brought more attention to the true crime book than any other. Because Capote's book was masterfully written and because he chose to do it at all, the true crime book was elevated to the level of literature.

## What Is a True Crime Book?

So, *In Cold Blood* is what we mean when we say a true crime book. We also mean *Helter Skelter, The Stranger Beside Me, Bad Blood, The Boston Strangler, The Hillside Strangler, Son, Nutcracker, At Mother's Request* and *Fatal Vision* to name just a few of the best-known ones. There are hundreds more, because true crime has long been one of the most popular types of book. In fact, as I write this we are in the midst of a true crime boom. *Bitter Blood*, by Jerry Bledsoe, and *Small Sacrifices*, by Ann Rule, have only recently departed from the best-seller lists, each after residing there for many months. The same can be said for *The Mormon Murders*, by Steven Naifeh and Gregory White Smith; *Blind Faith*, by Joe McGinniss; *Perfect Victim*, by Christine McGuire and Carla Norton; and *Missing Beauty*, by Teresa Carpenter. My own book, *Without Mercy*, has been on some regional best-seller lists and has been featured on several national television programs. *Small Sacrifices* and *Blind Faith* have been television movies in the past season, and I'm sure that some of the others will be showing up on the tube.

"We're going through a huge surge in the popularity of the true crime book, both paperback and hardcover, right now," said Charles Spicer of St. Martin's Press, one of the editors I interviewed on this subject. Other editors agreed. They also agreed with Spicer's prediction that, "Like any other boom, there will be a winnowing out process."

So maybe when you read this book, true crime books will still be as fabulously popular as they are right now, or maybe they won't. But some high level of popularity is assured. The enormous audience for good true crime books and stories may shrink and swell over the years like the audience for any kind of book, but it has remained large and enthusiastic for decades and will continue that way for a long time. That audience of readers will welcome you with open arms and they will gladly pay the price of a book if you can write one that is exciting, compelling, fascinating and frightening. In order to do that, of course, you first need to know just what a true crime book is.

The term "true crime" represents a genre in publishing. That is, it's a type of book. Romance is a genre. Thriller is a genre. Private detective is a genre. These genres are labels that are put on books so that the publisher can assess and target the audience. When the publisher's salesperson goes into a bookstore, he can say *"Fatal Rain* is a new true crime by Scooter McElroy," which tells the bookstore owner a lot more about the potential sales than, *"Fatal Rain* is a new book by Scooter McElroy."

Obviously, the content of a book is going to be the prime indicator of what genre it is. A story about mice who can fly is never going to be mistaken for a political thriller. But since books don't always fall neatly into a category, the publishers have to do a bit of arbitrary defining. So, to a certain extent, a book is whatever genre the publisher says it is. A novel about a young man who solves his father's murder, for example, might be a mystery to one publisher, a psychological novel to another, and a young adult novel to a third.

What all this means to you is that not all books that are true and have crime in them are "true crimes" to the publisher. And if a book is not regarded as a true crime, then the publisher can't assume that it will appeal to that vast true crime audience. Thus, he might not buy your book, or might not offer you as much money for it as he would for a true crime.

So you can see where it would be handy for you to know what a publisher means when he says "true crime." Don't despair, I've looked into that for you.

I've talked to several editors about this and, not surprisingly, they all agreed that *All the President's Men*, for example, was certainly not a true crime book, even though it was true and was, to a large extent, about some crimes. They also agreed that a book about a Mafia hit man would not be a true crime.

"That," says Charles Spicer, "would be a 'mafia book,' a separate genre."

My own book, *Finder: The True Story of a Private Detective*, deals with a good many crimes, but it is not really considered to be a true crime book. It is the biography of Marilyn Greene, the woman who finds missing people, and it is usually placed in the biography section in bookstores.

So not all books that are true and about crimes are necessarily part of the genre called "true crime." Then what is it that makes a book a true crime?

Charles Spicer at St. Martin's says, "I define a true crime book as one involving a murder. It's not about art theft, it's not about governmental cover-up. It's really a case involving a murder in which there's an investigation and usually a trial." Spicer says that among his favorite true crimes are Joe McGinniss's *Blind Faith* and Linda Wolfe's *Wasted*.

"I'm looking for a true crime where there's a story," he says. "I'm looking for something that's not just a magazine piece. If somebody just goes up to West Forty-second Street and shoots somebody, that's not really the stuff of a book. There just isn't enough there. You have to have layers. The best of the true crimes give you some insight into characters, usually the character of the killer, and the situation that produced the crime. I'm doing a book right now about a woman from a well-to-do Virginia family who murdered her parents. The author dug into the past of the family and that of the girl and the result is that while we may not sympathize with her we have an understanding that we didn't have before."

Spicer, like all the editors I quote in this piece, reads dozens of true crime proposals and manuscripts every year. He buys and publishes several, and he also reads the true crimes of other publishers to keep up with the field.

Another editor I spoke to is a woman at Putnam whom we will call Betsy, because she does not want her real name used. Putnam, like St. Martin's Press, is one of the top publishers of true crime books. Betsy says, "To me a true crime is the nonfiction equivalent of a mystery. It has interesting people involved and there's a good investigation." Her favorite true crime is *Blood Will Tell*, by Gary Cartwright, which she says is "one of the best true crime books ever written.

"Cartwright's book is great," Betsy says, "because he spends sixty pages setting the scene in Texas and explaining what Texas is and what Fort Worth is and who these people are. A sense of place is a very big factor in that book. I think if your book takes place in a great place and you evoke it well, it helps a lot."

Hyperion senior editor Brian DeFiore (while an editor at Avon Books) told me, "I don't think a true crime has to have a murder. But it has to have an illegal act, and victims, and it needs some sort of investigation that brings the criminal to justice." DeFiore is an editor both for paperback reprints and hardcover and softcover original true crimes. One of his reprints, the best-seller *Perfect Victim*, is a good example of a true crime that has no murder. (It is the story of a woman who went hitchhiking one day in 1977 and was kidnapped by a man who kept her prisoner in a coffinlike box under his bed for seven years.) DeFiore's idea of a great true crime book? *Fatal Vision*, by Joe McGinniss, and *Blood and Money*, by Thomas Thompson.

DiFiore says, "I like to see real psychological insight into a character, both of the victim and of the criminal. I like to see real in-depth research into the place where the crime happened. A strong sense of place is important so that the reader can almost understand how such a crime could happen in such a place."

In an article in *Publishers Weekly*, Carolyn Reidy, then president of Avon books, currently president and publisher of trade books at Simon & Schuster, noted what she saw as three themes common in true crime books: (1) there are murderers among us; (2) money can't hide evil or buy happiness; and (3) I may have the potential for this evil in me, too. Of these themes, Reidy says, "People these days feel threatened by their perception of increasing violence all around. There is both a desire to understand and a vicarious thrill in reading about violence."

## What Does Allan Say?

The publishing industry is notoriously unsophisticated about market research. There are no reliable surveys on just who buys and reads true crimes, and no one really knows if the audience is predominantly male or female, young or old, or anything else. We know which books have sold well, but beyond that we don't really know what the readers like and what they hate. So in the absence of a survey of thousands, I have conducted my own survey of one: Allan Provost, who, as it happens, is my brother.

Allan is an avid reader of true crimes. They are, by far, his favorite books. He has read hundreds of them and he knows what makes him turn pages and what bores him silly. He is the quintessential reader of true crimes, and so we will turn to him to see what at least one reader thinks.

As for what makes a good true crime, Allan has some definite preferences:

> To me a good true crime is about people doing things which, if put in a novel, nobody would believe. Like the book Beyond Belief, about people who were kidnapping children and making

*recordings of them. Also, these books are about people who can't see what's happening around them, and it seems inconceivable that they couldn't see it. Like in Jack Olsen's* Son, *it's so hard to believe that a woman can live with this man and not have a clue that he's going out and raping people every day.*

*Also I like a book where the victim is chosen for a reason. I don't like books where the victims are picked at random and could be anybody. For example, I would not be interested in a book about the guy who did the shooting at the McDonald's. On the other hand, if it's about a postal worker who went back to work and murdered his fellow employees because he had a grudge against them, that would be okay. For me, there must be a reason for the victim to be the victim.*

*There doesn't have to be a murder, and there doesn't have to be a lot of money. For me these books are a pyschological study. They are about the way people behave, and the good ones make you say, "Aren't people amazing?"*

## Q&A With Marcia Muller
*by Robin Gee*

In the early 1970s when Marcia Muller began writing, women characters in mystery, with few exceptions, were limited to two basic types: genteel old ladies who solved crimes between cups of tea and sultry dames who happened to be victims, girlfriends, murderers or all three. An avid reader of private eye novels a la Ross Macdonald and Raymond Chandler, Muller decided it was high time for a female P.I., and, dry-witted, quick-thinking, legal investigator Sharon McCone was born. Some fifteen books later McCone is still kicking about San Francisco, in and out of danger, and Muller has been credited with breaking the male-only barrier and opening the door to the likes of Sara Paretsky and Sue Grafton. In the following interview Muller describes her career and imparts some well-earned wisdom of interest to new and experienced mystery writers alike.

Q: *Did you read much mystery when you were growing up? Which authors or books made an impact on you then?*
MARCIA MULLER: When I was young, I read a lot of girls' series books. I especially liked the Judy Bolton series, by Margaret Sutton. Unlike some of these series, the Bolton books were not written by consensus of a group of people, but by one woman.

**Q:** *Were there any that you feel may have led directly to your interest in writing?*

**MULLER:** Sutton's books were so well-written I think I learned to write from reading them. Later I read a lot of Ross Macdonald's novels, which gave me the idea that I wanted to write mystery.

**Q:** *When was your first book published?*

**MULLER:** My first book was published in 1977 and it was a direct over-the-transom sale to the David McCay Company, a firm that published one mystery a month.

**Q:** *Did it star Sharon McCone? How was she "born"?*

**MULLER:** *Edwin of the Iron Shoes*, my first book, was a Sharon McCone mystery, but I first put Sharon on paper in 1973. It was the beginning of a long, four-year process. I knew from the start my manuscript would feature her, but I kept reworking the story. *Edwin* was actually the third complete manuscript written.

**Q:** *I notice you have several books to your credit. After your first sale, did you become a full-time writer right away?*

**MULLER:** I've been a full-time writer since 1984. Before that I was a partner in an editorial consulting firm with two other women. Both of them, by the way, are now mystery writers too.

**Q:** *Many say you are a pioneer in the field—one of the first to introduce a female private investigator. Was this a conscious decision and did you or Sharon have any problems being accepted in this (until recently) male-dominated field?*

**MULLER:** I had always liked Ross Macdonald and read many mysteries featuring private eyes. At the time I started writing, however, none of these featured women detectives. I just knew I couldn't write as a male in first person. I noticed, too, at that time, I began seeing more female police and district attorneys (in real life). Women were slowing starting to move into those nontraditional fields.

I don't think of myself as a pioneer, but just that I tried to do something a little different. I did get a lot of responses to my manuscripts saying no one was going to believe this character in this role, but that changed very, very quickly. Publishers began to catch up to reality and realized that a great deal of their readers were women.

**Q:** *I notice some of your books feature another protagonist. Tell me about Elena Oliverez. Do you plan to do more books about her?*

**MULLER:** Elena was a curator of Mexican art in an art museum. It was a limited, three-book series. Joanna Stark was a three-book series too. She was partner in a security firm that dealt exclusively with museums and art galleries. I don't have plans for any more of these right now.

I've been continuing with the McCone series. In fact, I've just completed one, *Wolf in the Shadows*, due out in July (1993). The one after that, the one I'm working on, is also in the series. For now I call it *Turnaround Man*, but that may change.

**Q:** *Does having a title in mind help you keep your focus on the work?*

**MULLER:** Sometimes I find a title will restrain my writing. Once I was working on a book titled *The Butcher Cut Him Down*. Once I got into the book I just couldn't make it fit that title. It was not the same book it was when I started. Now I like to remain as flexible as possible about titles.

**Q:** *A few of your books are collaborations with your husband, Bill Pronzini. How was that?*

**MULLER:** I coauthored *Beyond the Grave*, an Elena Oliverez book, with my husband. He also writes mystery, and his protagonist is a private investigator, so it was just inevitable that our characters would meet and we'd work together on a mystery. We also collaborated on two anthologies. One was a volume of mystery short stories. The other dealt with the Western field.

**Q:** *What was putting together an anthology like?*

**MULLER:** It wasn't hard. It's just a matter of establishing a theme for the book and reading and selecting stories. After that there's the mechanics of writing an introduction and securing permissions. We also did a five-pound critical work on mystery and detective novels, *1001 Midnights*. Putting together a book of reviews like that was a horrible project. We had to coordinate a large group of people doing all the reviews. The problem was by the time we got it done, it was already becoming out-of-date. Soon after we finished it, there was such an explosion of new mysteries.

**Q:** *I notice most of your books are with Mysterious Press. How are they to work with and what made you decide to go with them and stay with them?*

**MULLER:** Otto Penzler started his press with the backing of Warner Books, and three years ago it was sold to them. Now Mysterious Press is one of their imprints. It was nice to start with a small publisher because of the personal attention I received, and I had a terrific editor there. Actually, I ended up there because of editor hopping. Sara Ann Freed, my editor at the time, had been at Walker and we had such a good relationship. When she ended up at Mysterious, so did I.

**Q:** *Are you contracted to do a certain number of books for them?*

**MULLER:** I'm committed to two, but I try to have a new book out each July.

Q: *That sounds like a lot of pressure, even if it is self-imposed.*

MULLER: It doesn't put me under that much pressure, but all the personal appearances that go with a new book can. My publisher and I work well together, and I can discuss my concerns with them, which helps. So far, the schedule has not been a really big problem.

> ## *"I think at different points in your career you need a different agent, a different type of sales."*

Q: *Did you have an agent for your first book? Do you have the same agent now?*

MULLER: I've had several agents since I started. Immediately after my first sale, I got an agent. My first agent was good, but my second book was very hard to sell and she lost interest. Then I had another agent for a number of years. I think at different points in your career you need a different agent, a different type of sales. Right now I'm very happy with my latest one.

Q: *What would you say to a beginning writer about agents? Any tips on how to go about finding one?*

MULLER: Anyone who is serious needs an agent. They do so much more than just sell your work. They check your contract, negotiate it, and keep on top of things with the publisher. This is important because it frees up time for the writer to write.

My advice is to get to know other writers. An established author may be willing to read your work and may even recommend an agent. And an agent is more likely to look at your work if it comes recommended from a client. In this business, personal connections pay off.

Q: *Which of your books would you consider your favorite, or do you have a favorite?*

MULLER: Usually the last book I completed is my favorite one. I always feel my books are getting better, but not until after they're delivered. For some reason I can't seem to feel this way about the one I'm currently working on. I'm very insecure about it until it's finished.

Q: *I know you live in California and are very familiar with the West Coast, but your vivid scenes and settings go beyond a simple working knowledge of the area. What kind of research do you do for your settings?*

MULLER: I'm not a native of California, but, still, I'm fascinated by the state. My books don't always take place in California. Some happen in other parts of the West, like Nevada.

I try to visit a place and take notes on tape. I also take lots of photos and cover my wall with them. More importantly, I read the history of the area. I think, if you've read the history, it's a good bet it will tell you lots about how a place is and how it got to be that way.

Q: *How do you keep track of your settings, especially the part that is fictional?*

MULLER: I create maps if I'm working on a fictional version of a real place. You have to be careful about using a real place, especially when it's a small town. You risk stepping on toes of people who live there. It's better to fictionalize it and move it. Sometimes I need a map to sketch out things like where the important places are. In the end it's like building a new town.

Q: *Your protagonist, Sharon McCone, works with a quirky bunch of characters at All Souls, a law cooperative. How and why did you choose to put your character in this nontraditional setting?*

MULLER: Before I started writing the McCone series, I attended a symposium at Berkeley called Women in the Law. There I met some women who were part of a law cooperative in Los Angeles. Cooperatives were popular at the time, the idea being to provide quality legal services at low cost. I chose this setting because I wanted Sharon to have more than the traditional, sleazy, private eye office with a bottle in the desk drawer. Over the years, All Souls has been fully developed within the series and from it I get lots of ideas for subplots.

> *". . . writers shouldn't be afraid to approach professionals like coroners or police. People love to talk and, if you offer to buy someone lunch, you'll have access to all sorts of information."*

Q: *How do you research the legal tactics and investigative techniques used in your books? Do you have any tips for writers interested in developing sources?*

MULLER: I have a large library in my home with books on true crime and crime text books. I also have a friend who is a private investigator. But writers shouldn't be afraid to approach professionals like coroners or police. People love to talk and, if you offer to buy someone lunch, you'll have access to all sorts of information.

When I started, I would have been terrified to approach those people, but I've found them to be tremendously helpful. I had one friend who was a financial advisor. I asked him about fraud and the guy turned out to be an armchair crook! It's amazing what people think about and how much they know.

## "Ideas can come from reading the newspaper, true crime accounts, even from other novels."

**Q:** *How do you get your ideas?*

**MULLER:** I do a lot of on-site research, and I read a lot in the genre. Ideas can come from reading the newspaper, true crime accounts, even from other novels. They can come from friends' experiences, too. The idea for Elena Oliverez, for example, came from a dinner with a friend who worked for a museum. With me it's not a problem of not having enough ideas. Instead, it's more that it's hard to use all the ideas that come to me.

**Q:** *To write a book a year, you must keep to a rigorous schedule. What is your day like?*

**MULLER:** I write every day, Monday through Friday, and sometimes over the weekend. I like to write in the morning for few hours, then come back to it late in the afternoon until about seven in the evening. Fortunately, my husband works the same odd schedule. I have a separate office in my home, so the commute is great!

**Q:** *Do you ever suffer from the dreaded "writers' block"? If so, how do you overcome it?*

**MULLER:** There are two kinds of writers' block. The first one is serious and stems from psychological problems such as clinical depression. But the second, more common, is just getting stuck. When I get stuck, I know I've somehow taken a misstep in the book, so I stop and play solitaire or something and try to just free associate for awhile. Other times, I have to get away from the work completely—get in car and drive, dig in the garden, anything. Eventually I'll come up with what the trouble is and be able to fix it.

**Q:** *How much revision do you do?*

**MULLER:** I do tons of revision. I do a first draft initially, but then I immediately rework it at the next sitting, making changes as the plot is progressing. When I do the final draft about 10 to 20 percent is still changed. It's an ongoing process.

**Q:** *Do you work from an outline?*

**MULLER:** I know other writers who do very detailed outlines which are almost full drafts, but I like to leave my plots very open-ended. I have a general idea how the story is going to end up, but even that is flexible. This is because a great deal of it stems from the characters. The plot evolves from them. I can't put it any other way. I'd be hard put to teach someone how it happens, but it does.

**Q:** *How do you handle clues?*

**MULLER:** It's a mixed bag. Sometimes clues come to me while I'm writing. Sometimes things in the story turn into clues. Other times I might go back and put something in. In other words, some clues are deliberately planted and others just surprise me.

**Q:** *Do you belong to a writers' group? Do you find them helpful?*

**MULLER:** I did belong to a writers' club in the beginning. I wrote my first novel while in a writing workshop. Writers' groups are helpful in that they force you to write something, but it all depends on the people involved.

## *"For new writers a conference is a good place to make connections."*

**Q:** *Do you attend conferences? How can they help a writer?*

**MULLER:** Yes, I do. For new writers a conference is a good place to make connections. For established writers conferences can be refreshing. You get feedback from readers and other writers and see old friends.

**Q:** *You helped open the door for so many women who write detective fiction, and now women sleuths and their authors are considered "hot." Where do you see the mystery field going in the next few years?*

**MULLER:** I don't follow trends, but I have noticed one thing that's extremely strong right now. It's an overall expansion and diversification of the field. There's literally something for everyone from extremely realistic novels of character, to tricky puzzle-type mysteries, with every kind of possible protagonist. I think this will continue.

**Q:** *Are there any particular books or authors you feel budding mystery writers should know?*

**MULLER:** I'm hesitant to name names, but I can say writers should have a good overview from Poe to the current mysteries. It's invaluable to know all the different types of mystery there are and to be able to place oneself in historical context. For private eye writers, they should especially know the greats like Chandler, Macdonald, etc. Visit a library mystery section and select books you want to read. They will give you a good indication of what you should be writing.

**Q:** *What nonfiction books or reference books would you recommend?*

**MULLER:** There are several nonfiction books on every aspect of the genre. One very helpful reference in my library is Allen J. Hubin's *Bibliography of Crime Fiction*. It contains information on almost everything published in mystery and there's a new edition every ten years. Also, for the beginning writer in general, I'd recommend a new book by Michael Seidman, a Walker Books editor, called *Living the Dream*. It's published by Carroll & Graf, and it gives a lot of good practical advice.

**Q:** *What would you say to an aspiring mystery author today?*

**MULLER:** The first thing I'd say is write the kind of book you want to read. You have to care a great deal about it—you can't just imitate someone else. Secondly, I'd say, sit down and write everyday. It's the only way to make it.

# The Markets

## Marketing the Mystery
*by Robin Gee*

You wouldn't think of writing a police procedural about a Los Angeles police detective without first finding out how real-life L.A.P.D. detectives operate. In addition to interviewing detectives and those associated with them, you'd probably spend several hours at the library. You owe it to your readers to give them an honest, well-researched novel. You also owe it to yourself to spend as much time researching the field to locate markets for your work. Finding just the right publisher for your mystery is as important as learning the ins and outs of a homicide investigation.

Marketing the mystery is similar to marketing any other commercial fiction. Most mysteries are published by large commercial publishing houses and, while these publishers may do many mysteries, the competition is stiff. For every book published, there are hundreds of manuscripts that will be rejected for a variety of reasons and many more that will not even be read.

A quality manuscript, polished to perfection, is a good first step, but it is far from the last step on the road to publication. In this age of fierce competition, writers must spend as much time and care on marketing their work as they do writing it. A well-developed marketing plan can mean the difference between rejection and publication.

## Types of Mystery Markets

Before beginning your search for markets, it's a good idea to determine what types interest you. Of all the different categories of commercial fiction, mystery is the most versatile. It is because of that versatility that you'll find a wealth of both traditional and nontraditional markets.

Traditional markets include book publishers and magazines. As noted above, large commercial publishers comprise the largest sector of the mystery publishing field. These publishers may produce hardcover, trade paperback or mass market paperback mysteries.

## Novel Markets

Hardcover mysteries are often books by established writers and are usually one-shot titles. Lately, the books of some well-known series mystery writers' have made it to hardcover. Suspense, thrillers, and mystery books with mainstream appeal or popularity among hard-core mystery fans can be found in hardcover.

Trade paperbacks present an attractive option for publishers unwilling to take the expensive risks involved in hardcover publishing, but want to sell to bookstores rather than retail chain stores or other mass market outlets. Established and new writers who have hardcover potential may be published in this form.

The bulk of mysteries published are mass market paperbacks. These are the ones found in grocery and chain store racks as well as some bookstores. Writers on all career levels are published in this format, but mass market is an especially good place for newer authors to start. Mysteries with broad appeal and mystery series do well as mass market titles. Today, many publishers prefer hard/soft deals in which they contract to bring a book out in both hardcover and mass market paperback form.

Small presses and independent publishers offer opportunities for mystery publication. Some independents are devoted solely to mystery and have built strong reputations with fans. Yet many small presses interested in fiction will consider mystery publishing. The financial rewards may not be as great with a small or independent press, but writers say the personal attention and control they have over their books make these publishers very attractive. Small presses are often more receptive to new writers and writers whose work might be considered too literary or experimental for commercial houses.

While only a handful publish fiction, book packagers and producers can offer opportunities for mystery writers. Packagers produce books for other publishers and quite often work on book series. Either the publisher or the packager will come up with the idea for the book or series, but it is the packager who develops the book, hires the writer and artist, and produces the finished product. Most work done for packagers is work-for-hire—writers are paid a flat fee and the copyright belongs to the publisher. Quite often the writer will receive no credit for the book and will write under a pseudonym. New writers may find book packagers are a nice way to ease into publishing. The editors who work for book packagers play an important role in the development of the book and provide writers with background information and other help along the way.

## Short Story Markets

A few commercial magazines are devoted entirely to mystery. Many got their start as cheap pulp publications, but today these markets have excellent reputations for publishing some of the best mystery available. In addition to these, several other commercial magazines will consider mystery. Smaller publications are good markets too, especially for the new mystery writer. Look in mystery and general writers' organization newsletters and magazines for "calls for submissions" from publishers of mystery anthologies and other announcements regarding short fiction.

## Other Markets

As mystery continues to expand its audience, the number of nontraditional markets grows. BePuzzled and other puzzle and game manufacturers are looking for mystery stories that can be transferred to a puzzle format. The growing popularity of mystery dinner theaters and mystery train rides has opened up a small, but exciting market for mystery scripts. Comic book companies also look for mysteries with graphic appeal and a small but growing number of audio book publishers are looking for original fiction including mysteries.

No discussion of mystery markets is complete without mentioning scripts and screenplays. More mysteries are making it to the big screen these days, and television continues to offer opportunities for mystery episode and series scripts. For more information on script writing and marketing, see *Writer's Market* or the industry insider newsletter, *The Hollywood Scriptwriter* (Suite 385, 1626 N. Wilcox, Hollywood CA 90028). For script agents see the special section in *Guide to Literary Agents and Art/Photo Reps.*

## Choosing a Market

Any mystery editor will tell you the first place to learn about publishers and their needs is at the library or bookstore. Read as many mysteries as you can outside your interest area as well as within it. The more you read in the field, the more you will be able to determine which publishers might be interested in your work.

Mystery bookstores carry a wide variety of mystery and suspense books, and their owners are an excellent source of knowledge about the field. These booksellers are on the cutting edge of the mystery business and can direct you to exciting new authors and publishers. They also are privy to industry gossip and may be able to alert you to new publishers and changes within existing houses. This book includes an extensive list of mystery bookstores and a geographic index to help you find one near you. Even if you have to travel to another part of your state, a trip to a mystery bookstore can be a worthwhile eye-opener.

Don't ignore other independent bookstores in your search, especially if you are a new writer. Independent stores are most likely to stock books by small press and literary publishers, some of whom are open to mystery. These publishers are often very willing to work with new writers and many accept unagented submissions.

Next take a look at the market listings and read the interviews presented in this book. These offer insider views and information specific to the needs and interests of writers. See "How to Use This Book," starting on page 3, to find out exactly how you can use this book as a tool to help you target promising markets for your work.

After you've come up with a list of potential markets, the next step is to contact the publishers for additional information. Many have writers' guidelines available for a self-addressed, stamped envelope. Some offer catalogs for postage for a minimal charge. Study the guidelines for specific information on the publisher's needs and how best to approach them.

## About Agents

Not much more can be said about targeting publishers for your mystery manuscript without discussing agents. More and more commercial publishing houses are turning to agents as their sole source of submissions. The sheer volume of work, as well as cutbacks in many publishers' staffs, has forced them to use agents as first-readers to screen out inappropriate and unpublishable manuscripts.

Unfortunately for a new writer, getting an agent these days is almost as hard as getting published. Many writers try to market their first book themselves, because it's much easier to find an agent once you have at least one published novel under your belt. Some large publishers are willing to look at queries with sample chapters from new writers. If interested, they will request a complete manuscript. Independent and small presses tend to be more willing to look at unsolicited manuscripts, but check first before you waste your time and money.

If you are interested in publishers who require agented submissions, as do many of the large houses, take a look at the agents listed in this book selected from the *Guide to Literary Agents and Art/Photo Reps* (Writer's Digest Books); detailed information on these agents is available in the *Guide*. R.R. Bowker's *Literary Market Place* is another good source of agent names and addresses.

Approach agents as you would a publisher, with a query and sample chapters or a complete manuscript, depending on the agent's guidelines. It is generally acceptable to query more than one agent at a time, but avoid sending complete manuscripts to more than one agent for consideration.

Many writers get their agents through networking. For new mystery writers, joining Mystery Writers of America, Private Eye Writers of America, or another professional mystery writers' organization can be a good career move. You can make important contacts, particularly with published mystery writers, who may be willing to refer you. These groups hold regular conferences around the country offering opportunities to meet agents. Information on many of the mystery organizations and conferences is included in section four of this book.

Above all, remember your agent is your business partner. Take your time when looking for an agent and do not hesitate to ask questions. A good agent will not only get you the best deal, but will also act as a business liaison between you and the publisher. For more on how to find and work with an agent, read "Clues to the Literary Agent" starting on page 193.

## Manuscript Mechanics

Whether you approach an agent first or submit directly to a publisher, a professional presentation is essential. Granted, a poorly written manuscript will not make it out of a publisher's slush pile no matter how dazzling its presentation. Yet, on the other hand, a well-written piece will never be read if it's not presented properly. As one publisher says, "If it looks as though you don't care about your manuscript, why

Emma Slooth
222C Baker Street
New London, CT 02332

January 5, 1993

Ms. Abigal Baxter
Crabtree Publishing
112 86th Street, Sixth Floor
New York, NY 10101

Dear Ms. Baxter:

I am a mystery writer who recently sold two short stories to <u>Doyle's Mystery Magazine</u>. I am also a local historian for Farham county and use my expertise in post-war Connecticut history as background for my stories.

Both of my short stories feature amateur sleuth Elsie Boyd, a small-town newspaper reporter and antiques enthusiast. She is also the heroine of <u>A Perfect Time for Murder</u>, a 50,000-word novel I have completed. Elsie has a penchant for old clocks and is fairly good at repairing them, although there's not much call for her services in modern-day Fairport, Connecticut. While tinkering with an old mantle clock, Elsie finds a note inside the casing. It's a cry for help, and it's signed by Alice Horn, a woman whose remains were discovered last year in the trunk of a 1944 Ford excavated from Fairport Bay. Could the note lead to her killer, and is he or she still alive and residing in Elsie's hometown?

Your successful series by Barbara Smith and the bestseller <u>Forever Danger</u>, by Margaret Allan, both point to the continued popularity of female sleuths. <u>A Perfect Time for Murder</u> would bring a small-town perspective to your already strong line.

Enclosed are the first three chapters of my novel and a brief synopsis. May I send you the complete manuscript?

I look forward to hearing from you.

Sincerely,


Emma Slooth

Encl.: Three sample chapters
        Synopsis
        SASE

About the Author

Emma Slooth

Emma Slooth has been publishing both fiction and nonfiction since 1989. Her mystery stories have appeared in <u>Doyle's Mystery Magazine</u> and the <u>Mystery Place</u>, and she has published several nonfiction articles in a number of historical journals, including <u>Connecticut Historian</u> and the <u>World War II Journal</u>.

The star of Slooth's mysteries is Elsie Boyd, a reporter and antiques enthusiast. This love of antiques is shared by Slooth who operates a successful antiques and clock restoration business in upstate Connecticut. A history buff, Slooth is resident historian for Farham county.

<u>A Perfect Time for Murder</u> is Slooth's first full-length novel. She is currently working on a second Elsie Boyd novel, <u>Behind the Beveled Glass.</u>

Ms. Slooth lives with her husband and daughter in New London, Connecticut.

should I? I've got too many manuscripts to waste my time with one I can't read."

Ensure that your manuscript will be read and your talent has a fighting chance by making your manuscript as easy for the editor to read as possible. Manuscripts should be double-spaced with wide margins and relatively free of errors and cross outs. Before typing or computer printing, make sure you have a dark ribbon. Choose paper that will withstand being passed around — white bond rather than onion skin. Photocopies are fine as long as they are clear — and always keep a copy for yourself. Do not fax queries, submissions or other correspondence unless you have cleared it with the publisher first. For the most part, fax submissions are discouraged.

A word about computers: When sending a query with sample chapters or a complete unsolicited manuscript, send a hard copy, not a disk. Unless otherwise noted, publishers do not want unsolicited disk submissions. If a publisher has requested a complete manuscript, check to find out if disk submissions are acceptable.

## Queries, Cover Letters and Manuscript Formats

If you are asked to query a publisher first, chances are you will need to include a sample of your writing and some form of story outline. In fiction, the query letter should be as brief as possible (see sample A, page 56). You are simply asking the publisher if they would be interested in seeing your complete manuscript. Keep the letter to one page, preferably only a few paragraphs. You may choose to start the letter with a hook — something that will catch the editor's eye, but keep the hard sell to a minimum (one or two lines).

Be sure to identify the type of mystery you've written, how long it is, and where it might fit in this particular publisher's line. Information about yourself that may lend credibility to your work also should be included, but avoid giving a lot of extraneous personal information. For example, if your novel is about a dentist who happens to be an amateur sleuth in his off-hours and you are a dentist, by all means mention it. Beyond this, avoid giving details about your family or pets if they have nothing to do with your story. Other information to include in the query would be an estimated word count and a few of your publishing credits, if you have any. Occasionally, you'll be asked to send a "bio," short for "biographical statement." This is simply a brief description of your achievements (see sample B, page 57).

When sending sample chapters, always send the first three consecutive chapters. Editors want to know how your work flows and how you move from one chapter to the next. Include a cover sheet (see sample C, page 60) with either a partial or complete manuscript. Put your name, address and phone on the upper left-hand corner of the page and the word count in the right. Agented authors often leave the right-hand corner open for the agent's name and address, but some agents prefer their information should be the only material included on the cover sheet.

Center your title and byline about halfway down the page. Start your first chapter on the next page. If your chapter has a title, include it about one-third of the way down the page. Include your last name and page number in the upper right-hand corner of this and all subsequent pages. Be sure to carry page numbers all the way through to the end of the material.

Along with a query and sample chapters, you may be asked to include a synopsis, outline or summary. Unfortunately, publishers tend to use the terms interchangably, so when in doubt, check with the publisher. A synopsis is a brief summation of your story, condensed into a page or page-and-a-half, single spaced. An outline can run from five to twenty pages, double-spaced. An outline usually follows the chapters throughout the book, listing chapter headings and a few lines about what happens in each chapter. A summary is the most subjective of the terms, best defined by the particular publisher.

When sending a complete manuscript, include a cover letter (see sample D) rather than a query. Cover letters are simple and, again, should be kept very short. Don't tell much about the story—after all, it's all there for the editor to read. Basically, you are saying: "Here I am. Here is my mystery novel." You should include what type of mystery it is, how long it is, any pertinent information about yourself that lends credibility to the work, and why you selected this particular publisher.

For more information, several books by Writer's Digest Books can be helpful. For information on submitting to publishers, see *Writer's Market* or *Novel and Short Story Writer's Market*. For specifics on manuscript format see *The Writer's Digest Guide to Manuscript Formats*, by Dian Dincin Buchman and Seli Groves, and *Manuscript Submission*, by Scott Edelstein, a part of the Elements of Fiction writing series.

## More About Submission

In general, the above information applies to short fiction as well as to novels. Prepare your manuscript with care and research the magazines that interest you. Most of the time, magazine and anthology editors want to see the complete manuscript with a cover letter. Agents

Emma Slooth                                    50,000 words
222C Baker Street
New London, CT 02332

A Perfect Time for Murder

by Emma Slooth

Emma Slooth
222C Baker Street
New London, CT 02332

January 5, 1993

Ms. Abigal Baxter
Crabtree Publishing
112 86th Street, Sixth Floor
New York, NY 10101

Dear Ms. Baxter:

I am a mystery writer who recently sold two short stories to Doyle's Mystery Magazine. I
am also a local historian for Farham county and have used my expertise in post-war
Connecticut history as background for my stories.

Both of my short stories feature amateur sleuth Elsie Boyd, a small-town newspaper reporter
and antiques enthusiast. She is also the heroine of A Perfect Time for Murder, the 50,000-
word traditional mystery novel enclosed.

Your successful series by Barbara Smith and the bestseller Forever Danger, by Margaret
Allan, both point to the continued popularity of female sleuths. A Perfect Time for Murder
would bring a small-town perspective to your already strong line.

I look forward to hearing from you.

Sincerely,


Emma Slooth

Encl.: manuscript
      SASE

hardly ever handle short fiction (there just isn't enough money in it for them), unless as a favor to an author already under contract.

Most publishers are willing to look at simultaneous queries, and an increasing number consider simultaneous manuscripts. Keep in mind, however, that if more than one publisher expresses interest in the project, you will have to make a decision. It's common courtesy to let other publishers know if your manuscript has been sold.

Response time varies greatly with agents and publishers. It's best to wait two to three weeks after the stated response time before checking on the status of your submission. A follow-up letter should be courteous and brief, and you should include a SASE for a reply. Some writers prefer to call, but calls should be brief and kept to a minimum.

Keep careful records of your submissions. In addition to the name of the publisher and the nature of the submission, include the date you mailed it and dates of any correspondence. Record the date on which you receive a reply from the publisher. If accepted, keep track of your rewrite and other deadlines. If rejected, record any notes or encouragements accompanying the rejection. Not only will this information help you manage your submissions, but it can also help you make an informed decision when making future submissions.

Once you've sent your query or manuscript out, all you can do is wait. Unfortunately, the waiting can be the most grueling part. According to many writers, the best remedy for submission anxiety is to begin work on a new project.

## Short Story Markets
### Primary Markets
(Circulations over 5,000, or primarily mystery magazines)

The following markets were chosen as "primary" based on their circulations (over 5,000), their involvement with mystery, or whether they are paying markets. These factors also contribute to the competition a writer faces when submitting to these markets.

Many of the following magazines are available at newsstands and bookstores. It is advisable to become familiar with a magazine before querying. In addition to familiarizing yourself with the market, you also get to read some great mysteries.

Although many of these markets publish beginning writers, the competition is stiff, so they are probably not the best markets for new writers trying to break in. Those that are more suited to beginners, "secondary" markets for our purposes, follow this section.

# The Armchair Detective

▶ **Considers:** short stories
▶ **Categories:** private eye
hard-boiled detective
police procedural
cozy
amateur sleuth
malice domestic

**Address:** 129 W. 56 St., New York NY 10019, (212) 765-0902
**Contact:** Kate Stine, Editor
**Profile:** *The Armchair Detective* is "a magazine devoted to mystery and crime fiction. Every issue features an interview with a well-known mystery writer, portraits of little-known writers, historical overviews, criticism, book reviews and short fiction." Established 1967. Magazine: 8½ × 11; 128 pages. Published quarterly. Circulation: 4,500.
**How to Contact:** Send complete ms with cover letter. SASE preferred for query and ms response. Simultaneous submissions are OK. Receives 25 unsolicited mss/month. Accepts 2 mss/issue. Reports on queries in 2 months; on mss in 3 months. Sometimes comments on mss. Guidelines available for #10 SASE. Sample copy available for $7.50.
**Terms:** Pays $100-1,000 on publication. Buys all rights. Publishes ms 6 months after acceptance. Author reviews galleys.
**Tips:** "Writers eager to publish in *The Armchair Detective* have a better chance getting a nonfiction article accepted than a short story."

# Bepuzzled

▶ **Considers:** short stories (length:
4,000-5,000)
▶ **Categories:** young adult
juvenile
private eye
hard-boiled detective
cozy
amateur sleuth
romantic suspense
light horror

**Address:** Lombard Marketing, Inc., 45 Wintonbury Ave.,
Bloomfield CT 06002, (203) 286-4222
**Contact:** Sue Hardersen
**Profile:** *Bepuzzled* is a mystery puzzle, using verbal and
visual clues. Established 1987, 12 pages.
**How to Contact:** Query for submission guidelines. SASE
required for query and ms response. Simultaneous submissions are OK. Receives 3 unsolicited mss/month. Accepts 10-15 mss/year. Reports on queries in 1 week; on
mss in 2 months. Sometimes comments on mss. Guidelines available for SASE.
**Terms:** Pays $200 minimum on delivery of final ms. Buys
all rights. Publishes ms 6-18 months after acceptance.
**Tips:** It is advisable to become familiar with the product
before submitting.

# Boys' Life

▶ **Considers:** short shorts (length:
650 words)
short stories (length:
1,200 words)
▶ **Categories:** young adult
juvenile

**Address:** Boy Scouts of America, P.O. Box 152079, Irving TX 75015-2079, (214) 580-2000 Fax: (214) 580-2079
**Contact:** Kathleen DaGroomes, Fiction Editor
**Profile:** "Editorial content covers practically every interest of all boys." Established 1911. Magazine: 8 × 11; 65 pages. Published monthly. Circulation: 1,300,000.
**How to Contact:** Submit complete ms with cover letter. SASE required for query and ms response. Agented and electronic submissions are OK. Receives 160 unsolicited mss/month. Accepts 1-2 mss/issue. Reports on queries and mss in 6 weeks. Rarely comments on mss. Guidelines available; sample copy available for $2.50.
**Terms:** Pays $500 and up on acceptance. Buys first rights. Publishes ms up to 2 years after acceptance.
**Tips:** "No set of guidelines can substitute for careful reading of as many back issues as possible. *Boys' Life* can be found in the children's section of most libraries."

---

# ByLine

▶ **Considers:** short stories (length: 1,500-4,000)
▶ **Categories:** private eye
hard-boiled detective
police procedural
cozy
amateur sleuth
malice domestic
romantic suspense

**Address:** P.O. Box 130596, Edmond OK 73013, (405) 348-5591
**Contact:** Kathryn Fanning, Managing Editor
**Profile:** "We're aimed at helping writers succeed. Our fiction may be any kind of good story—general or mystery. Our readers are writers and therefore appreciate skillful writing." Established 1981. Magazine: 8½ × 11; 28

pages. Published 11 times/year. Circulation: 3,000.

**How to Contact:** Send complete ms with SASE. SASE required for query and ms response. Simultaneous submissions are "reluctantly accepted." Receives 100-125 unsolicited mss/month. Accepts 1 ms/issue. Reports on mss in 2-6 weeks. Comments on mss if writer requests. Guidelines available for SASE. Sample copy available for $3.50.

**Terms:** Pays $50 and 2 contributor's copies on acceptance. Buys first North American rights. Publishes ms 3 months after acceptance. Author gets bio notes.

**Tips:** "No excessive gore or explicit sex and violence. We do have student readers. Write well. Read a few back issues. Keep trying."

---

# Dagger of the Mind, Beyond the Realms of Imagination

▶ **Considers:** short shorts
short stories
novelettes

▶ **Categories:** private eye
hard-boiled detective
police procedural
amateur sleuth
malice domestic
romantic suspense
surrealistic mystery

**Address:** K'yi-Lih Productions, 1317 Hookridge Dr., El Paso TX 79925, (915) 591-0541

**Contact:** Arthur William Lloyd Breach

**Profile:** *"Dagger of the Mind*, from the onset, was a publication dedicated to the intellectual reader. As both a reader and writer I concern myself predominantly with the moral of the story rather than its trappings. I want *good* fiction that moves and makes you think. Don't retell old trite themes (the butler did it, ghosts, vampires and werewolves), *you* lead the way. Be a leader—not a follower. *That's* what gets my attention." Established 1990. Magazine: 8½ × 11; 62-86 pages. Published quarterly. Circulation: 5,000.

**How to Contact:** Send complete ms with cover letter. SASE required for query and ms response. Electronic submissions are OK. Receives 250 unsolicited mss/ month. Accepts 8-15 mss/issue. Reports on queries in 2 weeks; on mss in 3-4 months. Comments on mss. Guidelines available for 1 first-class stamp. Sample copy available for $3.50 and 5 first-class stamps.

**Terms:** Pays ½-1 cent/word plus 1 contributor's copy on publication. Buys first rights. Publishes ms 1 year after acceptance.

**Tips:** "Familiarize yourself with the market. I receive so many manuscripts per month that I don't have the time to read material that doesn't fit into my guidelines. Send in *only* your very best and make sure you send a good, clean copy. If you have a manuscript, be it fiction or nonfiction, and you're uncertain if what you've got will fit in with what I have, query with the idea."

# Ellery Queen's Mystery Magazine

▶ **Considers:** short shorts (length: 250 words minimum)

short stories (length: 9,000 words maximum, occasionally longer)

novelettes (length: 18,000 words — established authors only)

▶ **Categories:** private eye
hard-boiled detective
police procedural
cozy
amateur sleuth
malice domestic
psychological suspense
suspense
humorous mystery

**Address:** Dell Magazines, 1540 Broadway, New York NY 10036

**Contact:** Janet Hutchings

**Profile:** "The best of all types of mystery and suspense fiction. No sex, no violence and no sensationalism, please. We look for good writing as well as a good story." Established 1941. Magazine: Digest-sized; 160 pages (single issues) 288 pages (double issues). Published 13 times/year. Circulation: 350,000.

**How to Contact:** Send complete ms with SASE. In cover letter include bio and credits, but keep letter short. SASE required for query and ms response. Simultaneous submissions are OK. Receives 300 unsolicited mss/month. Accepts 10-15 mss/single issue; 20 mss/issue for double issue. Reports on mss in 2 months. Rarely comments on mss. Guidelines available for SASE. Sample copy available for $2.75.

**Terms:** Pays 3 cents/word and up on acceptance. Buys first North American serial rights. Publishes ms 6-12 months after acceptance.

# Hardboiled

▶ **Considers:** short shorts (length: 500-1,000 words)
short stories (length: under 3,000 words)
novelettes
novel excerpts (query first)

▶ **Categories:** private eye
hard-boiled detective
police procedural
crime
urban horror

**Address:** Gryphon Publications, P.O. Box 209, Brooklyn NY 11228-0209

**Contact:** Gary Lovisi

**Profile:** "I am looking for hard, cutting-edge crime tales, private-eye stories and hard-boiled material under 3,000 words with *impact*. No satire, Chandler-clones. Realistic, gritty, trench warfare." Established 1988. Magazine: Digest sized; 100 pages. Published quarterly. Circulation: 1,000.

**How to Contact:** Query first or send complete ms with cover letter. In cover letter include "a little bit about the story and author—1 paragraph." Must query for novelette, novella and novel excerpts. SASE required for query and ms response. Receives 40-50 unsolicited mss/month. Accepts 9-12 mss per/issue. Reports on queries in 2-4 weeks; on mss in 2-6 weeks. Comments on mss "most of the time." Guidelines available for SASE. Sample copy available for $6.

**Terms:** Pays $5-25 and 2 contributor's copies (higher in some cases) on publication. Buys first North American serial rights. Publishes ms 6 months to 2 years after acceptance.

**Tips:** "I want lean fiction, cut to the bone. I try to work with new writers and have published many in each issue of *Hardboiled*. Let me see a story, and try an issue to get a feel for what I'm after."

---

# Alfred Hitchcock Mystery Magazine

► **Considers:** short shorts (no minimum)
short stories (length: 14,000 words maximum)

► **Categories:** private eye
police procedural
amateur sleuth
cozy
hard-boiled detective
suspense

**Address:** Dell Magazines Fiction Group, 1540 Broadway, New York NY 10036

**Contact:** Cathleen Jordan

**Profile:** Established 1956. Magazine: 5¹⁄₁₆ × 7³⁄₈; 160 pages. Published 13 times/year. Circulation: 225,000.

**How to Contact:** Send complete ms and SASE. Receives 300 unsolicited mss a month. Accepts 7-8 new stories and 1 reprint/issue.

**Terms:** Pays 6½ cents/word on acceptance.

# Interview

*Cathleen Jordan, Editor*
Alfred Hitchcock Mystery Magazine

*"I'm convinced everything you can find in a novel, you can find in a short story," says Cathleen Jordan, editor of Alfred Hitchcock Mystery Magazine. While she admits the short story is a challenging art form simply because of its brevity, she says "it is possible, even if it is in miniature, to have fully-realized characters and a complicated plot."*

*Jordan has experience with both long and short mystery fiction. Before coming to the magazine 12 years ago, she edited mysteries for Doubleday for what used to be called the Crime Club line. "When I was at Doubleday the conventional wisdom was that short story collections did not sell very well, so I wasn't aware of the market for mystery short stories. When I came here, I found the short story market was much more alive than I thought."*

*Still, Hitchcock and its sibling publication, Ellery Queen's Mystery Magazine, are two of the strongest in only a handful of mystery magazines that feature short fiction. The biggest change in the marketplace for mystery short stories, says Jordan, has been with book publishers rather than magazines. Publishers seem much more willing today to publish anthologies featuring original mystery fiction.*

*As far as the different types of mystery, Jordan says, "There's always been considerable variety in the short fiction market. At Hitchcock we are interested in all subgenres, every possible type of mystery and crime story, even some with supernatural, occult or science fiction overtones."*

*Jordan's criterion for selecting a story for publication is simple. "It's always a matter of the quality. One can tell very quickly whether the author is in control of the writing. However interesting a story might be it's useless to us if the writing is not good. On the other hand, although we don't take stories that need a lot of revision, a first-rate writer might be able to work on a story to improve it."*

*Although Jordan has no absolute taboos, one mistake writers make is in thinking mystery short stories must have surprise or trick endings. "A good surprise ending is very hard to do. A lot of writers get so excited about getting to the surprise*

*at the end that they neglect the rest of the story. There's more
to it than a punch line."*

*The magazine receives about 3,800 unsolicited submis-
sions each year. Jordan and one assistant read all submissions,
selecting about 100 of them for publication. She is particularly
proud of the number of new writers published in* Hitchcock.
*"Many of our stories have received the Robert L. Fish Memorial
Award from Mystery Writers of America for Best First Original
Short Story. About 20 stories each year are first publications."*

*Jordan says talented new writers have an excellent chance
of being published in her magazine. "We have a number of
established writers who have been writing for our magazine for
awhile, but we even turn them down once in a while. It's not as
though all the slots are filled. There's a very real market here,
and I'm sure today publishers of mystery anthologies would tell
you the same thing."*

*Her advice: "Don't be discouraged by the competition. If
your writing is good, your chances are good in this market."*
—Robin Gee

## Mystery Notebook
**Address:** Box 1341, FDR Station, New York NY 10150-
1341
**Contact:** Stephen Wright
**Profile:** "Our publication publishes *very* little fiction."
See listing in *Markets for Reviews and Articles*, page
188.

## Mystery Street

▶ **Considers:** short shorts (length:
350 words)
short stories (length:
5,000 words pre-
ferred; 10,000 maxi-
mum)

> ▶ **Categories:** hard-boiled detective
> police procedural
> cozy
> espionage
> malice domestic
> suspense

**Address:** Pulphouse Publishing, Inc., P.O. Box 1378, Eugene OR 97440, (503) 435-6822
**Contact:** O'Neil DeNoux, Editor
**Profile:** A new mystery fiction magazine from Pulphouse Publishing, Inc. Established 1992. Magazine: 8½ × 11; 64 pages. Published bimonthly.
**How to Contact:** Send complete ms with cover letter. Cover letter should include estimated word count, 50-word bio, social security number, list of publications, list of organizations. SASE required for ms response. Simultaneous submissions OK if noted. Reports on queries in 1 week; mss in 1 month. Sometimes comments on mss. Guidelines available #10 SAE and 1 first-class stamp. Sample copy available for $3.95, 9 × 12 SAE, and 4 first-class stamps.
**Terms:** Pays 4-7 cents/word, subscription and 3 contributor's copies. Pays on publication for first rights. Sends galleys to author.

# Mystery Time, An Anthology of Short Stories

> ▶ **Considers:** short stories (length: 1,500 words maximum)
> ▶ **Categories:** private eye
> police procedural
> cozy
> amateur sleuth
> malice domestic

**Address:** Hutton Publications, P.O. Box 2907, Decatur IL 62526

**Contact:** Linda Hutton

**Profile:** "We aim to satisfy mystery readers who lack the time to savor a full-length book." Established 1983. Magazine: 5½ × 8½; 44 pages. Published annually. Circulation: 200.

**How to Contact:** Send complete ms with SASE. SASE required for ms response. Does not read mss in December. Simultaneous submissions and reprints are OK. Receives 10-15 unsolicited mss/month. Accepts 10-12 mss/issue. Reports on mss in 1 month. Sometimes comments on ms. Guidelines available for a #10 SASE. Sample copy available for $3.50.

**Terms:** Pays ¼ cent/word minimum on acceptance. Buys first or all rights.

**Tips:** "Study a sample copy. Emphasize your characters and inject a bit of humor; don't take yourself too seriously."

---

# New Mystery, The Best New Mystery Stories

▶ **Considers:** short shorts—1 per issue (length: 500-1,250 words)
short stories (length: 3,000-5,000 words)

▶ **Categories:** private eye
hard-boiled detective
police procedural
cozy
amateur sleuth
malice domestic

**Address:** Suite 2001, 175 5th Ave., New York NY 10010, (212) 353-1582 Fax: (212) 353-1582

**Contact:** Linda Wong

**Profile:** Features mysteries dealing with contemporary

themes. Established 1990. Magazine: 8½ × 11; 64 pages. Published quarterly. Circulation: 50,000.

**How to Contact:** Send complete ms with cover letter. Cover letter should include short bio. SASE required for ms response. Simultaneous and electronic submissions and reprints are OK. Occasionally comments on mss. Receives 400 unsolicited mss/month. Accepts 1-5 mss/issue. Reports on mss in 1-3 months. No writer's guidelines — "study an issue." Sample copy available for 4 first-class stamps.

**Terms:** Pays $25-500 on publication. Buys all rights. Publishes ms 1 year after acceptance. Author reviews copyedited ms and galleys and gets bio notes.

**Tips:** "Write your best story. Make it personal. Cut it back and rewrite until it is a clear narrative.

# P.I. Magazine

▶ **Considers:** short shorts (occasionally)
short stories (length: 500-5,000)
▶ **Categories:** private eye
hard-boiled detective

**Address:** 755 Bronx, Toledo OH 43609, (419) 382-0967
**Contact:** Bob Mackowiak
**Profile:** "Fact and fiction about the world of private investigators. America's consumer private eye magazine." Established 1988. Magazine: 8½ × 11; 50 pages. Published quarterly. Circulation: 1,300.

**How to Contact:** Send complete ms with cover letter. SASE required for query and ms response. Simultaneous submissions are OK. Receives 15-20 unsolicited mss/month. Accepts 4-6 mss/issue. Reports on mss in 4 months. Almost always comments on mss. Guidelines available for SASE. Sample copy available for $4.75.

**Terms:** Pays $25 or more, plus contributor's copies on

publication. Buys one-time rights. Publishes ms
2-3 months after acceptance. Author gets bio notes.
**Tips:** "Avoid the cliché. Don't start the story in the private eye's run-down office. Most parodies tend to fall flat—instead add humor to a great story."

# Potpourri

▶ **Considers:** short shorts (length: under 1,500 words) short stories (length: 2,500 words maximum)

▶ **Categories:** private eye hard-boiled detective amateur sleuth romantic suspense

**Address:** P.O. Box 8278, Prairie Village KS 66208, (913) 642-1503
**Contact:** Candy Schock
**Profile:** "*Potpourri* accepts a broad range of material; hence its name. Guidelines specify no religious, confessional, racial, political, erotic, abusive or sexual preference materials unless fictional and necessary to plot. Potpourri is sent to over 400 publications, some of which do publish mystery genre." Established 1989. Magazine: 12 × 14; 28 pages. Published monthly. Circulation: 6,000.
**How to Contact:** Send complete ms with cover letter, which should include phone number, brief summary statement and short bio; include complete name and address on ms. SASE required for query and ms response. Simultaneous submissions are OK. Receives 75-80 unsolicited mss/month. Accepts 8-10 mss/issue. Reports on queries in 3-6 weeks; on mss in 2-4 months. Comments on mss. Guidelines available for #10 SAE and 1 first-class stamp. Sample copy available for SAE and 3 first-class stamps or for $1.

**Terms:** Pays in contributor's copies on publication. Acquires first rights. Publishes ms 3-6 months after acceptance. Author "usually" reviews copyedited ms and "sometimes" galleys.

**Tips:** "We look for the unusual twist. Is the story idea different? Does the story hold the reader's interest from beginning to end? The introduction should spark interest and set the mood. Action in dialogue and narration tell the story. Build the conflicts. The conclusion should leave something with the reader to be long remembered. Work on humor and suspense."

---

# PSI

▶ **Considers:** short stories (length: 10,000 words average)
novelettes (length: 30,000 words average)

▶ **Categories:** young adult
private eye
police procedural
amateur sleuth
romantic suspense

**Address:** Suite 856, 1377 K Street NW, Washington DC 20005

**Contact:** A.P. Samuels

**Profile:** Publishes "good, entertaining stories for a general audience." Established 1987. Magazine: 8½ × 11; 32 pages. Published bimonthly.

**How to Contact:** Send complete ms with cover letter. SASE required for query and ms response. Does not read mss in December. Electronic submissions are OK. Receives 35 unsolicited mss/month. Accepts 1-2 mss/issue. Reports on queries in 2 weeks; on mss in 1 month. Guidelines available for #10 SASE.

**Terms:** Pays 1-4 cents/word on acceptance. Buys first North American serial rights. Time between acceptance and publication of magazine varies. Author reviews copyedited ms, if requests.

**Tips:** "Just (use) good, clean writing."

---

# 2 AM Magazine

▶ **Considers:** short shorts
short stories (length: 500-5,000 words)
▶ **Categories:** police procedural
romantic suspense

**Address:** 2 AM Publications, P.O. Box 6754, Rockford IL 61125-1754

**Contact:** Gretta M. Anderson

**Profile:** Uses "suspense-filled stories of horror, sf, fantasy, mystery, suspense-romance or action-adventure with a believable (though not necessarily realistic) threat to interacting characters readers can identify with and care about." Established 1986. Magazine: 8½ × 11; 60 pages. Published quarterly. Circulation: 1,500.

**How to Contact:** Send complete ms with cover letter. SASE required for query and ms response. Simultaneous submissions are OK. Receives 500 unsolicited mss/ month. Accepts 12-14 mss/issue. Reports on queries in 1 month; on mss in 3 months. Sometimes comments on mss. Guidelines available. Sample copy available for $5.95.

**Terms:** Pays ½ cent/word minimum plus 1 contributor's copy on acceptance. Buys one-time rights with non-exclusive anthology option. Publishes ms 6-9 months after acceptance. Author reviews copyedited ms and galleys and gets bio notes.

**Tips:** "Write the kind of story you love to read. Write the story you wish someone else would have written so you could read it—but no one else has, so *you* must."

## Secondary Markets

The markets listed here may not pay or may have small circulations, but they are valuable publications for mystery writers. Some markets included here do not focus specifically on mystery. These publications are included because they are open to writers of all stripes.

---

# Advocate

► **Considers:**  short shorts (length: less than 1,000 words)
short stories (length: 1,000-2,500 words)
► **Categories:**  young adult
juvenile
private eye
hard-boiled detective
amateur sleuth
romantic suspense

**Address:** PKA Publications, 301A Rolling Hills Park Prattsville NY 12468, (518) 299-3103
**Contact:** Remington Wright
**Profile:** Tabloid-style newsprint magazine with line drawings. Established 1987. Magazine: 11¼ × 13¾; 32 pages. Published bimonthly. Circulation: 12,000.
**How to Contact:** Send complete ms. SASE required for query and ms response. Receives 36 unsolicited mss/ month. Accepts 7-8 mss/issue. Reports on queries in 2 weeks; on mss in 2 months. Sometimes comments on mss. Guidelines available for SAE and 1 first-class stamp. Sample copy available for $2.
**Terms:** Pays in contributor's copies. Acquires first rights. Publishes ms 2 months-1 year after acceptance.
**Tips:** "The highest criterion in selecting a work is its entertainment value. It must first be enjoyable reading. It must, of course, be original. To stand out, it must be thought-provoking or strongly emotive, or very cleverly

plotted. We will consider only previously unpublished works by writers who do not earn their living principally through writing."

---

# Alabama Literary Review

► **Considers:** short shorts (length: 1,000 words)
short stories (length: 2,000-3,000 words)
► **Categories:** private eye
hard-boiled detective

**Address:** Troy State University, Troy AL 36082, (205) 670-3286, ext. 330
**Contact:** Jim Davis
**Profile:** "We look mainly at artistic literary quality; whether a story is a mystery is of no consequence to us." Established 1987. Magazine: 6 × 9; 100 pages. Published semiannually. Circulation: 700.
**How to Contact:** Send complete ms with cover letter or submit through agent. "Cover letter should include: previous credits, whether we have corresponded with you about this ms before, and some background info about the author. No synopsis—the story will speak for itself, or not." SASE required for query and ms response. Simultaneous submissions are OK. Receives 50 unsolicited mss/ month. Accepts 3 mss/issue. Reports on queries in 2 weeks; on mss in 2-3 months (response time is longer in summer and December). Sometimes comments on mss. Guidelines available for SASE. Sample copy available postpaid for $4.50.
**Terms:** Pays in contributor's copies upon publication. Acquires first rights; rights returned to author upon publication. Manuscript published 5-6 months after acceptance. Author reviews copyedited ms and gets bio notes.
**Tips:** "Read, read, read; write, write, write."

# Arnazella

▶ **Considers:** short stories (length: 3,500 words)
unagented novel serializations (length: 3,500 words)

▶ **Categories:** private eye
hard-boiled detective
malice domestic

**Address:** English Department, A255, Bellevue Community College, 3000 Londerholm Circle SE, Bellevue WA 98007, (206) 641-2373

**Contact:** Laura Burns-Lewis

**Profile:** "Staff is comprised of students. We select our pieces according to quality." Established 1976. Magazine: 9 × 8; 80 pages. Published annually. Circulation: 500.

**How to Contact:** Send complete ms with cover letter. Cover letter should include 25-word bio, name, address, phone number. SASE required for query and ms response. Does not read mss from June through October. Receives 100 unsolicited mss/month. Accepts 5-6 mss/issue. Reports on queries between October and May; on mss in spring. Guidelines available for SASE. Sample copy available for $5.

**Terms:** Pays in contributor's copies. Acquires first North American serial rights. Publishes ms 2 months after acceptance. Author gets bio notes.

**Tips:** "Send in high-quality material; avoid clichés and formula plots."

# The Belletrist Review

▶ **Considers:** short stories (length: 2,500-5,000)

▶ **Categories:** police procedural
amateur sleuth
malice domestic

**Address:** Marmarc Publications, Suite 290, 17 Farmington Ave., Plainville CT 06062, (203) 793-9509
**Contact:** Marc Saegaert
**Profile:** "We are not limited to any particular genre and our first issue featured works by beginning writers as well as published writers. The editorial panel accepts high-quality fiction that impacts us in some way and leaves a lasting impression." Established 1992. Magazine: 8½×11; 70 pages. Published semiannually. Circulation: 500.
**How to Contact:** Send complete ms with cover letter. Cover letter should include brief bio note and any previous publications. SASE required for query and ms response. Simultaneous submissions and reprints are OK. Receives 100 unsolicited mss/month. Accepts 10-12 mss/issue. Reports on queries in 1 month; on mss in 2 months. Comments on mss. Guidelines available for 4×9 SAE and 1 first-class stamp. Sample copy available for $3.95.
**Terms:** Pays in contributor's copies upon publication. Acquires one-time rights. Publishes ms within 1 year after acceptance. Author gets bio notes.
**Tips:** "Too many writers simply narrate events rather than tell a story. Cut out material that does not further the plot or the characters."

---

# Chapter One, For the Unpublished Writer in All of Us

▶ **Considers:** short shorts (length: 100 words)
short stories (length: 100-6,000 words)
novelettes (length: 10,000 words maximum)

► **Categories:** young adult
juvenile
private eye
hard-boiled detective
police procedural
cozy
amateur sleuth
malice domestic
romantic suspense

**Address:** JAB Publishing, 12018 State Route 45, Lisbon OH 44432
**Contact:** Belinda J. Puchajda
**Profile:** "We are geared to the unpublished writer and (include) a variety of stories." Established 1989. Magazine: 5¼ × 8; 100-280 pages. Published quarterly. Circulation: 600.
**How to Contact:** Send complete ms with cover letter that includes biographical info. SASE required for query and ms response. Simultaneous submissions are OK. Receives 800-3,000 unsolicited mss/month. Accepts 25-35 mss/issue. Reports on queries in 2-4 months; on mss in 4-6 months. Sometimes comments on mss. Guidelines available for #10 SASE and 1 first-class stamp. Sample copy available for $1 and 2 first-class stamps.
**Terms:** Pays up to $50 plus contributor's copies on publication. Buys one-time rights. Publishes ms 1-2 years after acceptance.
**Tips:** "Submit. We try to help people break into print for the very first time."

## Cochran's Corner

► **Considers:** short shorts (length: 1,000 words)
short stories (length: 1,500 words)

> ▶ **Categories:** young adult
>   juvenile
>   private eye
>   romantic suspense

**Address:** 225 Ralston, Converse TX 78109
**Contact:** Debra G. Tompkins
**Profile:** Publishes fiction, nonfiction and poetry for a family audience. Established 1986. Magazine: 5½ × 8; 52 pages. Published quarterly. Circulation: 500.
**How to Contact:** Subscribers only. Send complete ms with cover letter. SASE required for ms response. Simultaneous submissions are OK. Receives 50 unsolicited mss/month. Accepts 4 mss/issue. Reports on queries in 3 weeks; on mss in 3 months. Comments on mss. Guidelines available for #10 SAE and 1 first-class stamp. Sample copy available for $5.
**Terms:** Pays in contributor's copies. Acquires one-time rights. Publishes ms by the next issue after acceptance.

---

# Eagle's Flight, A Literary Magazine

> ▶ **Considers:** short shorts
>   short stories (length:
>     1,000-2,000 words)
>   novel excerpts
>     (length: 1,000-2,000
>     words)
> ▶ **Categories:** considers all
>   categories

**Address:** 2501 Hunters Hill Drive, #822, Enid OK 73703, (405) 233-1118
**Contact:** Rekha Kulkarni
**Profile:** "We try to encourage our writer friends, give them some platform so they can keep improving and thus someday can contribute to classic literature that will stand

the test of time and be read forever." All stories published in previous year are entered into *Eagle's Flight* Best Story Award competition. Established 1989. Magazine: 8½ × 11; 8-12 pages. Published quarterly. Circulation: 200.
**How to contact:** Query first. SASE required for query and ms response. Does not read mss from July through December. Receives 7-8 unsolicited mss/month. Accepts 1-3 mss/issue. Reports on queries in 6 weeks; on mss in 3 months. Guidelines available for $1, #10 SAE and 1 first-class stamp. Sample copy available for $1.
**Terms:** $5-20 or free subscription to magazine on publication. Buys first North American serial rights or one-time rights. Publishes ms 1-3 years after acceptance.
**Tips:** "Read previous issues, know what we like and be part of our family. Don't get discouraged."

---

# Epiphany, A Journal of Literature

▶ **Considers:** short shorts (length: 1,200 words maximum)
short stories (length: 10,000 words maximum)
novel excerpts (length: 10,000 words maximum)

▶ **Categories:** considers all categories

**Address:** University of Arkansas, P.O. Box 2699, Fayetteville AR 72701, (401) 524-3326
**Contact:** Dora Rainey
**Profile:** "Good, literary writing. Literary stories that just happen to be mysteries, if there is such a thing." Established 1990. Magazine: 8½ × 11; 86-120 pages. Published quarterly. Circulation: 300.
**How to Contact:** Submit complete ms, no cover letter.

SASE required for ms response. Simultaneous submissions accepted "begrudgingly. Inform us if taken elsewhere." Receives 300 unsolicited mss/month. Reports on mss in 2 months. Comments on mss. Guidelines available for #10 SASE. Sample copy available for $4.

**Terms:** Pays 1 contributor's copy on publication. Acquires one-time rights. Publishes ms 3-6 months after acceptance. Author gets bio notes.

**Tips:** "Be as good as Poe, only better."

# His Garden

► **Considers:** short shorts
short stories (length: 2,000 words maximum)

► **Categories:** considers all categories

**Address:** 216 N. Vine Street, Kewanee IL 61443

**Contact:** Margi Washburn, Editor

**Profile:** "You'll find many different items planted in an ordinary garden. You'll find a variety of works to inspire you in *His Garden*." Established 1992. Published three times/year.

**How to Contact:** Reports in 2 months on mss; 3 weeks on queries. Guidelines available for #10 SASE. Sample copy available for $3.50.

**Terms:** Pays $5 plus contributor's copy on publication. Buys one-time rights. Ms published 4-6 months after acceptance.

**Tips:** "I want to work with new/unpublished writers. Be open to suggestion. Bring some light into the world. Bring some creative variety to the magazine."

# Grasslands Review

► **Considers:**  short shorts (length:
100-150 words)
short stories (length:
100-3,500 words)
► **Categories:**  private eye
hard-boiled detective
police procedural
amateur sleuth
malice domestic
romantic suspense

**Address:** University of North Texas, P.O. Box 13706, #14200 Kennelly, Denton TX 76203
**Contact:** Laura B. Kennelly
**Profile:** "We look for new writers of promise, but also publish established writers." Established 1989. Magazine: 6 × 9; 80 pages. Published biannually. Circulation: 200.
**How to Contact:** Send complete ms in October or March. SASE required for ms response. Reads mss only in October or March. Accepts 4-5 mss/issue. Reports on mss in 3 months, on queries "right away." Sometimes comments on mss. Guidelines available for SASE. Sample copy available for $2.
**Terms:** Pays in contributor's copies on publication. Acquires one-time rights. Publishes ms 6 months after acceptance. Author sometimes reviews copyedited ms and galleys; author gets bio notes.
**Tips:** "Be original. Have a sense of humor."

# Green's Magazine, Fiction for the Family

► **Considers:**  short stories (length:
1,500-4,000 words,
2,500 preferred)

► **Categories:** considers all
categories

**Address:** Green's Educational Publications, P.O. Box
3236, Regina, Saskatchewan, S4P 3H1 Canada
**Contact:** David Green
**Profile:** "Aims to be exemplary of first-class writing.
Strong characterization in complex conflicts, generally
with strong plots." Established 1972. Magazine: 5¼ × 8;
100 pages. Published quarterly. Circulation: 300.
**How to Contact:** Send complete ms. SASE required for
query and ms response; IRC needed for U.S. mss. Receives 20-30 unsolicited mss/month. Accepts 10-12 mss/
issue. Reports on mss in 2 months. Sometimes comments
on ms. Guidelines available for #10 SAE and IRC. Sample
copy available for $4.
**Terms:** Pays in contributor's copies. Acquires first North
American serial rights. Publishes ms within 3-6 months
of acceptance. Author gets bio notes.
**Tips:** "Study the publication."

# Hawaii Pacific Review

► **Considers:** short shorts; short
stories (length:
5,000 words maxi-
mum)
► **Categories:** considers all
categories

**Address:** Hawaii Pacific University, 1060 Bishop St.,
Honolulu HI 96813, (808) 544-0214
**Contact:** Elizabeth Fischel
**Profile:** "*HPR* is not primarily a mystery magazine. We
will consider mysteries, however, if they show ingenuity
or innovative themes or narrative techniques." Estab-

lished 1988. Magazine: 6×9; 100-150 pages. Published annually. Circulation: 600.

**How to Contact:** Send complete ms with cover letter and brief bio. SASE required for ms response. Does not read mss in summer. Simultaneous submissions are OK. Receives 50 unsolicited mss/month. Accepts 4-8 mss/issue. Reports on mss in 3 months. Sometimes comments on mss. Guidelines available for #10 SAE and 1 first-class stamp. Sample copy available for $4.

**Terms:** Pays in contributor's copies upon publication. Acquires first North American serial rights. Publishes ms 3-12 months after acceptance.

---

# Housewife-Writer's Forum

> ► **Considers:** short stories (length: 500-2,000, 1,500 preferred)
> ► **Categories:** considers all categories

**Address:** P.O. Box 780, Lyman WY 82937, (307) 786-4513

**Contact:** Bob Haynie

**Profile:** "Magazine of networking and how-to's for women writers. All fiction we accept is critiqued in print. We publish stories based on their quality in writing, voice, plot and pacing rather than on genre." Established 1988. Magazine: 6½ × 10; 32-48 pages. Published bimonthly. Circulation: 1,200.

**How to Contact:** Submit complete ms. SASE required for ms response. "Prefer not to" accept simultaneous submissions; accepts some reprints. Receives 100-200 unsolicited mss/month. Accepts 2 mss/issue. Reports on mss in 2-4 months. Sometimes comments on mss. Guidelines available for SASE. Sample copy available for $4.

**Terms:** Pays 1¢/word on acceptance. Acquires North American serial rights and one-time rights. Publishes ms

6 months-1 year after acceptance. Author gets bio notes.

---

# Innisfree

> ► **Considers:** short shorts
> short stories (length:
> 3,000 words maxi-
> mum)
> ► **Categories:** private eye
> hard-boiled detective
> amateur sleuth

**Address:** P.O. Box 277, Manhattan Beach CA 90266, (310) 545-2607 Fax: (310) 546-5862
**Contact:** Rex Winn
**Profile:** *"Innisfree* attempts to publish new writers who take pride in their work and have some talent." Established 1981. Magazine: 8½×11; 50+ pages. Published bimonthly. Circulation: 350.
**How to Contact:** Send complete ms with cover letter. SASE required for query and ms response. Does not read mss in November and December. Simultaneous and electronic submissions and reprints are OK. Receives 150 unsolicited mss/month. Accepts 12-15 mss/issue. Reports on queries in 1 month; on mss in 1-2 months. Comments on mss. Free guidelines available. Sample copy available for $4.
**Terms:** No pay—prizes offered. Acquires one-time rights. Publishes ms 1 year after acceptance. Author reviews copyedited ms and galleys and gets bio notes.
**Tips:** "Begin with strong hook, entertain, pay attention to the craft of writing. Inspire or enlighten."

---

# Monthly Independent Tribune Times Journal Post Gazette News Chronicle Bulletin

> ► **Considers:** short shorts (length:
> 400 words pre-
> ferred)
> short stories (length:
> 1,200 words maxi-
> mum)

► **Categories:** private eye
hard-boiled detective
amateur sleuth
parody
satire
absurdist

**Address:** 1630 Allston Way, Berkeley CA 94703
**Contact:** Denver Tucson
**Profile:** "We are not devoted solely to mysteries, but we frequently publish short and short-short mystery stories, all of which are excessively peculiar or funny in some way: mysteries without a mystery, incredibly stupid and/or eccentric detective stories and parodies of any and all genres." Established 1983. Magazine: 5½ × 8; 8 pages. Published irregularly. Circulation: 500.
**How to Contact:** Send complete ms with cover letter. SASE required for query and ms response. Simultaneous submissions are OK. Receives 15 unsolicited mss/month. Accepts 1-2 mss/issue. Reports on queries in 1 week; on mss in 1 week. Sometimes comments on mss. Sample copy available for 50¢.
**Terms:** Pays 3 contributor's copies on publication. Not copyrighted. Publishes ms 1 week-10 months average after acceptance.
**Tips:** "Keep it short, keep it funny."

---

# Oak

► **Considers:** short shorts (length: 200 words)
short stories (length: 500 words maximum)
► **Categories:** considers all categories

**Address:** 1530 7th St., Rock Island IL 61201, (309) 788-3980
**Contact:** Betty Mowery
**Profile:** "We are read by fiction and nonfiction writers and poets college age and up. I use anything that strikes me, but will not even look at erotica." Established 1991. Magazine: 8½ × 11; 8-16 pages. Published bimonthly. Circulation: 385.
**How to Contact:** Send complete ms. SASE required for ms response. Simultaneous submissions and reprints are OK. Receives 12 unsolicited mss/month. Accepts 6 mss/issue. Reports on mss in 1 week. Comments on mss. Sample copy available for $2.
**Terms:** Pays in contributor's copies. Acquires first rights. Publishes ms 3 months after acceptance.
**Tips:** "Send a tight story that doesn't exceed suggested word length."

# Oxalis

> ► **Considers:**  short shorts (length: 1,000 words)
> short stories (length: 3,000 words maximum)
> novel excerpts (length: 3,000 words maximum)
>
> ► **Categories:**  considers all categories

**Address:** Stone Ridge Poetry Society, P.O. Box 3993, Kingston NY 12401, (914) 687-7942
**Contact:** Mildred Barker
**Profile:** "We like stories with social significance, humor and brilliant writing. Our test: if we can't forget it, it's probably good." Established 1988. Magazine: 8½ × 11; 48-60 pages. Published 3-4 times/year. Circulation: 350.

**How to Contact:** Query first to determine status of backlog, or send complete ms with cover letter. SASE required for query and ms response. Simultaneous submissions are OK. Receives 10 unsolicited mss/month. Accepts 2-7 mss/issue. Reports on queries in 2 weeks; on mss in 1 month. Sometimes comments on mss. Guidelines available for #10 SASE. Sample copy available for $4.

**Terms:** Pays 2 contributor's copies on publication. Acquires first rights or one-time rights. Publishes ms 6-15 months after acceptance.

**Tips:** "Send something other than (typical) genre fiction. We have never published a mystery but can't say that we wouldn't if it were exceptional — and one that would appeal to people who don't usually read mysteries."

---

# The Pinehurst Journal

▶ **Considers:** short stories (length: 750-4,000 words)
▶ **Categories:** hard-boiled detective

**Address:** Pinehurst Press, P.O. Box 360747, Milpitas CA 95036, (510) 440-9259

**Contact:** Michael K. McNamara

**Profile:** "We are a literary magazine that contains some 'good reads.' Try to make the story upscale and unique for a well-read, educated subscriber." Established 1990. Magazine: 8½ × 11; 44 pages. Published quarterly. Circulation: 250.

**How to Contact:** Send complete ms with cover letter and short bio. SASE required for query and ms response. Simultaneous submissions are OK. Receives 80 unsolicited mss/month. Accepts 17 mss/issue. Reports on queries in 1 month; on mss in 2 months. Comments on mss. Guidelines available for #10 SASE. Sample copy available for SAE and $4.75.

**Terms:** Pays $5 and 1 contributor's copy on publication.

Buys one-time rights. Publishes ms 1-4 months after acceptance. Author gets bio notes.

**Tips:** "It's hard to be distinctive in such a competitive genre but the better writers are. Study your craft and try to excel."

# Post

▶ **Considers:** short stories (length: 10,000 average)
▶ **Categories:** private eye
suspense
romantic suspense

**Address:** Publishers Syndication International, Suite 856, 1377 K St., Washington DC 20005
**Contact:** A.P. Samuels
**Profile:** Established 1988. Newspaper: 8½ × 11; 32 pages. Published monthly.
**How to Contact:** Send complete ms with cover letter. Receives 75 unsolicited mss/month. Accepts 1 ms/issue. Reports on mss in 5 weeks.
**Terms:** Pays ½-4¢/word on acceptance. Buys all rights. Time between acceptance and publication varies.

# Pulphouse: A Fiction Magazine

▶ **Considers:** short stories
▶ **Categories:** considers all categories

**Address:** Pulphouse Publishing, Inc., P.O. Box 1227, Eugene OR 97440-1227
**Contact:** Dean Wesley Smith, Editor

**Profile:** Established 1988. Magazine: 8½ × 11; 48 pages.
**How to Contact:** Send complete ms with cover letter.
SASE required for query and ms response.
**Terms:** Pays on acceptance for first serial rights.

---

# Short Story Digest

▶ **Considers:**   short shorts (length: 500 words minimum)
short stories (length: 3,000 words maximum)

▶ **Categories:**   private eye
hard-boiled detective
amateur sleuth
malice domestic
romantic suspense

**Address:** Caldwell Publishing, P.O. Box 1183, Richardson TX 75083
**Contact:** Jack T. Hess, Senior Editor
**Profile:** "Looking for short fiction (under 3,000 words), tightly written with a strong surprise ending. We want the reader to remember the stories read and come back for more." Runs a yearly contest — SASE for details. Established 1991. Magazine: 5⅛ × 8½; 40-50 pages. Published quarterly. Circulation: 1,000.
**How to Contact:** Send complete ms with cover letter including name, address, name of ms and number of words. SASE required for ms response. Electronic (ASCII or Microsoft Word) submissions are OK. Receives 50-100 unsolicited mss/month. Accepts 8-12 mss/issue. Reports on mss in 8-10 weeks. Guidelines available for #10 SAE and 1 first-class stamp. Sample copy available for $3.
**Terms:** Pays 1¢/word on publication. Buys first North American serial rights and one-time reprint rights. Publishes ms 2 months-1 year after acceptance.

**Tips:** "Hook the reader early and have a good surprise ending."

---

# Short Stuff Magazine for Grown-ups

> ▶ **Considers:** short shorts (length: 1,500 words maximum)
> ▶ **Categories:** private eye
> hard-boiled detective
> police procedural
> cozy
> amateur sleuth
> romantic suspense

**Address:** Bowman Publications, P.O. Box 7057, Loveland CO 80537, (303) 669-9139
**Contact:** Donna Bowman
**Profile:** "We are seasonal in terms of holidays and somewhat regional. Designed for people who are in a waiting mode in professional offices, our stories must be punchy and a little upbeat. Who wants gore when waiting to see a doctor?" Established 1989. Magazine: 8½ × 11; 40 pages. Published monthly. Circulation: 5,400.
**How to Contact:** Send complete ms with cover letter and bio. SASE required for ms response. Simultaneous submissions and reprints are OK. Receives 100 unsolicited mss/month. Accepts 9-12 mss/issue. Reports on mss in 3-6 months. Comments on mss. Guidelines available for SASE. Sample copy available for 98¢ postage.
**Terms:** Pays $10-50 and subscription to magazine on publication. Buys first North American serial rights. Publishes ms up to 3 months after acceptance. Author gets bio notes.
**Tips:** "Write a good story with beginning, middle and end with dialogue. Many are merely essays."

# Skylark

▶ **Considers:**  short shorts (length: up to 600 words maximum)
short stories (length: 4,500 words maximum)
novel excerpts (length: 3,000 words)

▶ **Categories:**  private eye
hard-boiled detective
amateur sleuth
malice domestic
romantic suspense
young author's fiction

**Address:** Purdue University, 2200 169th St., Hammond IN 46323, (219) 989-2262
**Contact:** Pamela Hunter
**Profile:** "We are a literary arts annual that likes to work with both published and unpublished writers as long as [the submitted] work is honest, original and unpublished." Established 1971. Magazine: 8½ × 11; 100 pages. Published annually. Circulation: 500-1,000.
**How to Contact:** Send complete ms. SASE required for ms response. Does not read mss from June 1-December 1. Simultaneous submissions are OK. Receives 15 unsolicited mss/month. Accepts 12-15 mss/issue. Reports on mss in 2 months. Comments on mss. Guidelines available for SASE. Sample copy available for SAE and $5 for current issue; back issue for $3.
**Terms:** Pays 1 contributor's copy. Acquires first rights. Publishes ms 4 months maximum after acceptance. "If we want to hold a ms longer, we contact the author."
**Tips:** "Be original. All well-written work is considered, regardless of the author's past publishing (or academic) credentials."

# Snake River Reflections

> ► **Considers:** short shorts (length: 500 words)
> short stories (length: 1,200 words)
> ► **Categories:** young adult
> juvenile
> private eye
> hard-boiled detective
> police procedural
> cozy
> amateur sleuth
> malice domestic
> romantic suspense

**Address:** 1863 Bitterroot Dr., Twin Falls ID 83301, (208) 734-0746 (evenings)
**Contact:** Bill White
**Profile:** Established 1990. Magazine: 5½ × 8½; 8 pages. Published 10 times/year. Circulation: 300.
**How to Contact:** SASE required for ms and query response. Receives 3-5 unsolicited mss/month. Accepts 1 mss/issue. Reports on queries in 1 month. Sometimes comments on mss. Guidelines available for #10 SASE. Sample copy available for 55¢.
**Terms:** Pays in 2 contributor's copies. Acquires first rights. Publishes ms 1 month after acceptance.

# Square One, A Magazine of Fiction

> ► **Considers:** short stories (length: 3,000-5,000 words preferred)
> novelettes (length: 20,000 maximum)

► **Categories:** private eye
hard-boiled detective
police procedural
amateur sleuth
malice domestic
romantic suspense

**Address:** Tarkus Press, P.O. Box 11921, Milwaukee WI
53211-0921
**Contact:** William D. Gagliani
**Profile:** "We have been an all-genre fiction forum since
the beginning and remain committed to variety in styles
and genres, but we are actively seeking to increase our
horror and dark fantasy content (including urban fantasy,
magic realism, splatterpunk and traditional). We would
also like to see alternate history SF and mystery, as well
as steampunk SF/F/H/M and other genre-blending." Established 1984. Magazine: 7 × 8½; 75-90 pages. Published
irregularly. Circulation: 250.
**How to Contact:** Send complete ms with cover letter.
Cover letter should include "brief bio, *selected* credits, and
*no description of story*." Query for novel excerpts or anything over 7,500 words. SASE required for query and ms
response. Does not read mss between May and Septem-
ber unless labelled "keep on file." Simultaneous (if so
labeled) and electronic (3.5″ HD Macintosh disk or 3.5″
2S2D Atari disks) submissions are OK. Receives 50-75
unsolicited mss/month. Accepts 9-15 mss/issue. Reports
on queries in 1-3 months; on mss in 1-14 months "due to
irregular schedule." Sometimes comments on mss.
Guidelines available for SAE and 1 first-class stamp. Sample copy available for $3.50, 9 × 12 SAE and 6 first-class
stamps.
**Terms:** Pays 2 contributor's copies on publication. Buys
one-time rights. Publishes ms 1-14 months after acceptance. Author gets bio notes.
**Tips:** "We are tiny, part-time, barely financed and
swamped . . . but we are also proud of our product. Please
be patient when submitting or contacting us and always
enclose a SASE. Again, please don't describe your story
in the cover letter."

# Thema

| | |
|---|---|
| ▶ **Considers:** | short shorts (length: 300-500 words) short stories (length: 2,700-6,000 words) |
| ▶ **Categories:** | private eye cozy amateur sleuth malice domestic |

**Address:** THEME Literary Society, P.O. Box 74109, Metairie LA 70033-4109, (504) 887-1263

**Contact:** Virginia Howard

**Profile:** "Each issue of *Thema* is based on a different unusual theme. Prefer stories free of bedroom-bathroom profanity." Established 1988. Magazine: 5½ × 8½; 200 pages. Published quarterly. Circulation: 500.

**How to Contact:** Send complete ms and cover letter, which should include "specification for target *theme* for the ms." SASE required for query and ms response. Simultaneous submissions are OK. Receives 70 unsolicited mss/month. Accepts 10-12 mss/issue. Reports on queries in 1 week; on mss 2-3 months after deadline for specified issue. Comments on mss. Guidelines available for SASE. Sample copy available for $5.

**Terms:** Pays $25 on acceptance. Buys one-time rights. Publishes ms 3-4 months after acceptance. Author gets bio notes.

**Tips:** "Know what themes are upcoming and slant story towards theme. It's best to consider theme first, then write story to fit theme — not to adapt a previously-written story to fit theme. Please don't submit a story unless you know the theme. Specify theme. Themeless story = instant rejection."

# Tucumcari Literary Review

▶ **Considers:** short shorts (length: 200 words)
short stories (length: 400-1,200 words)
novel excerpts (length: 1,200 words)

▶ **Categories:** private eye
police procedural
amateur sleuth

**Address:** 3108 W. Bellevue Ave., Los Angeles CA 90026
**Contact:** Troxey Kemper
**Profile:** *"Tucumcari* is old-fashioned and nostalgic." Established 1988. Magazine: 5½ × 8½; 32 pages. Published bimonthly. Circulation: 100-200.
**How to Contact:** Send complete ms; cover letter optional. SASE required for query and ms response. Simultaneous submissions and reprints are OK. Receives 100 unsolicited mss/month. Accepts 2-3 mss/issue. Reports on queries in 1-2 days; on mss in 2 weeks. If ms is accepted, author is sent copy of magazine and SASE is returned. Sometimes comments on mss. Guidelines available for #10 SASE. Sample copy available for $2.
**Terms:** Pays in contributor's copies on publication. Acquires one-time rights. Publishes ms 2-4 months after acceptance.
**Tips:** "Write something interesting."

# The Ultimate Writer

▶ **Considers:** short shorts (length: 99 words minimum)
short stories (length: 99 words minimum; more than 5,000 words will be serialized)
novel excerpts (length: open)

► **Categories:** young adult
juvenile
private eye
amateur sleuth
romantic suspense

**Address:** Perry Terrell Publishing, 1617 Newport Place 24, Kenner LA 70065, (514) 465-9412
**Contact:** Perry Terrell
**Profile:** "The editorial slant of *The Ultimate Writer* and Perry Terrell Publishing is to bring people with the same interests together, encourage them to communicate with each other, and present the different styles of expressions that can and should be appreciated." Established 1990. Magazine: 8½ × 11; 40-60 pages. Published monthly. Circulation: 632.
**How to Contact:** Query first or send complete ms with cover letter. SASE required for query and ms response. Simultaneous, photocopied and electronic submissions and reprints are OK. "If no trouble to writer, send either 5.25" or 3.5" disks, WordPerfect, any version, or ASCII or IBM compatible." Receives 35-45 unsolicited mss/month. Accepts 6-8 mss/issue. Reports on queries in 1 week; on mss in 4-6 months. Comments on mss. Guidelines available for #10 SAE and 1 first-class stamp. Sample copy available for $3.75.
**Terms:** Pays 3 contributor's copies or 3-month subscription upon publication. Purchases one-time rights. Publishes ms 4-8 months after acceptance, depending on length.
**Tips:** "Believe in your ability to express yourself whether in fiction or nonfiction. If you feel the need to write something down and/or have used some of your valuable time to write something down, there is a strong possibility that some of us will learn, appreciate and grow from your eloquence, experiences and creative ability. Envision the confidence you are giving others that are reluctant to share their thoughts, ideas, opinions, creative expressions, and of course, humor. In other words, some of us out here need to hear from you whether you are making

us laugh, cry, frown, or amazing the heck out of us. Believe in yourself and share."

---

# The Veneration Quarterly

> ▶ **Considers:** short shorts (length: 99 words minimum) short stories (length: 99 words minimum; more than 5,000 words will be serialized)
> ▶ **Categories:** considers all categories

**Address:** Perry Terrell Publishing, 1617 Newport Pl 24, Kenner LA 70065, (514) 465-9412
**Contact:** Perry Terrell
**Profile:** *The Veneration Quarterly* has as a goal to "showcase 20 ultimately talented and distinguished writers that have emerged in the literary arena." Established 1992. Magazine: 8½ × 11; 100-110 pages. Published quarterly. Circulation: 150.
**How to Contact:** Query first or send complete ms with cover letter. SASE required for query and ms response. Simultaneous, photocopied and electronic submissions and reprints are OK. Receives 25-40 unsolicited mss/month. Accepts 20 mss/issue. Reports on queries in 1 week; on mss in 2-3 months. Sometimes comments on mss. Guidelines available for SASE. Sample copy available for $6.50.
**Terms:** Acquires one-time rights. Manuscript published 4-8 months after acceptance.
**Tips:** "Establish your distinguished talent with Perry Terrell Publishing."

# The Village Idiot

▶ **Considers:** short stories
▶ **Categories:** considers all
  categories

**Address:** Mother of Ashes Press, P.O. Box 66, Harrison
ID 83833-0066
**Contact:** Joe M. Singer
**Profile:** The *Village Idiot* is "idiosyncratic." Established
1970. Magazine: 5½ × 8⅜"; 48 pages. Published 3 times/
year. Circulation: 200.
**How to Contact:** Send complete ms. SASE required for
query and ms response. Receives 100 unsolicited mss/
month. Accepts 20 mss/issue. Reports on queries in 3
months; on mss in 2 months. Guidelines available for
SASE. Sample copy available for $3.
**Terms:** Pays 2 contributor's copies on publication. Acquires one-time rights. Publishes ms 2-4 months after
acceptance. Author reviews copyediting or galleys on request.

# Vintage Northwest

▶ **Considers:** short stories (length:
  1,000 words maxi-
  mum)
▶ **Categories:** considers all
  categories

**Address:** P.O. Box 193, Bothell WA 98041, (206) 487-
1201
**Contact:** Lawrence T. Campbell
**Profile:** "If you have a writer, over 55, who has ability,
but has not yet had stories widely accepted, we could possibly be a place to get a start. I can visualize an appealing

senior super-sleuth doing his stuff among the seniors with aplomb and dash." Established 1980. Magazine: 7 × 8½; 64 pages. Published biannually. Circulation: 500.

**How to Contact:** Send complete ms. SASE required for ms response. Simultaneous submissions are OK. Receives 6-7 unsolicited mss/month. Accepts 2 mss/issue. Reports on mss in 3-4 months. Sometimes comments on mss. Guidelines available for SAE. Sample copy available for $2.50.

**Terms:** Pays 1 contributor's copy on publication. Acquires first North American Serial rights.

**Tips:** "Be over 50. Eliminate any mental reservation about seniors being over the hill — take a tip from Dorothy Gilman. We're looking out from the top of the hill, not over it. Keep a sense of humor. Write simply; use a 'fog index.' Get to the point fast, make it fun, don't take yourself too seriously. Take a different tack. Be droll, astute, human, and filled with the love of living."

# Writer's Guidelines: A Roundtable for Writers and Editors

▶ **Considers:** short shorts (length: 200-500 words)
▶ **Categories:** "All as long as writer stays within our length requirements."

**Address:** Salaki Publishing, HC77 Box 608, Pittsburg MO 65724

**Contact:** Susan Salaki

**Profile:** Publishes any genre, based on quality. Established 1988. Magazine: 8½ × 11; 26 pages. Published bimonthly. Circulation: 750.

**How to Contact:** Send complete ms with cover letter. SASE required for query and ms response. Simultaneous

submissions are OK. Receives 30 unsolicited mss/month.
Accepts 1 ms/issue. Reports on queries in 1 week; on mss
in 1 month. Comments on mss. Guidelines available for
SASE. Sample copy available for $4.98.
**Terms:** Pays in contributor's copies. Acquires first North
American serial rights and one-time rights. Manuscript
published within 2 months of acceptance. Author gets bio
notes.

### Novel Markets

The following system of symbols has been devised to help you
distinguish the submission interests of the publishers listed in this section. The ⟿ indicates a publisher that is a big market for mysteries
or that is entirely devoted to mystery publication. The ✎ indicates a
mystery market that is most open to established or agented authors.
The ✍ indicates a market that is open to unagented or unpublished
authors.

---

# Accord Communications Ltd.

▶ **Considers:** novels
▶ **Categories:** hard-boiled detective
private eye
police procedural
cozy
amateur sleuth
malice domestic
(strong preference)
romantic suspense

**Address:** Suite B, 18002 15th Ave. NE, Seattle WA
98155-3838, (206) 368-8157 Fax: (206) 368-7968
**Contact:** Karen Duncan, Managing Editor, Mysteries
**Profile:** Established in 1987, Accord launched its mystery
line, A.K.A. Books, in 1993. The company has been publishing 3-4 titles each year. The new mystery line repre-

sents an expansion into the national market. Plans 4 mystery novels in first year of new mystery line.

**How to Contact:** Query first with outline and sample chapters. SASE required for query and ms response. Simultaneous submissions are OK. Receives 20-30 unsolicited mss/month. Reports on queries in 1 month; mss in 2-3 months. Sometimes comments on mss.

**Terms:** Average royalty 12% on net. No advance. Author receives 10 copies of printed book; additional copies at 50% discount. Rights bought vary. Publishes ms 12-18 months after acceptance. Author reviews copyedited ms. Author receives bio note.

**Tips:** Looks for "skillfully crafted prose, tight plotting, well-drawn characters. For the first three years, Northwest writers will be given preference, although we are open to quality work from other regions as well." Will be concentrating on "developing series detectives by new writers, including a strong backlist program." Taboos and tired topics: "No gratuitous sex or violence. We're pretty tired of cartoonish serial killers. . . ."

---

# Aladdin Books

▶ **Considers:** novels
▶ **Categories:** young adult
juvenile
hard-boiled detective
private eye
police procedural
cozy
amateur sleuth
romantic suspense

**Address:** Macmillan Children's Book Group, 866 3rd Ave., 25th Floor, New York NY 10022, (212) 702-6895
Fax: (212) 605-3099

**Contact:** Julia Sibert or Leslie Ward, Associate Editors

**Profile:** Aladdin is a paperback imprint of Macmillan Children's Books. Established 1986. Publishes 450 books/year. Number of mysteries published varies, depending on what is received.

**How to Contact:** Query. SASE required for query and ms response. 50% of accepted mss are agented. Reports on queries in 2-6 weeks; mss in 3-4 months. Guidelines available for SASE. Catalog available.

**Terms:** Pays advance and royalties. Publishes ms 1-2 years after acceptance.

# Archway Paperbacks

▶ **Considers:** novels
▶ **Categories:** young adult

**Address:** Pocket Books, 1230 Avenue of the Americas, New York NY 10020, (212) 698-7000

**Contact:** Patricia MacDonald, Executive Editor

**Profile:** Archway is a paperback imprint of Pocket Books and is aimed at children age 11 and up. Pocket Books publishes 300 books/year and about one-third are mysteries spread across several lines and imprints. In other words, each imprint, including Archway, publishes mystery books as part of their list, but the number varies.

**How to Contact:** Submit query with first outline. SASE required for query and ms response. Simultaneous submissions are OK. Receives 200-300 unsolicited mss/month. Guidelines available.

**Terms:** Pays in royalties. Author reviews galleys; usually reviews copyedited ms. Author receives bio note.

# Atheneum Publishers

▶ **Considers:** graphic novels
novels
▶ **Categories:** considers all
categories

**Address:** Macmillan Publishing Co., Macmillan, Inc., 866 Third Ave., New York NY 10022, (212) 702-2000 Fax: (212) 605-3099
**Contact:** Susanne Kirk, Executive Editor
**Profile:** Atheneum is a division of the large commercial publisher Macmillan. Established 1959. Publishes 310 books/year (for all adult trade lines). Publishes 20 mystery hardcovers/year. Mystery imprints include Otto Penzler Books and Scribner Crime Novels (see separate listings).
**How to Contact:** Send outline and 3 sample chapters. SASE required for query and ms response. Simultaneous submissions are OK. 40% of accepted mss are agented. Reports on queries in 3-4 weeks; mss in 6-8 weeks. Guidelines available for SASE. Catalog available for 6 first-class stamps.
**Terms:** Average royalty 10-12%. Average advance $3,000. Author receives 10 copies of printed book.

# Avon Books

▶ **Considers:** novels
▶ **Categories:** hard-boiled detective
private eye
police procedural
cozy
amateur sleuth
malice domestic

**Address:** The Hearst Company, 1350 Avenue of the Americas, New York NY 10019, (212) 261-6800

**Contact:** Mystery Editor

**Profile:** Avon Books is a large paperback publisher with several lines in all fiction genres. Established 1942. Publishes 300 books/year. Publishes 36 mystery mass market paperbacks/year.

**How to Contact:** Submit through agent only with outline and 2 sample chapters. SASE required for query and ms response. E-mail queries and simultaneous submissions are OK, if indicated. Receives over 60 unsolicited mss/month. Reports on mss in 12-18 months.

**Terms:** Pays advance and royalties. Rights bought are negotiable.

**Tips:** Looks for "good writing and characterization." Taboos and tired topics: "none if book is fabulous, if not, then hard-boiled detective."

## Interview

*Margery Bramen, Senior Editor*
*Avon Books*

*For mystery writers looking for a publisher, Margery Bramen has one piece of unqualified advice: Get an agent. Bramen, a senior editor at Avon Books, offers this as a word of friendly caution to aspiring novelists who want to submit unsolicited manuscripts to major publishing houses.*

*"Unagented submissions take a very long time to be looked at—they don't get priority," Bramen says. "If you don't have an agent, you're going to make mistakes. In a high-volume business like the editorial process of looking at submissions, the people who make mistakes are the people who are going to be rejected on the basis of those mistakes."*

*Bramen should know. Some 600 mystery manuscripts—agented and otherwise—come through her department at Avon Books each year, 36 of which are eventually published. A dozen of those authors will be new to Avon Books this year, Bramen says, and authors who want to count themselves among that exclusive group should take great care in how and to whom they submit their work. Knowing how to package and target submissions is critical to getting your work a prompt first* reading, and agents are invaluable in that area, she says.

"If you don't have an agent you may be wasting your time," Bramen says, "You may be sending the wrong work to the wrong editor at the wrong house if you don't have the expertise of an agent who knows the houses and knows the market."

The mystery manuscripts that do get the attention of Bramen and other editors at Avon Books have two things in common, she says — well-crafted characters that create empathy in the reader and writing that evokes a strong sense of atmosphere.

"The books I really like to edit are the books where I really respond to the characters," Bramen says, adding that characters readers can relate to are more important than those that are strictly realistic. She cites a recently rejected series set in Victorian times in which the protagonist, a woman, "is a second-class citizen, and she has to work behind the scenes — without credit — in order to make her somewhat bumbling husband look good. Now that's more realistic, but it's totally unappealing to me."

Female protagonists are becoming increasingly popular among mystery readers, Bramen says, noting a marked rise in readership for cozies that predominantly feature women. Mysteries featuring female private eyes ("cunningly referred to in the business as 'soft-boiled' private eyes," Bramen says) is another up-and-coming genre, as demonstrated by the popularity of authors such as Sara Paretsky and Sue Grafton.

Whether a manuscript is anchored by a male or female protagonist, it must meet a second important criterion to catch the eye of an Avon editor, Bramen says — a strong evocation of atmosphere.

"No matter what subgenre you're talking about, atmosphere is really important," she says. "One of the things I think the mystery audience responds to is a sense on continuity . . . they want to get to know a place. If you're talking about a cozy, and creating that small-town atmosphere and the readers can see it and smell it and picture the characters operating in that setting, I think they'll come back."

Readers are coming back in increasing numbers for mystery series, according to Bramen, because of the desire for continuity both in characters and atmosphere. She notes that

*while mystery series have had a history of popularity — Sam
Spade and Philip Marlowe being two hard-boiled notables —
lately there has been a resurgence of reader interest in following
a character through ongoing exploits. Strong characters and
atmosphere, now more than ever, can enable an author to create
and maintain a loyal reader base.*

*Bramen cautions against heavy reliance on the traditions
of mystery writing as a model. Derivative dialogue is an absolute
taboo. "It's that sort of clipped, hard speech of L.A. detectives
of the forties that [authors] just copy," she says. "Unrealistic
and bad dialogue always turns me off."*

*Bramen offers two final pieces of advice to aspiring
mystery writers: Read what's being published ("if you want to
be a professional, you've got to see what works") and take great
care in constructing the first half of the book.*

*"The beginning of the book is so important," she says.
"Even in a mystery, when you're talking about a book that needs
suspense to sustain it throughout, I really think the first half of
the book is more important than the second." Overwriting — or
using an excess of overblown words to grab the reader's
attention rather than relying on a premise, concept or dialogue —
is a trap new authors too often fall into, she says, "but if the
first chapter grabs you, you're off to a good start."*

—Anne Bowling

---

# Avon Books/Books for Young Readers

▶ **Considers:** novels
▶ **Categories:** young adult
juvenile

**Address:** The Hearst Co. (Juvenile Div.), 1350 Avenue
of the Americas, New York NY 10019, (212) 261-6800
**Contact:** Juvenile Editor
**Profile:** The juvenile division of Avon Books publishes
books for both middle readers and young adults. Estab-

lished 1942. Publishes 300 books/year. Publishes "very few" mystery trade paperbacks/year; 36 mystery mass market paperbacks/year.

**How to Contact:** Submit through agent only with outline and 2 sample chapters. SASE required for query and ms response. Simultaneous submissions are OK, if indicated. 60% of accepted mss are agented.

**Terms:** Pays advance and royalties. Rights bought are negotiable.

**Tips:** Looks for "good writing and good characterization."

---

# Baker Book House

> ► **Considers:** novels
> ► **Categories:** contemporary Christian fiction and mysteries

**Address:** P.O. Box 6287, Grand Rapids MI 49516-6287, (616) 676-9185 Fax: (616) 676-9573

**Contact:** Director of Publications

**Profile:** Baker Book House is a midsize Evangelical book publisher specializing in Christian fiction. Its mystery program is new. Established 1939. Publishes 130 books/year.

**How to Contact:** Does not accept unsolicited submissions. Query with outline/synopsis and sample chapters. 100% of accepted mss are agented.

**Terms:** Sometimes pays advance. Pays royalty.

# Ballantine Books

▶ **Considers:** novels
▶ **Categories:** considers all
categories

**Address:** Random House, 201 E. 50th St., New York NY
10022, (212) 751-6500
**Contact:** Pamela D. Strickler, Vice President and Senior
Editor
**Profile:** This large commercial publisher is a division of
Random House and includes several imprints including
Ivy, Fawcett and Columbine in addition to Ballantine ti-
tles. Publishes hardcover, trade paperback and mass mar-
ket originals and reprints. Publishes 120 books/year.
**How to Contact:** Submit brief outline/synopsis and com-
plete ms.
**Terms:** Pays advance and royalty.

## *Interview*

Joe Blades, Executive Editor
Ballantine Books

Joe Blades, executive editor of Ballantine Books, has long
been a mystery reader. Before moving to this imprint of Random
House, he was at Avon, where he was known as the "inveterate
mystery reader on the premises" and eventually went on to
shape their mystery list for several years. At Ballantine he does
the "lion's share" of the house's mysteries, which average about
twelve mass market paperbacks and six to seven hardcovers a
year. The other 50 percent of his energies go into general fiction
and some nonfiction.

Ballantine, he says, is a "general purpose, mass market
purveyor of crime fiction. We do try to run the gamut — hard-
boiled and cozy or body-in-the-library are two ends of the
spectrum. We do several series that involve history mysteries —
a Roman and Victorian series and a number that involve specific
professions like the priesthood or forensic anthropology, and

*particular locales. I think it's good to get a mix of geography in our list."*

*Blades is a hands-on editor who acquires, line edits and shepherds his manuscripts through all stages of production. Perhaps more than anything he enjoys working closely with his authors and watching them develop both as writers and as marketing entities. When speaking of Ballantine's marketing program, he points to its "really muscular distribution. We get the books out there," he says, "and we keep them out there longer than most other places." He adds that in the last few years the house has developed a hardcover mystery program. "We were struggling with having wonderful paperback originals, which, because of the prejudice against [this format] didn't get many reviews. This program presents an opportunity to collect good reviews in hardcover, get the press attention, and then twelve to sixteen months later, have its most profitable life as a paperback."*

*Blades is open to publishing all types of mysteries but says, "After a lifetime of reading mysteries, I started to get burned out on most hard-boileds. There seems to be a sameness about the writing, the kinds of detectives and the locales. I think there's a richness in the cozy mystery; it seems to be a way for writers to explore professions and places that are far more diverse." The keys though, he says, are tasteful and high-quality writing, interesting and believable characters and well-constructed narratives. A recent manuscript sent to Blades that he says was immediately attractive was* Dead Folks Blues, *by Steven Womack. "His first-person narrator, a private eye from Nashville, has a voice so appealing, welcoming and warm that it instantly pulls you into the story—the hope of every writer and reader."*

*A trend that is "awakening" within mysteries, he says, is gay and lesbian literature. He gives as examples Michael Nava, a Los Angeles-based lawyer, and Sandra Scoppettone, of New York City, who respectively have introduced a gay detective and a lesbian private eye. As Blades says, these new writers do "bring a wider band to the party" of mystery readers, for the books have also been targeted to gay and lesbian feminist bookstores. "I think any shrewd mystery publisher now is trying to widen the doors a bit. It's a really attractive period from that standpoint." He mentions how the audience has also grown to include history enthusiasts, for example, who are drawn to period mysteries.*

*The last time Blades bought a manuscript that wasn't submitted by an agent was two years ago. Now he is about to publish a third novel by that writer and adds that she has subsequently acquired an agent. "Probably the longer one stays in this business and gets to know agents, the higher the percentage [of agented manuscripts he sees] will go," he says.*

*Blades warns that "neatness really does count. In this increasingly difficult time of gaining acceptance as a first-time writer, it's increasingly important that the physical manuscript be impeccable." He adds that he doesn't wish to see overly elaborate proposals either. "For me just a page or two of what is going on is much preferable to 20-30 page outlines. I think outlines are tremendously vital for authors themselves, but I don't need them." In addition, he says, "the opening pages really have to be grabbers. There needs to be an immediate impact and an avoidance of cliché. If the manuscript is coming in unsolicited, I think that's where the most polished writing has to come. Oddly enough, that is usually where the worst writing is."*

*He adds, "Yet unpublished authors are going to have to go where no one has gone before. The time for emulating successes and being clones of, say, Robert Parker or Dick Francis or Mary Higgins Clark, is past. I think mystery lists are so glutted that to get into the door, you're going to have to really be somebody fresh and not appear to be a diminution, a watered-down version of any big-time writers. It's not enough for an editor to say this person is like X." He warns that now is "not the time to be an unpublished lawyer who wants to write mysteries" in the vein of "John Grisham or Scott Turow. It's late to jump on that bandwagon.*

*"I would advise unpublished writers," he says, "to let loose and be experimental and not try to be a copy of what's out there. Part of it is strictly luck — being in the right place at the right time with the right kind of book."*
—Lauri Miller

⌒ ✎

# Bantam Crimeline Books

► **Considers:** novels
► **Categories:** juvenile
hard-boiled detective
private eye
police procedural
cozy
amateur sleuth
malice domestic
romantic suspense

**Address:** Bantam Doubleday Dell Publishing Group, Inc., 666 5th Ave., New York NY 10103, (212) 765-6500 Fax: (212) 765-3869

**Contact:** Kate Miciak, Associate Publisher

**Profile:** The Bantam Doubleday Dell Publishing Group is one of largest commercial publishers. Established 1945. Bantam publishes 400 titles/year. Bantam Crimeline publishes about 40 books/year. Publishes 15-28 mystery hardcovers/year; 10-12 mystery mass market paperbacks/year. Publishes 2 first novels/year.

**How to Contact:** Does not accept unsolicited mss. Submit through agent only with a 4-page synopsis or outline with cover letter. SASE required for query and ms response and ms return. E-mail, fax queries and simultaneous submissions are OK. 100% of accepted mss are agented. Reports on queries in 3 months; mss in 3 months. Sometimes comments on represented mss. Catalog available for 5 first-class stamps.

**Terms:** Average royalty 4-15%. Buys English world rights. Publishes ms 18-24 months after acceptance. Average time to complete a book after contract signing is 1 year.

**Tips:** Looks for "good writing, suspenseful plot and unique characterization." Will be concentrating on "improving hardcover original releases."

# *Interview*

Kate Miciak, Associate Publisher
Bantam Doubleday Dell Publishing Group

"I didn't start out as a mystery enthusiast," explains Kate Miciak, associate publisher for Bantam. "It wasn't until after I'd finished helping put my husband through grad school. I decided I wasn't going to take a job that I wouldn't want to hold for a long time. This meant I was out of work for seven months. We were broke and what got me through that time was my discovery of secondhand exchange bookstores. I found I could get a mystery for a dollar. It wasn't long before I'd become a mystery fanatic."

At Bantam, Miciak found the job she intended to keep. It was her first job in publishing and she's been with the company for thirteen years. "Later I was told they knew I loved mystery because (unlike other candidates) I nodded my head at names my predecessor mentioned, names no one else knew." Miciak is now in charge of Bantam Crimeline, Doubleday Perfect Crime, and mysteries published in Bantam's other lines.

When Miciak came on board, Bantam's mystery list included mostly dead authors, men who wrote and died in the 1940s and 1950s. Her first change was to begin to sign new, living authors. Her next change, which reflected her own interests, was to include many more strong women authors. This was met with some skepticism by her superiors, but "we survived that," she says. Today Bantam is known as one of the first publishers to pay serious attention to women's detective and mystery fiction and Miciak is particularly proud of the number of authors who got their start with the company.

"When I started reading mystery, I read a lot of what was very classic British mystery, such as those written by Margery Allingham. I liked Ngaio Marsh because I could never guess who did it, but my first love has always been the depth of characterization in a mystery novel. I respond more to character than I do to the corpse or who did it." This interest carries over into her selection of manuscripts. "What I really fall for is voice. Other than that I have no innate criteria."

Bantam is open to all types of mystery. In addition to Bantam Crimeline, which is a paperback imprint, Miciak edits hardcover mysteries for Doubleday Perfect Crime. "This imprint gave us our hardback list and an important library subscription *base." Mysteries may also appear on Bantam's regular hardcover and paperback lists. Miciak points to author Elizabeth George as one who has done well in Bantam's regular line.*

*The mystery lines are not divided by particular types, Miciak explains. "The audience very much defines where I will put a book. Perfect Crime tends to be more traditional in venue, more literary, more psychological suspense, because this is what appeals to people who browse libraries. If I think the book will appeal to a broad audience, I might bring a book out in mass market paperback.*

*"A good example is Diane Davidson's book,* Dying for Chocolate, *which includes recipes. It appealed to lots of people in hardcover and we knew it would do well as a mass market paperback." On the other hand, "Michael Dibdin writes in a very literary style and his books are set in Italy. When I read it I thought 'people who find this book at the local library are going to love it.' "*

*Some books appeal to readers willing to pay $25 for a hardcover, and some appeal to readers who love mysteries but are on a limited budget. The latter make up the library readership.*

*Bantam only accepts manuscripts submitted through agents. Miciak is quick to add, however, that this does not mean she is not interested in new writers. "I've never been afraid of an author without a track record." Davidson had only one book when she approached Bantam and George had none, according to Miciak.*

*Miciak agrees it is difficult to get a good agent, yet insists it is very important in the mystery field. One way to get one, she says, is by referral. "Get to know published authors and ask other writers about their agents. If you develop a relationship, you might be able to get someone to refer you," she says.*

*Not only is an agent better able to get your work seen, Miciak says, "an agent plays an important role as someone with whom you can talk over the business aspects of your career. An author's primary focus should be on writing and an agent can help free up time for that."*

*In addition to a strong voice, Miciak looks for manuscripts that can hold up to the "double challenge of mystery. Mystery readers want to find out who did it but they also want to discover a new universe or world. I think today readers have a strong* sense of the importance of their time. They want their reading to have a purpose. A book is a ticket to another world and they want to learn about something else along the way."

This is one reason readers like mystery series. They become involved in the life of the main character. Once they know the series characters, they enjoy meeting them again. One reason Elizabeth George's books are so popular, says Miciak, is because people become involved with her characters, a circle of four friends. "That's why investing in character, rather than just who done it, is important."

Miciak passes on the advice she received as a young editor. "If you love it you must trust someone else will too. On the other hand, just because you love it, it may not be a success." Yet, she says, if it's an idea that sticks in your mind, write it. Then you'll know.

"Ultimately, what I want—whether it's a classic mystery, a psychological thriller or hard-boiled detective story—is a book that will haunt me. I want to be thinking of it on my commute home. I look for a story so moving people will still be talking about it three months after they've read it."
—Robin Gee

---

# Barricade Books

> ► **Considers:** novels
> ► **Categories:** hard-boiled detective
> private eye

**Address:** 61 4th Ave., New York NY 10003
**Contact:** Carole Stuart, Publisher
**Profile:** Established 1990. Publishes 40 books/year. Publishes 0-1 first novels/year. Average print run in hardcover 5,000. The number of mysteries published by this commercial publisher varies.
**How to Contact:** Query with 2 sample chapters. SASE required for query and ms response. Simultaneous sub-

missions are OK. Disk submissions acceptable. Reports on queries in 2 weeks; mss in 10 weeks. Guidelines available for SASE. Catalog available for 2 first-class stamps. **Terms:** Average royalty 6-12%. Average advance $1,000-5,000. Author receives 25 copies of printed book; additional copies at 40% discount. Buys world rights in all languages. Publishes ms 1 year after acceptance. Average time to complete a book after contract signing is 9 months. Author reviews galleys, copyedited ms and jacket copy. Author receives bio note. Sometimes conducts author tours.

# Berkley Publishing Group

▶ **Considers:** novels
▶ **Categories:** young adult
hard-boiled detective
private eye
police procedural
cozy
amateur sleuth
malice domestic
romantic suspense

**Address:** The Putnam Berkley Group Inc., 200 Madison Ave., New York NY 10016, (212) 951-8800 Fax: (212) 213-6706
**Contact:** Natalee Rosenstein, Senior Editor-in-Chief
**Profile:** Berkley publishes a large commercial category line. Any editor may work on mysteries, so there is no specific mystery imprint or line. Established 1954. The company publishes 70 books (total)/month. Publishes 50 mystery mass market paperbacks/year. Publishes 10 first novels/year.
**How to Contact:** Does not accept any unsolicited mss. Submit through agent only. E-mail, fax queries and simul-

taneous submissions are OK. 100% of accepted mss are agented. Reports on queries in 1 month.

**Terms:** Average royalty 4-10%. Publishes ms 24-30 months after acceptance.

**Tips:** Looks for "a combination of a distinctive voice, strong character, and the quality of writing. Open to all, whatever is good."

## *Interview*

Natalee Rosenstein, Senior Executive Editor
Berkley Publishing Group

Natalee Rosenstein, senior executive editor with Berkley Publishing Group, is a mystery enthusiast who enjoys reading all of Berkley's various authors and genres of mystery, as well as "everyone from Sue Grafton to Tom Cook." A vociferous reader as a child, Rosenstein didn't read strictly mysteries, but did average about four books a week.

She began her relationship with Berkley as a freelance copywriter, later moving into editorial work. Her first editorial position, ten years ago, involved working with reprints of Lawrence Block's books. Berkley bought Eight Million Ways to Die as well as Block's backlist, which Natalee worked on closely with the author.

"My first major acquisition was The Cat Who Saw Red, by author Lillian Jackson Braun. Without question the 'Cat Who' mysteries have been the most fun and the most memorable — every one has been more delightful than the one before and working with the author has been a wonderfully rewarding experience."

Berkley publishes across the genre: cozies, some women P.I.'s, some police procedurals. "For the last couple of years we've been stronger in the cozie-r area, though not strict cozies, but we do all kinds of mysteries." Rosenstein herself works on between fifteen and twenty mysteries per year.

"The most obvious development in the last years has been the phenomonal rise in women mystery writers and women heroines-private eyes or amateur sleuths — and we haven't seen the end of it. The growth is absolutely tremendous — the whole Sisters in Crime phenomenon; the majority of our new mystery writers are women as well.

"Pets seem to be hot — the 'Cat Who' mysteries made

*the* New York Times*' best-seller list. Dog-lover mysteries do well, so you think, are there any other pets?"*

Berkley garnered three Edgar nominations this year, among them was A Cold Day for Murder, *by Dana Stebenow, who was recently discovered by one of Berkley's young editors.* A Cold Day for Murder *has an Alaska setting. "Setting is another element to pay attention to," says Rosenstein.*

*"The book also features a husky dog named 'Mutt,' which adds to the appeal of the story. It's not a cozy, but has a strong woman lead, which is not exactly a new trend, but very much accepted now. People are interested in the character more than the puzzle aspect of the story. You can't get by with stereotypical or cardboard characters. Readers want to see flesh and blood and weaknesses."*

*Berkley doesn't accept unagented manuscripts. Of the manuscripts Rosenstein sees, nothing disqualifies them immediately other than not being in a readable form. "The main things I'm looking for are the voice, the specialness—how engaging the main character or characters are, if there's some kind of internal hook—what makes this book different, what's special about it? Unfortunately, a problem is the wealth of material out there; it can't be just another well-written mystery." The only taboos are blatant or gratuitous racism or sexism.*

*Rosenstein offers this advice to the unpublished mystery writer: "Keep writing. I know it's a cliché, but it's the first rule; don't get discouraged.*

*"Also, try to develop your idea with a series character in mind. We very rarely at this point buy one-shot mysteries; you don't have to have three books written, but have a character that you can see continuing, have some ideas when you submit of what the follow-up books could be.*

*"Try to really develop your own voice—don't try to imitate someone else." She stated that the unpublished writer has a good chance with Berkley. "We publish many first-time mystery writers," says Rosenstein.*
—Donna Collingwood

✍ ✎

# Carroll & Graf Publishers, Inc.

► **Considers:** novels
► **Categories:** hard-boiled detective
private eye
police procedural
cozy
amateur sleuth
malice domestic
romantic suspense

**Address:** 260 5th Ave., New York NY 10001, (212) 889-8772 Fax: (212) 545-7909
**Contact:** Margaret Norton, Editor
**Profile:** Any editor at this commercial publisher can work on mysteries, so there is no specific mystery line or imprint. Established 1983. Publishes 130 books/year. Publishes 10-12 mystery hardcovers/year; "very few" mystery trade paperbacks/year; 10-12 mystery mass market paperbacks/year. Publishes 5-6 first novels/year.
**How to Contact:** Query first or submit outline/synopsis and sample chapters. SASE required for query and ms response. E-mail queries are OK; prefers no simultaneous submissions. Receives 20-25 unsolicited mss/month. Reports on queries in 2 weeks. Sometimes comments on mss. Catalog available.
**Terms:** Average royalty 6-15%. Advance is negotiable. Buys world rights, all languages. Publishes ms 6 months-1 year after acceptance. Author reviews galleys.
**Tips:** "The first few pages must establish original characters, physical location offering unusual possibilities, and different kind of story."

## *Interview*
*Kent Carroll, Publisher and Executive Editor*
*Carroll & Graf*
  *For the folks at Carroll & Graf, finding the right manuscripts for their mystery line—those that are well written and interesting, with characters that breathe on the page—*

requires a bit of detective work. "Most everything is derivative
to some degree," says Kent Carroll, publisher and executive
editor. "But we look for something that has originality to it,
something that will involve the reader. The other considerations
become more objective in terms of publishing, and that has to
do with 'who is the audience?' " Although Carroll admires such
mystery writers as John D. MacDonald and Dashiell Hammett,
he observes that the audience has diversified, and that is
reflected in their expanded line. "Clearly, today there are many
more women readers. Therefore, if you get a good manuscript
that's a tough 'hard-boiled'—even if you like it—you know that
it is more difficult to sell, that there is a smaller audience for it.
However, there is nothing in the genre we are not open to
publishing. We are fairly broad-based."

In the seven years since Carroll and Graf began publishing
mystery originals, they have received praise and recognition for
their works. "This past season in the Los Angeles Times we
were credited with two of the top ten mysteries of the year, and
at Boucheron we also had three nominations," says Carroll of
the young company. "We may not be able to compete
commercially with Warner and a few places like that, but in
terms of quality, and certainly literary attention, we can compete
with anybody."

As for the large number of submissions received, Carroll
mentions some definite disadvantages that writers competing
for publication should avoid. "Manuscripts that come in single-
spaced or in a faint dot-matrix are uncomfortable. What generally
happens is that if there are four manuscripts and you can only
get to two straight away, those that are difficult to read are more
likely to be set aside. Another disadvantage is a manuscript that
attempts to emulate the style of established writers, making it
obvious where the ideas and approach come from.

"Also, there are certain areas—such as a character
discovering they had been abused at six years old—which have
been much accounted for. Usually there is a very clear
relationship between the quality of the book and the degree to
which it is derivative, and a 'hot' social topic tends not to be
very well done. A better writer will have something original to
say, with more imagination, and will be doing things on their
own." However, there are no "taboos" so long as the work is
engaging and well crafted. "There are a lot of possibilities, and

*you can write about almost any subject, any place, with any kind of character. It's pretty wide open. One of the things about mysteries is that they encompass such a variety of life experiences and people — you don't have to be twenty-four and beautiful to be a character.*

*"Mystery publishing will move in a direction that will be led by very good writers," Carroll adds. "It's difficult to predict who they will be and what they will want to do, but the new best people that come along will have an influence on this direction."*
—Michelle Moore

---

# Cliffhanger Press

▶ **Considers:** novels
▶ **Categories:** considers all categories

**Address:** P.O. Box 29527, Oakland CA 94604-9527
**Contact:** Nancy Chirich, Editor
**Profile:** Cliffhanger Press is a small, independent publisher of trade paperback originals, all mystery and suspense. Established 1986. Publishes 2-3 mystery trade paperbacks/year; 2-3 mystery mass market paperbacks/year. Publishes 2-3 first novels/year.
**How to Contact:** Does not accept unsolicited mss. Send synopsis, outline and first 3 chapters with cover letter. SASE required for query response. Simultaneous submissions are OK. Reports on queries in 2-4 weeks. Guidelines available for SASE.
**Terms:** Average royalty 10% hardcover, 8% paper. No advance. Author receives 20 copies of printed book; additional copies at 50% discount. Publishes ms a minimum of 2 after acceptance. Author reviews galleys and jacket copy. Author receives bio note.
**Tips:** "Get into the story right away with strong characters in an interesting situation. Good, unaffected story

writing is important. It's surprising how few manuscripts like this come from first novelists." Will be concentrating on "suspense fiction that is 'mysterious,' but we can't be pinned down to one or two subgenres within the mystery field." Taboos and tired topics: "drugs, spies and the KGB."

---

∞

# Council Oak Books

▶ **Considers:** novels
▶ **Categories:** cozy
                    amateur sleuth

**Address:** 1350 E. 15th St., Tulsa OK 74120, (918) 587-6454 Fax: (918) 583-4995
**Contact:** Andra Whitworth, Associate Publisher
**Profile:** Council Oak Books is a small, independent publisher. Imprints include Brown Bag Mystery Series and Council Oak/Hecate. Established 1984. Publishes 8-10 books/year. Publishes 2 mystery hardcovers/year. Publishes 1 first novel/year.
**How to Contact:** Query only; include sample chapters. No unsolicited manuscripts. SASE required for query response. Simultaneous submissions are OK. 95% of accepted mss are agented. Reports on queries in 1 month. Catalog available for 75¢.
**Terms:** Publishes ms 1 year after acceptance. Author receives galleys and copyedited ms.
**Tips:** "If we want to put it down, so will a reader. We make decisions based on the degree of excitement we feel about a book." Will be concentrating on "female amateur sleuths and cozies." Taboos and tired topics: "no graphic violence or male P.I.'s."
**Titles/Authors of Note:** *The Mark Twain Murders* and *The Glendower Conspiracy: A Memoir of Sherlock Holmes.*

# Crown Publishing Group

> ▶ **Considers:** novels
> ▶ **Categories:** hard-boiled detective
> romantic suspense
> true crime

**Address:** Random House Inc., 210 E. 50th St., New York NY 10022, (212) 572-6117 Fax: (212) 572-6192
**Contact:** Jane Meara, Mystery Editor
**Profile:** The Crown Publishing Group is a large, commercial publisher of both hardcover and paperback originals and reprints. Although there are several imprints, there is no separate one for mystery. Established 1933. Publishes 225 books/year. Publishes 25 first novels/year.
**How to Contact:** Query letters only. SASE required for query response. E-mail queries and simultaneous submissions are OK. Receives 25-30 unsolicited mss/month. 75% of accepted mss are agented. Reports on queries in 3-4 months. Usually comments on mss. Guidelines available for SASE.
**Terms:** Pays advance and royalty. Buys world rights, all languages. Publishes ms 12-18 months after acceptance.
**Tips:** "Originality" makes a ms stand out.

---

# Delacorte HC Mysteries

> ▶ **Considers:** novels
> ▶ **Categories:** hard-boiled detective
> private eye
> police procedural
> cozy
> amateur sleuth
> romantic suspense

**Address:** Bantam Doubleday Dell Publishing Group, Inc., 666 5th Ave., New York NY 10103, (212) 765-5000 Fax: (212) 765-3869

**Contact:** Jackie Farber, Fiction Editor

**Profile:** Bantam Doubleday Dell Publishing Group is one of the largest commercial publishers. Delacorte is one of their mystery hardcover imprints. Established 1965. Publishes 36 mystery hardcovers/year; 12 mystery trade paperbacks/year; 12 books are initially published as hardcover first, then as mystery mass market paperbacks. Publishes 2 first novels/year.

**How to Contact:** Does not accept unsolicited submissions. Submit through agent only. SASE required for query and ms response. E-mail queries and some simultaneous submissions are OK. Receives 25-30 unsolicited mss/month. 100% of accepted mss are agented. Reports on queries in 3 weeks; mss in 1 month.

**Terms:** Royalty percentage is negotiable. Publishes ms 1 year after acceptance. Average time to write book after contract signing is 9-12 months.

**Tips:** "The plot and the narrative" make a ms stand out. Will be concentrating on "thrillers, mostly medical or courtroom, but still interested in detective."

# Doubleday Perfect Crime

▶ **Considers:** novels
▶ **Categories:** juvenile
hard-boiled detective
private eye
police procedural
cozy
amateur sleuth
malice domestic
romantic suspense

**Address:** Bantam Doubleday Dell Publishing Group, Inc., 666 5th Ave., New York NY 10103, (212) 765-6500 Fax: (212) 492-9700

**Contact:** Kate Miciak, Associate Publisher

**Profile:** Doubleday Perfect Crime is a hardcover imprint of the Bantam Doubleday Dell Publishing Group. Established 1897. Publishes 30 mystery hardcovers/year. Publishes 2 first novels/year.

**How to Contact:** Does not accept unsolicited mss. Submit through agent only. E-mail and fax queries and simultaneous submissions are OK. Reports on queries in 3 weeks; mss in 1 month. Sometimes comments on represented mss.

**Terms:** Average royalty 4-15%. Buys English world rights. Publishes ms 18-24 months after acceptance. Average time to complete a book after contract signing is 1 year.

**Tips:** "Good writing—suspenseful plot, unique characterization"—makes a ms stand out. Will be concentrating on "improving hardcover original releases."

---

# Dutton Children's Books, Penguin USA

▶ **Considers:** novels
▶ **Categories:** young adult
juvenile

**Address:** 375 Hudson St., New York NY 10014, (212) 366-2000

**Contact:** Lucia Monfried, Editor-in-Chief

**Profile:** Dutton Children's Books, a juvenile imprint of the large commercial publisher Penguin USA. Established 1852. Publishes many picture books, about 4 young reader titles, 10 middle reader titles, and 8 young adult titles/year. Publishes 60 books/year. Publishes 3 mystery hardcovers/year.

**How to Contact:** Query first. SASE required for query and ms response. E-mail and fax queries and simultaneous submissions are OK; query first. Receives 500 unsolicited mss/month. Reports on queries in 2 months; mss in 2-3 months. Sometimes comments on mss. Guidelines available for SASE. Catalog available for 1 first-class stamp.

**Terms:** Pays advance and royalties. Buys English world rights.

**Tips:** Looks for "quality writing and unique ideas." Will be concentrating on "continuing with quality hardcover fiction and nonfiction.

## *Interview*

*Joseph Pittman, Editor*
Dutton (Penguin USA)

*"Agatha Christie sealed my fate," says Joseph Pittman, editor for Dutton, a division of Penguin USA. "I read a lot of mystery when I was young and have always had an interest in it." Thanks to authors like Christie, he says, he started on cozies and later discovered crime fiction. No matter the type of mystery, he says, "it had always been my aim to have a finger in the mystery field."*

*Pittman has been involved in publishing for seven years and editing mysteries for four. Pittman is new to Dutton, coming to them this year from Bantam where he edited mysteries for the Crimeline program. At Dutton he edits crime fiction including hard-boiled detective novels. However, Dutton's list, he says, is fairly broad and there are editors working on cozies and other subgenres.*

*Dutton has several mystery "stars" but is perhaps best known, says Pittman, for Joan Hess whose Maggody series has been a tremendous success. Dutton publishes about 20 titles per season, in which "we do a fair amount of mystery in all its forms," he says.*

*Pittman lists a number of big-name crime fiction authors as his personal favorites, including Jonathan Kellerman, Elmore Leonard and Robert B. Parker. He also likes many lesser-known authors such as Marc Savage, Karen Kijewski and Robert Cray. He likes courtroom thrillers and says they represent one of the biggest trends in mystery publishing today.*

*"There is a danger with trends, however," he warns. "Something is considered hot and you can find so many books in that area. Then suddenly there seems to be too many and the market becomes saturated. It happened with true crime and techno-thriller and it is beginning to happen with courtroom thrillers."*

*He's quick to add, however, that good books, regardless of their type, will survive market trends. "And as far as trends go, write what you want to write and don't pay much attention to trends. Besides, who knows, you may start the next trend."*

*Submissions to Dutton must be made through an agent, says Pittman, because there are just too many submissions to handle it any other way. In submissions, he appreciates the little things such as a neat manuscript presented in a professional manner. A concise, direct cover letter is also a plus.*

*"So many new writers try to say too much in their cover letters rather than letting the story speak for itself. A cover letter should not detail the plot. I don't want the plot. I want to go into it cold. Basically, the letter should just say what type of manuscript it is, who the author is and here it is."*

*Unlike some editors who look for something to grab them right away, Pittman says he likes to ease into a story. "When I read it usually takes me ten to twenty pages to decide if I'm 'into' a book. I like to get used to an author's style, so I give it a bit of time. However, I do like a good opening line, some twist of a phrase at the start that makes you go 'hmmmm . . .' "*

*A mystery writer as well as editor, Pittman knows the business from both sides. Being an editor gives him a sense of what sells, he says, but he follows his own advice and avoids following trends. He enjoys his job as editor. "I have a lot of fun. When a finished book comes in it's a great feeling." One of the books that made the biggest impact on him, he says, was a book he edited for Bantam, Flamingos by Marc Savage. "It came in pristine condition, beautifully written. It's the book that got me into crime fiction."*

*When asked what makes a good mystery, Pittman says, "The plot's the thing. Remember what you're writing. There's so much emphasis these days on the atmosphere and the characters that the mystery can suffer. I think readers buy these books initially for the mystery, for the story. The trick is to*

*tain a level of mystery while developing characters with whom the reader can identify."*
—Robin Gee

# Eclipse Books

▶ **Considers:** graphic novels
▶ **Categories:** hard-boiled detective
private eye

**Address:** Eclipse Enterprises Inc., P.O. Box 1099, Forestville CA 95436
**Contact:** Catherine Yronwode, Editor-in-Chief
**Profile:** Eclipse publishes both comics and graphic novels, some of which are mysteries. Publishes 10-20 comics and graphic novels/month. Established 1978.
**How to Contact:** Send cover letter, proposal and sample of script. SASE required for query and ms response. Simultaneous submissions are OK. Reports on queries in 3 months. Guidelines available for SASE.
**Terms:** Average royalty 8%. Average advance $35-55/page of comic script.

# Donald I. Fine, Inc.

▶ **Considers:** novels
▶ **Categories:** private eye
police procedural
cozy
amateur sleuth
malice domestic
romantic suspense
trial novels

**Address:** 19 W. 21st St., New York NY 10010, (212) 727-3270 Fax: (212) 727-3277
**Contact:** Sarah Gallick, Mystery Editor
**Profile:** Donald I. Fine, Inc., is a midsize independent publisher. Established 1983. Publishes 30 books total/year. The number of mysteries published varies depending on what is received. All mysteries published are hardcover.
**How to Contact:** Does not accept unsolicited mss. Query only. Submit through agent only. 100% of accepted mss are agented. Catalog available.
**Terms:** Average advance varies. Pays royalties. Buys world rights, all languages. Publishes ms 1 year after acceptance.
**Tips:** Will be concentrating on "mystery suspense, women's fiction."

---

# Foul Play

> ► **Considers:** novels
> ► **Categories:** private eye
> police procedural
> cozy
> hard-boiled detective
> amateur sleuth
> malice domestic

**Address:** Countryman Press, P.O. Box 175, Woodstock VT 05091-0175, (802) 457-1049
**Contact:** Louis F. Kannenstine, President
**Profile:** Foul Play is the mystery imprint of Countryman Press, a small independent publisher. Established 1978. Publishes 6 mystery hardcovers (originals)/year; 8 mystery paperbacks (reprints)/year.

**How to Contact:** Does not accept unsolicited mss. Query with proposal and sample chapters. Agented mss preferred. Reports on queries in 3 months.
**Terms:** Pays advance and royalty.

---

# Gallopade Publishing Group

▶ **Considers:** novels
▶ **Categories:** young adult
juvenile

**Address:** 235 E. Ponce de Leon Ave., Suite 100, Decatur GA 30030, (404) 370-0420
**Contact:** Michele Youther
**Profile:** Gallopade publishes adult trade books and children's books. Mystery imprint is Carole Marsh Mystery Books. Established 1981. Publishes 5 mystery hardcovers/year; 2 mystery trade paperbacks/year; 3 mystery mass market paperbacks/year. Publishes 5 first novels/year.
**How to Contact:** Submit through agent only. SASE required for query and ms response. E-mail queries are OK. Receives 5 unsolicited mss/month. Reports on queries in 1 week. Guidelines available.
**Terms:** Occasionally pays advance and royalties, but most often buys book outright. Work is copyrighted by the publisher (all rights). Buys world rights, all languages.
**Tips:** "Originality and good artwork" make a ms stand out. Will be concentrating on "geographic mysteries."

# Harcourt Brace Jovanovich, Inc.

▶ **Considers:** novels
▶ **Categories:** considers all categories

**Address:** 1250 6th Ave., San Diego CA 92101, (619) 699-6810 Fax: (619) 699-6777

**Contact:** Manuscript Submissions Editor

**Profile:** Harcourt Brace Jovanovich is a large commercial publisher of hardcover originals and paperback reprints. The publisher does not have a separate mystery imprint. Established 1919. Publishes 75-100 books/year. Publishes "very few" first novels/year.

**How to Contact:** Send outline/synopsis and 2-4 sample chapters. SASE required for query and ms response and ms return. E-mail queries are OK. Disk submissions acceptable with hard copy. Receives 800 unsolicited mss/month. Reports on queries in 6-8 weeks; mss in 6-8 weeks. Sometimes comments on mss. Guidelines available for SASE. Catalog available for 4 first-class stamps.

**Terms:** Pays advance and royalties. Rights bought vary. Author reviews galleys, copyedited ms and jacket copy. Author receives bio note. Conducts author tours.

**Titles/Authors of Note:** *The Weirdo*, by Theodore Taylor (winner, Edgar Allan Poe award 1992).

# HarperPaperbacks

▶ **Considers:** novels

▶ **Categories:** young adult
juvenile
hard-boiled detective
private eye
police procedural
cozy
amateur sleuth
malice domestic
romantic suspense

**Address:** Caedmon, HarperCollins, 10 E. 53rd St., New York NY 10022, (212) 207-7000

**Contact:** Carolyn Marino, Senior Editor

**Profile:** Harper Paperbacks is the paperback division of the large commercial publisher, HarperCollins. Established 1960. Publishes 350-400 books/year. Publishes 12 mystery mass market paperbacks/year.

**How to Contact:** Query first. SASE required for query and ms response. Simultaneous submissions are OK, if stated. Disk submissions are acceptable with hard copy. Reports on queries in 2 months. Sometimes comments on mss.

**Terms:** Pays advance and royalties. Rights bought are negotiable. Publishes ms "about one year" after acceptance. Author receives galleys and copyedited ms. Author receives bio note.

**Tips:** Looks for "a fresh, individual voice."

**Titles/Authors of Note:** Tony Hillerman, Susan Isaacs, William F. Buckley, Jr., Len Deighton, Stuart Woods.

## *Interview*

Carolyn Marino, Senior Editor
HarperPaperbacks

The novel that hits the ground running with a gutsy female private investigator, or yanks readers into a tangled web of courtroom drama, may be destined to find a publisher in 1993, says Carolyn Marino, senior editor at HarperPaperbacks, a division of HarperCollins Publishers.

But trends come and go, Marino says, so she sticks to what works. "We try to publish the strongest stories, the ones with tight writing, strong character development, and plots that hold up," says Marino, who specializes in crime fiction and women's fiction.

Marino joined HarperPaperbacks in 1990, shortly after it was formed. By then she was hooked on mysteries. "That's how I ended up doing a lot of mysteries here," says Marino, who has bachelor's degrees in history and English and a master's degree in history. "When a suspense manuscript would come in, I would volunteer to read it." Marino gravitated to the publishing field after working as a newspaper reporter and editor. "I was very interested in editing," she says.

Harper is one of the oldest publishers of mysteries, bringing readers The Moonstone by Wilkie Collins, in 1868 and the Sherlock Holmes stories by Arthur Conan Doyle in the early 1890s. "Bringing out the best in suspense fiction is a tradition we want to continue," Marino says in Deadline, the new Harper newsletter for mystery readers.

What does that mean? "We consider all mystery categories," Marino says. Anything from amateur sleuth to psychological suspense to medical mystery has a chance. "I look for the ones that have pizzazz, that are unusual and keep me reading to the end," she says. While all mysteries are welcome, Harper is strong on cozies and hard-boiled detective novels.

Writers should be their own first editors, advises Marino. "One of my pet peeves is misused verbs in dialogue, for instance, 'he smiled' instead of 'he said.' You can't smile words."

The senior editor is constantly looking for new talent. "Often I find new writers through agents and query letters," she says. Other sources include the mystery newsletter, her own writers and yearly conferences, such as the ones held by Mystery Writers of America.

Of the nearly forty suspense manuscripts received each week, only a few are unagented, and the count is split between male and female writers. "Writers should send a query letter first," Marino says. "If we're interested, we'll ask to see the entire manuscript." Response time is about two months, but if a writer hasn't received a reply by then, he may want to write again. "We try our best to be prompt," Marino says. "Sometimes a delay happens. Right now, we're moving to a

*different floor, so our day-to-day activities are being
interrupted."*

*Marino says writers who want to succeed should keep
submitting their work. "If a writer believes in what he or she has
written and has tried and tried to sell it, I believe it's important
for the writer to stay committed to it. There's no accounting for
taste. What doesn't appeal to one editor may appeal to another."*
—Dorothy Maxwell Goepel

---

# HarperCollins Publishers

▶ **Considers:** novels
▶ **Categories:** private eye
police procedural
amateur sleuth
suspense
thrillers
true crime

**Address:** 10 E. 53rd St., New York NY 10022, (212) 207-
7000
**Profile:** HarperCollins is one of the largest commercial
publishers. Established 1817. Publishes more than 400
books/year. Publishes 5-10 first novels/year.
**How to Contact:** Does not accept unsolicited queries or
mss. Submit through agent only. Receives 75-100 unsolicited mss/month. 100% of accepted mss are agented. Catalog available for 6 first-class stamps.
**Terms:** Royalty percentage negotiable. Buys world
rights, all languages. Publishes ms 9-18 months after acceptance. Author reviews galleys, copyedited ms and
jacket copy. Author receives bio note.
**Tips:** "It's not enough just to have a female detective
anymore. All our mysteries have strong central characters and are well plotted." Taboos and tired topics: "Ho-
mophobic and misogynistic hard-boiled detectives."

**Titles/Authors of Note:** *In Broad Daylight,* by Harry MacLean. Also, mysteries by Tony Hillerman, Stuart Woods and Patricia Wentworth.

---

∞

# Alfred A. Knopf, Inc.

▶ **Considers:** novels
▶ **Categories:** considers all
categories

**Address:** Random House Inc., 201 E. 50th St., New York NY 10022, (212) 751-2600
**Contact:** Editors
**Profile:** This publisher has become known for publishing many literary and commercial best-sellers. Publishes some suspense as a small part of its line. Established 1915. Publishes 45 books/year. Publishes 6-10 first novels/year.
**How to Contact:** Submit complete ms. SASE required for ms response. Simultaneous submissions are OK. 70% of accepted mss are agented. Reports on ms in 6 weeks. Catalog available for 5 first-class stamps.
**Terms:** Average royalty 10-15%. Author receives 10 copies of printed book; additional copies at 40% discount. Publishes ms 1 year after acceptance. Author reviews prepublication galley and copyedited ms. Author usually receives bio note.

---

∞

# Little, Brown & Company, Inc.

▶ **Considers:** novels

▶ **Categories:** considers all
categories

**Address:** 34 Beacon St., Boston MA 02108, (617) 227-0730
**Profile:** Little, Brown & Company publishes adult and juvenile hardcover and paperback originals. Publishes very little mystery and publishes established authors only (no new authors). Publishes 200-225 books/year.
**How to Contact:** Does not accept unsolicited submissions. Query only.
**Terms:** Pays advance and royalty.

---

# Lodestar Books

▶ **Considers:** novels
▶ **Categories:** young adult
juvenile

**Address:** Penguin USA, 375 Hudson St., New York NY 10014, (212) 366-2627
**Contact:** Virginia Buckley, Editorial Director or Rosemary Brosnan, Senior Editor
**Profile:** Lodestar is an imprint of Dutton Publishing, part of Penguin USA. "We do a whole range of books for juveniles and young adults." Established 1979. Publishes 25 books/year. Publishes 1-2 mystery hardcovers/year. Average print run in hardcover 5,000. Publishes 3-6 first novels/year.
**How to Contact:** Query first. SASE required for query and ms response. Simultaneous submissions are OK. 50% of accepted mss are agented. Reports on queries in 1-2 months; mss in 2-4 months. Sometimes comments on mss.
**Terms:** Average royalty 10%. Advance varies. Author receives 20 copies of printed book; additional copies at 40%

discount. Buys world rights, all languages. Publishes ms 18 months after acceptance. Author reviews copyedited ms. Author receives bio note.

**Titles/Authors of Note:** *Second Fiddle*, by Ronald Kidd (Edgar nominee).

---

# Mega-Books

▶ **Considers:** novels
▶ **Categories:** considers all
categories

**Address:** 116 E. 19th St., New York NY 10003, (212) 598-0909 Fax: (212) 979-5074
**Contact:** Carol Gilbert, Managing Editor
**Profile:** Mega-Books is a book packager producing trade and mass market originals, including mystery and mystery series. Produces 95 books/year.
**How to Contact:** Does not accept unsolicited mss. Write for writer's guidelines before contacting. Submit résumé, publishing history and writing samples. 25% of accepted mss are agented. Guidelines free.
**Terms:** Buys ms outright for $3,000 and up.

## *Interview*
Carol Gilbert, Managing Editor
Mega-Books

Writing mystery books for children and young adults means acquiring a certain skill. Rather than just writing down to children, writers should be aware of their audience, says Carol Gilbert, managing editor at Mega-Books of New York. A combination of degrees from Penn State in English and secondary education and her publishing experience help Gilbert understand the components that make a good children's mystery book. For one thing, she says, young readers want to get into the story right away. "Start out running," says Gilbert. "Open up and grab their attention quickly."

As a book packager, Mega-Books operates a little differently than a publishing company. The company produces books for publishers, hiring writers to work on specific projects for which they are paid a flat fee. Packagers are also more likely than publishers to use new writers. The focus at Mega-Books is on ideas that will make a book series and on continuing their established series. Therefore, the company is always looking for new writers and material.

Most everyone is familiar with the Nancy Drew and Hardy Boys books. Mega-Books produces these two well-known children's mystery series for Simon & Schuster, owner of the series and characters. Both of the original Nancy Drew and Hardy Boys series, popular in the 1920s and 1930s, were created by Edward Stratemeyer. The Mega-Books continuance of these series has been successful, says Gilbert, because the publisher has managed to bridge the gap in time by updating the characters and making them attractive to today's children.

Both the Nancy Drew and Hardy Boys series include "digest-size" and "mass market" books. The story lines for both formats are not always the same and each book may be written by a different writer. The digest-size books are aimed at an audience of eight- to twelve-year-olds, basically the same audience for the original series. These contain simplified relationships and plots that children of those ages can understand. The mass market books are for a slightly older audience of ten to fourteen years of age. For these books, the nature of the crime is more complex as are the character relationships.

Mystery plots for children require writers to work carefully, paying particular attention to consistency, says Gilbert. The setting and other elements should be easily intertwined with the main action of the mystery. Characters should be "easily distinguishable from each other," she says, and should act with "logical motives." Blood and gore are not permitted in the books, she adds, except for a slight trace in the Hardy Boys racks or similar young adult books.

If you're interested in writing for either series, you should request a copy of the mass market or digest "bible," Gilbert explains. Series "bibles" are reference books for the series *that include vital information such as character names, dispositions, occupations, relationships, etc. In other words the "bibles" provide the background information you will need to continue the series' story, format and style. For those who would like to invent a new series, other options are available. Gilbert says you can either send a few chapters or a letter stating your idea along with a curriculum vitae and a sample chapter.*

*When asked about the current market for children's and young adult mystery, Gilbert said she is confident of its strength. The mystery, whether it's juvenile or adult, says Gilbert, "is always going to be a viable and robust form and medium."*
—Sheri Toomey

---

# William Morrow and Company, Inc.

▶ **Considers:** novels
▶ **Categories:** considers all categories

**Address:** 1350 Avenue of the Americas, New York NY 10019
**Contact:** Editor
**Profile:** This large publisher has several imprints and publishes both hardcover and paperback originals. About one-fourth of their books are fiction, including some mystery and suspense. Established 1926. Publishes 200 books/year.
**How to Contact:** Does not accept unsolicited submissions. Submit only through agent.
**Terms:** Pays advance and royalty.

---

# Mysterious Press

▶ **Considers:** novels

▶ **Categories:** hard-boiled detective
private eye
police procedural
cozy
amateur sleuth
malice domestic

**Address:** Warner Books, 1271 Avenue of the Americas,
New York NY 10020, (212) 522-5144 Fax: (212) 522-7991
**Contact:** Sara Ann Freed, Executive Editor
**Profile:** As the name implies, Mysterious Press is a mystery imprint of the large commercial publisher, Warner Books. Publishes both hardcover and paperback originals. Established 1976. Publishes 40-60 books/year. Publishes 1-3 first novels/year.
**How to Contact:** Query first. SASE required for query response. Simultaneous submissions are OK. Receives 20-50 unsolicited mss/month. 95-100% of accepted mss are agented. Reports on queries in 6-8 weeks. Sometimes comments on mss.
**Terms:** Pays advance and royalties.

## Interview
*Sara Ann Freed, Executive Editor*
*Mysterious Press*

*Sara Ann Freed has loved reading mysteries all of her life. As executive editor of Mysterious Press, which publishes fifty to seventy mysteries per year, she indulges her love of the whodunit every working day.*

*"I started reading Nancy Drew and Agatha Christie, like everyone else, but I never stopped," Freed says. From there she moved to the great British mystery writers, such as Julian Symons, Josephine Pey and Michael Gilbert. She now prefers the American mystery, particularly the work of Sara Paretsky, Elmore Leonard, Sue Grafton, Tony Hillerman and Elizabeth Peters.*

*"I fell into editing mysteries as a fan," she says. Her career in publishing began with religious and children's books, in the subsidiary rights department. In the late seventies, while working at Walker Publishing, she made the leap to editing,*

*mostly because her colleagues, knowing her great love of the genre, encouraged her to do it. She has been a full-time editor for the past three years at Mysterious Press, which began in 1976 as an independent publisher and is now an imprint of Warner Books.*

*She has worked with a number of popular authors, including Ellis Peters, Marcia Muller, Charlotte MacLeod and Aaron Elkins. But she takes little credit for their success. "You can't really edit books," she says. "You can just help the writer reach his vision of the work. Editing is an eye—and a respect for what the writer does."*

*According to Freed, the goal of Mysterious Press is to publish "a good range of well-thought-out crime fiction." The press is open to all types of mysteries and does not specialize in or stress any subgenre. "We do anything that relates to crime," Freed explains. "None are emphasized over others."*

*The novels she personally acquires often involve strong female protagonists, an area which she came to Mysterious Press to develop. Since she is best known for acquiring this type of book, she tends to see more of them than her colleagues, to whom agents send the thrillers and the more male-oriented stories. But she quickly adds that she is open to all types, from cozies to hard-boiled.*

*Though Freed loves romantic-suspense novels, that area is rarely represented on Mysterious Press list. Likewise, espionage novels seldom find a home there. "Espionage is tough," Freed explains, "because it often seems so contrived and doesn't engage us." Most espionage novels rely too heavily on coincidence and on a simplistic worldview of good guys and bad guys, she says. "Things aren't so black and white in real life."*

*Though she keeps an open mind, considering every manuscript that lands on her desk, she admits to being quickly turned off by worn-out drug plots, overly politically correct stories in which everything is very proper and very dull, and by conventional private detective plots that strongly echo the work of Raymond Chandler and Mickey Spillane.*

*"We've seen that character over and over and over," she says. She's also tired of misogynistic stories. "There's always going to be violence against women, but if the author doesn't handle it in an honest way, I don't want to read about it." Her*

*biggest turnoff? "Colorless, tedious prose—and unfortunately
we see much of it."*

*Biggest turn-on? "Character, character, character," she
proclaims. "If I don't care about the characters, I won't care
about anything else. Old-fashioned puzzle books don't interest
me because the characters are so flat. The books we really enjoy
have very strong characters."*

*Novels that offer "bits of unusual information" also will
grab and hold her attention. "Ellis Peters tells us a lot about
medieval life and culture, Aaron Elkin uses forensic anthropology
in his books, Emma Lathen looks at different kinds of businesses.
People like to think they're learning something new while
reading crime fiction, and I'm no different."*

*Fresh and unusual settings are another key element of
her favorite mysteries. Since many readers share this feeling,
she believes the regional mystery has a great future. "And it
should," she says. "When I started reading crime fiction, people
thought the stories had to be set in big cities or in England.
Now people like to read about other places." She cites the work
of Tony Hillerman as a major catalyst for this change, adding,
"and God bless him for that."*

*This trend toward regional settings should bode well for
the new mystery writer who doesn't live in a coastal metropolis.
Other trends may make it harder for the beginner, according to
Freed. First, publishers are focusing more on finding (and
promoting) The Big Book, the potential best-seller, and less on
cultivating a large number of authors and books. New writers
and writers whose books have achieved only modest sales will,
of course, enjoy fewer opportunities for publication.*

*Second, fewer and fewer publishers are reading
unagented manuscripts. Mysterious Press does not employ
freelance or part-time readers, and the small staff is simply
unable to handle a heavy load of unsolicited material.*

*The good news is that they try to find and publish at least
two new writers a year. Freed advises aspiring mystery writers
to read widely, polish their prose, and to have realistic
expectations about the money they can make through
publication.*

*"Don't expect the first book to be like winning the lottery,"
she says, adding that mystery novels (and novelists) can take
time to attract an audience. This often means slower sales for*

*early novels but, unlike many types of fiction, the mystery enjoys a long life on the publisher's backlist. When an author finally hits with a popular book, readers will find and read the earlier ones, often reading an author's complete body of work.*

*The key, finally, to success? According to Freed, it's no great mystery: "We're just looking for good writing."*

—Jack Heffron

# Naiad Press, Inc.

▶ **Considers:** collections
graphic novels
novels (all lesbian)
▶ **Categories:** hard-boiled detective
private eye
police procedural
cozy
amateur sleuth
romantic suspense

**Address:** P.O. Box 10543, Tallahassee FL 32302, (904) 539-5965 Fax: (904) 539-9731

**Contact:** Barbara Grier, Chief Executive Officer

**Profile:** "Naiad is the oldest and largest lesbian publisher in the world. Books written by and for lesbians." The publisher does not have a separate mystery imprint. Established 1973. Publishes 24 books/year. Publishes 8 mystery trade paperbacks/year. Average print run in trade paperback is 12,000. Publishes 6-8 first novels/year.

**How to Contact:** SASE required for query and ms response. Receives 75-80 unsolicited mss/month. Reports on queries in 2-3 weeks; mss in 2-3 weeks. Usually comments on mss. Guidelines available. Catalog available for 1 first-class stamp.

**Terms:** Average royalty percentage varies. No advance.

Author receives 25 copies of printed book. Buys world rights, all languages. Publishes ms 2 years after acceptance. Author reviews copyedited ms. Author receives bio note.

**Tips:** "I look for good craft writing and an author with some idea of internal editing." Will be concentrating on "series mysteries with strong lesbian protagonists." Taboos and tired topics: "exploitative material, S&M, incest, abuse — all have been done to death."

**Titles/Authors of Note:** *The Beverly Malibu*, by Katherine V. Forrest (won the Lamda Literary Award for best mystery of 1989); *Ninth Life*, by Lauren Wright Douglas (won the Lambda Literary Award for best mystery of 1990); *Murder by Tradition*, by Katherine V. Forrest (won the Lambda Literary Award for best mystery of 1991). "Katherine V. Forrest is becoming a well-known author, and one of her books is being made into a movie."

# NAL/Dutton, Penguin USA

► **Considers:** novels
► **Categories:** considers all
categories

**Address:** 375 Hudson St., New York NY 10014, (212) 366-2000

**Profile:** This large commercial publishing division of Penguin USA has several imprints and publishes hardcovers, trade paperbacks and mass market paperbacks. NAL mystery imprints are Onyx and Signet, but other imprints also publish mystery and suspense. Established 1948.

**How to Contact:** Does not accept unsolicited mss. Submit through agent only. 100% of accepted mss are agented.

**Terms:** Pays advance and royalty.

# *Interview*

*Michaela Hamilton, Editorial Director*

*NAL/Penguin USA*

   *Michaela Hamilton, editorial director for NAL's mass market program, has been editing mysteries, as well as a wide variety of other books, for 20 years. Over the years, she says, she's worked on almost every type of mystery book and is hard-pressed to choose a favorite. In fact, when asked to list her favorite mystery authors, she rattles off dozens of names, authors working in everything from cozies to hard-boiled detective novels. All of them, she adds, are NAL authors, and many she has worked with personally.*

   *A division of Penguin USA, NAL publishes mass market mysteries under either the Signet or Onyx imprints, but which of those a book appears under is more a matter of scheduling than any other criteria, explains Hamilton. If you count traditional categories only, she says, NAL publishes two to four mysteries every month. Yet, if you add suspense categories such as serial killer and legal thriller novels, the list grows to five to eight titles per month — "nearly 50 percent of our list," she says.*

   *NAL, says Hamilton, is known for publishing a very diverse mystery list. "I think right now we're best known for our female authors and mysteries, but that might just be because they've become so popular. Two of our women authors have become very well known — Lydia Adamson and Joan Hess, and I know in the future Sharyn McCrumb will be very important to our list. Our legal thrillers, cozies, cat mysteries, and serial killer versus cop novels are also very popular areas."*

   *In addition to the increased interest in novels by female authors featuring female sleuths, Hamilton says the greatest change she's witnessed in the mystery market in recent years has been its tremendous growth. "I don't think mystery is moving in any one direction. It's moving in all directions, diversifying all over the place. That's what gives the mystery field so much vitality. There are so many different kinds of mystery for so many different levels of taste."*

   *When speaking of mystery, Hamilton is careful to mention suspense as a separate but related area. Legal thrillers have done very well at NAL, she adds. In fact, she says, she's very excited about the publication of* Mitigating Circumstances, *a book by Nancy Taylor Rosenberg. "The book has received tons of attention. It's a national best-seller. We've sold rights in fifteen other countries. Columbia/TriStar bought the film rights, and Jonathan Demme is already committed to the project. This level of success has made acquiring that book a real milestone in my career."*

Hamilton is also proud of her role in developing a very different type of mystery. *"I noticed many mystery readers seemed also to be cat lovers, so I decided to search for an author who could develop a series involving cats."* She found the perfect author for the job in Lydia Adamson. Adamson's sleuth is cat-sitter Alice Nestleton. Her series was an instant hit and now includes nine books.

Although NAL accepts manuscripts only through agents, Hamilton is always on the lookout for new talent. *"The main thing I look for is surprise. I want to see things I haven't seen before. I want to see the work of an author who can give me something fresh. One who can take a standard formula and make it new."*

This goes hand-in-hand with Hamilton's pet peeve. *"I want no clichés. That means no cliché of writing, plot or character."* While this seems like a tall order coming from an editor who has been working in the field as long as Hamilton, she's confident that *"there are authors out there making mystery new all the time."*

One of the biggest mistakes some new mystery authors make is skipping around within the genre, Hamilton says. *"Don't go from doing one private eye novel to a cozy and then on to something else. People who jump all over the place penalize themselves. Try instead to identify an audience and write to that audience consistently, over a number of books. In the mystery area it can take six to twelve books before your name has any clout. You must develop your own niche in the market and stay with it."*

To be successful, she says, writers must keep in mind that they are writing for someone else. *"You have to think about the reader you are trying to reach. Get to know and respect that reader's taste."*

—Robin Gee

# New Victoria Publishers

► **Considers:** novels (all lesbian/
feminist)
► **Categories:** private eye
hard-boiled detective
amateur sleuth
romantic suspense

**Address:** P.O. Box 27, Norwick VT 05055, (802) 649-5297
**Contact:** Claudia Lamperti, Fiction Editor
**Profile:** This small press specializes in feminist and lesbian fiction, including mystery and thrillers. Established 1976. Publishes 6 books/year. Publishes 2-3 mystery trade paperbacks/year. Publishes 3-4 first novels/year.
**How to Contact:** Query first with outline and sample chapters. SASE required for query and ms response. E-mail queries are OK. Receives 4-6 unsolicited mss/month. Sometimes comments on mss, only if SASE included. Reports on queries in 2-4 weeks; mss in 4-6 weeks. Guidelines for SASE.
**Terms:** Pays royalty. Buys world rights, all languages. Publishes ms 1 year after acceptance. Average time to complete a book after contract signing is 1 year.
**Tips:** Looks for "good writing, good characterization, well-drawn-out scenes and good story line. Prefer strong women characters, definitely no sexism."

# W.W. Norton & Co., Inc.

► **Considers:** novels
► **Categories:** considers all
categories

**Address:** 500 5th Ave., New York NY 10110, (212) 354-5500 Fax: (212) 869-0856
**Contact:** Liz Malcolm, Editor
**Profile:** W.W. Norton is a large commercial publisher. Established 1923. Publishes 250 books/year. Publishes "very few" mystery paperbacks. Publishes 2 first novels/year.
**How to Contact:** Submit outline/synopsis and first 50 pages. SASE required for query and ms response. Simultaneous submissions are OK. Receives 300 unsolicited mss/month. 90% of accepted mss are agented. Reports on queries in 8-10 weeks. Sometimes comments on mss. Guidelines available for SASE. Catalog available for 2 first-class stamps.
**Terms:** Average royalty 7½-10%. Author receives 15 copies of printed book. Buys all rights.

---

# Otto Penzler Books

▶ **Considers:** novels
▶ **Categories:** considers all categories

**Address:** 129 W. 56th St., New York NY 10019, (212) 765-0923 Fax: (212) 265-5478
**Contact:** Kate Stine, Editor-in-Chief
**Profile:** "Small to midsize commercial publisher devoted to the world's most distinguished mystery-crime-suspense fiction." Established 1993. Publishes 24 new titles, 24 reprints/year. Publishes 36 mystery hardcovers/year; 12 mystery trade paperbacks/year.
**How to Contact:** Does not accept unsolicited submissions. Submit through agent only. 100% of accepted mss are agented. Reports on 4-6 weeks. Seldom comments on rejected mss.
**Terms:** Average advance varies. Average royalty 10-15%.

Author receives 15 copies of printed book; additional copies at 50% discount. Rights bought vary widely. Publishes ms 8-12 months after acceptance. Average time to complete a book after contract signing is 1 year. Author reviews galleys, copyedited ms and jacket copy (if requested). Author receives bio note.

**Titles/Authors of Note:** John Gardner, Stephen Solomita, William Tapply.

---

# Pocket Books

> ► **Considers:** collections
> novels
> ► **Categories:** hard-boiled detective
> private eye
> police procedural
> cozy
> amateur sleuth
> malice domestic

**Address:** Simon & Schuster Trade Division, The Simon & Schuster Bldg., 1230 Avenue of the Americas, 13th Floor, New York NY 10020, (212) 698-7000 Fax: (212) 632-8084

**Contact:** Jane Chelius, Mystery Editor

**Profile:** Pocket Books, a large commercial house, publishes hardcover and paperback originals and reprints. The publisher does not have a separate mystery imprint. Publishes 300 books/year. Publishes 8-10 mystery hardcovers/year; a varying amount of mystery trade paperbacks/year; 24 mystery mass market paperbacks/year. Publishes 1-4 first novels/year.

**How to Contact:** Query with outline. SASE required for query response. Simultaneous submissions are OK. Receives 50 unsolicited mss/month. 90% of accepted mss are agented. Reports on queries in 6 months. Sometimes comments on mss. Catalog available.

**Terms:** Pays advance and royalties. Author receives 25 copies of printed book; additional copies at 40% discount. Conducts author tours. Buys U.S., Canadian or world rights in English language. Publishes ms 18-24 months after acceptance. Average time to write book after contract signing is 7-9 months. Author reviews galleys, copyedited ms and jacket copy. Author usually receives bio note.

**Titles/Authors of Note:** *Maze*, by Tom Adcock (Edgar for Best Original Paperback Mystery of 1991); *The Staked Goat*, by Jeremiah Healy (Private Eye Writers of America Best Novel of 1986); *Devil in a Blue Dress*, by Walter Mosley (John Creasy won the United Kingdom's Award for Best Crime Novel of 1990).

## Interview

Jane Chelius, Senior Editor
Pocket Books

Growing up in a family of avid mystery readers, Jane Chelius, senior editor at Pocket Books, collected all the books in the Nancy Drew series. "For many years it was the favorite birthday present," recalls Chelius, who graduated from Duke University in the late sixties. Although she knew she wanted to go into publishing, she never guessed that she'd find her niche as a mystery editor.

"I wanted to be more of a literary editor," says Chelius, "but as it happened, the first job I got was at Fawcett Gold Medal Books which did a lot of suspense and mystery in those days — and I discovered that I had a knack for it."

Seven years later, Chelius left to raise a family, freelancing for various houses. She joined Pocket Books six years ago at the onset of their mystery program, which began with one paperback mystery a month. In 1989, they began to publish mystery in hardcover.

For those fortunate enough to sell their manuscript to Pocket Books, the relationship is quite often a long-lasting one because of the house's interest in developing series writers, enabling them to use one book to sell another. "Once we take on a mystery writer, we expect to have a new book roughly once a year," says Chelius. The downside is that most of the slots are filled with Pocket Books' established writers, making it difficult to take on a new author unless someone drops out.

Although Chelius admits an affinity for mysteries on the cozy side, as well as the hard-boiled detective story, she's hesitant to say what might turn her off about a novel. "If I said I absolutely couldn't bear to read a book that had pink petunias in the first paragraph, the very next day someone would send me a perfectly wonderful novel that had pink petunias in the first paragraph," she says. "I do, however, think the world has had enough drug plots for one century."

Pocket Books will review unsolicited materials but for the most part "it's pretty much agents only" through whom Chelius receives twenty five to thirty manuscripts a month. For those interested in sending unsolicited manuscripts, however, Chelius prefers a letter of inquiry first, including a brief description of the plot and main character (along with whatever secondary characters seem appropriate), and a few words about the writer's background, particularly as it pertains to what he or she is writing about.

In crafting your mystery, advises Chelius, it's important to come up with a fresh approach. Don't imitate even the best, because it's already been done. Be imaginative about the setting. "What's wonderful about mystery now is that virtually any kind of setting can be made suitable. We're now seeing a lot of historical mysteries going back centuries, so if you know something about a particular period in history you should write a mystery set there."

As for the future of mystery, Chelius says it seems to be moving in a great many directions. "I think that there are probably fewer private eye novels; mystery seems to be expanding much more in the area of amateur sleuth, particularly the female sleuth." But Pocket Books, adds Chelius, is interested in continuing to appeal to a broad range of readers.

Success as a mystery writer is often the result of a combination of talent, luck and perseverance. "I think you have to go into this realizing that you're not picking the easiest thing in the world to do, and decide you're going to take your lumps and keep going."

Accordingly, if your proposal doesn't receive a rave review from an editor don't be disheartened. "Every book deserves an editor who loves it, and editors are as different from one another as anybody else," she says. "If the person who

*it first hates it and rejects it, that doesn't mean that it's a bad book. It just means it hasn't found the right editor yet."*
—Kathleen M. Heins

# G.P. Putnam's Sons

▶ **Considers:** novels
▶ **Categories:** young adult
juvenile
hard-boiled detective
private eye
police procedural
romantic suspense

**Address:** The Putnam Berkeley Group Inc., 200 Madison Ave., New York NY 10016, (212) 951-8700 Fax: (212) 532-3693

**Contact:** Editor

**Profile:** G.P. Putnam's Sons is a division of the large commercial publisher, Putnam Berkley Group. Both Putnam's and Grosset & Dunlap (also associated with the Putnam Berkley Group) publish mysteries, but there is no separate mystery imprint. Established 1838. Publishes 150 mystery hardcovers/year (adult and juvenile).

**How to Contact:** Does not accept unsolicited mss. Query only. E-mail and fax queries and simultaneous submissions OK. Sometimes comments on mss.

**Terms:** Pays advance and royalties. Rights bought are negotiable.

**Tips:** Looks for "strong story, good dialog, memorable characters." Will be concentrating on "building relationships with authors with series as a goal."

# Q.E.D. Press

► **Considers:** novels
► **Categories:** private eye
hard-boiled detective
amateur sleuth

**Address:** 155 Cypress St., Ft. Bragg CA 95437, (707) 964-9520
**Contact:** John Fremont, Senior Editor
**Profile:** This small press publishes hardcover and paperback originals. Established 1985. Publishes 10 books/year. Publishes 0-1 mystery hardcover/year; 1-2 mystery trade paperbacks/year. Publishes 1 first novel/year.
**How to Contact:** Submit outline/synopsis and 3 sample chapters. SASE required for query and ms response. Simultaneous submissions are OK. Disk submissions preferred. Receives 500 unsolicited mss/month. 10% of accepted mss are agented. Reports on queries in 2 months; mss in 3-4 months. Catalog for 2 first-class stamps.
**Terms:** No advance. Average royalty 8-15%. Author receives 25 copies of printed book; additional copies at 40-50% discount. Buys world rights, all languages. Publishes ms 6-24 months after acceptance. Average time to complete a book after contract signing is 3-6 months. Author reviews pre-publication galleys. Author receives bio note.

# Random House, Inc.

► **Considers:** novels
► **Categories:** considers all
categories

**Address:** 201 E. 50th St., New York NY 10022, (212) 751-2600

**Profile:** This large publisher has several imprints and publishes hardcover and paperback originals. Mystery and suspense are included in many Random House lines including Ballantine (see Ballantine listing and interview with Elisa Wares of Fawcett and Ivy Books below). Trade division publishes 120 books/year.

**How to Contact:** Query with outline/synopsis and 3 sample chapters. SASE required for query response. Agented mss recommended.

**Terms:** Pays advance and royalty.

## *Interview*

*Elisa Wares, Editor*
*Fawcett and Ivy Books, division of Ballantine, division of Random House*

*Julie Smith, Joyce Christmas and Janet Dawson are a few of the mystery writers Fawcett and Ivy Books editor Elisa Wares has worked with during her three years at this Random House imprint. They are creators of women sleuths who exemplify what Wares seeks in characters — ordinary people who "use their heads more than their arms."*

*Although Fawcett still publishes hard-boileds, Wares says the list has generally evolved toward softer cozy mysteries, which is her area of concentration within mystery. Wares is particularly interested in women authors and envisions her audience as predominately female — women "who grew up with Agatha Christie, intelligent readers you can't pull anything over on."*

*In the two manuscripts Wares receives each week (usually from agents), she looks for good writing and dialogue, carefully constructed plots, close attention to detail, and "sometimes," she says, "I like a sense of humor." She won't even consider those mysteries in which the reader "can guess who the killer is very early on." Readers, she explains, "want to be challenged, to guess; they don't want to know who did it till the end." And, she adds, "I dislike gratuitous violence. Obviously there's going to be violence with murdered bodies all over, but I don't want my sleuth to be beating people over the head, and I don't want to see a lot of violence against women."*

*Wares says it is important for her to present a mix of geography and professions, and she tends to think in terms of series potential when considering these elements. "I have a great New Orleans mystery series. New Orleans is very atmospheric, and there are so many social levels. You can place the same character in different areas of this city and have a different kind of book each time. I have a Milwaukee hospital series, which I love." She cautions against using professions that don't have much scope. "I tried real estate, but it didn't work; it was too limited."*

*She believes that mysteries will continue to evolve as the country evolves and attitudes changes. "I think there will be more gay mysteries and more social mysteries," she says. "I have no African-American or Hispanic detectives, and I wish I did. And I would like them to be written by people who are African-American or Hispanic."*

*Because Wares feels an agented submission carries much more weight immediately, she strongly recommends getting an agent. Submissions from agents mean less work for the editor whose time is very tight. It means that the manuscript has had one reading, gone through the first stage already, and is cleaner as a result. For those who are unable to get an agent, an alternative, she says, is a reading group, a critique body that can help an author to rigorously work through a manuscript.*

*Her other advice is to read as many mysteries as you can. "See what's out there, see what the trends are. Have some fun with the sleuth. Find a good profession, and make it a real person. Keep going over it. If you don't have an agent or a reading group, make sure you go over it until everything is really precise. And, surprise yourself."*

—Lauri Miller

---

# St. Martin's Press, Inc.

▶ **Considers:** novels

**Categories:** hard-boiled detective
private eye
police procedural
cozy
amateur sleuth
malice domestic

**Address:** Macmillan Limited, U.K., 175 5th Ave., New York NY 10010, (212) 674-5151 Fax: (212) 420-9314
**Contact:** Editor (all editors look at mystery submissions)
**Profile:** St. Martin's, a large commercial publisher, has a very strong mystery program. There is no separate mystery imprint. Established 1952. Publishes 800 books/year. Publishes 100 mystery hardcovers/year; 8 mystery mass market paperbacks/year. Publishes first novels, but number varies each year.
**How to Contact:** Query or submit complete ms. SASE required for query and ms response. Simultaneous submissions are OK, but "we want to be told it's a simultaneous submission." Receives 35-50 unsolicited mss/month (for one editor). 50-75% of accepted mss are agented. Reports on queries in 1 month; mss in 2-2½ months. Mss should be "double spaced, typed or word processed; number pages consecutively, not by chapter."
**Terms:** Average royalty 10-15% on regular trade sales. Average advance $2,500+. Author receives 10 copies of printed bok. Publishes ms 8-12 months after acceptance. Average time to write book after contract signing is 1 year. Author reviews copyedited ms.
**Tips:** Looks for "fresh voice." Taboos and tired topics: "Personally, drug rings, psychic phenomena, but I'm only one editor."

## Interview
*Ruth Cavin, Senior Editor/Associate Publisher*
Thomas Dunne Books
St. Martin's Press
*The mystery program of St. Martin's Press is unusual in a couple of respects: It publishes more mysteries by first-time mystery writers (and more un-agented submissions) than any*

other major mystery publisher, and it publishes only hardcovers, which is particularly attractive to authors. Hardcovers garner the most press attention, and thus are at the greatest advantage when entering the paperback market. Ruth Cavin, senior editor and associate publisher of Thomas Dunne Books, tells a story that illustrates the excitement of bringing new writers into this strong mystery publishing program.

"St. Martin's is located in the Flatiron Building of New York City. Because it is a landmark, the elevators cannot be modernized. They're very slow—legendary. I was waiting for the elevator one day and this very attractive woman came up and asked what she should do with a mystery for St. Martin's; I told her to give it to me. It was a four- to five-chapter manuscript with only her name on it, no phone number or address. So I put in on the shelf with the eighty-five other books I had to read and didn't do anything about it." A month later Cavin received an indirect inquiry from her (the woman didn't know who she had given the manuscript to and contacted another editor), and so "took the manuscript off the shelf, read it and was absolutely thunderstruck. This woman is a real writer, an absolutely gripping, wonderful, marvelous writer. So I called her and told her I liked what I saw and that when she finished the book, I'd like to see it. In time it came. The plot needed some work; it was rather thin, but the writing was just out of this world. So I called and said I'd like to buy her book. She said, 'Just a minute.' I figured she was getting a pen or something. Then I heard her yell, 'whoo hoo.'" Cavin laughs as she remembers this emotional response from Mary Anne Kelly, whose second book, Foxglove, has since been published by the press and whose third is in the works.

As this anecdote shows, it is good writing that Cavin is after. As one who receives five unsolicited manuscripts a week, must see sixty books through publication each year, and has but one assistant, she must continually read ("at home, on the train, at baseball games") and be able to determine with relative speed whether a manuscript merits publication.

Although she is open to all mystery subgenres, she prefers fiction to nonfiction because "it is truer to life." Of course, she admits she has her prejudices. "I'm not fond of mysteries that are really thrillers about organizations like the C.I.A.," she says. "I'm much more interested in crimes involving real people with real passions. I think things that are not real or are super-real, such as visions of the future and ghosts, are a cop out in mystery."

What Cavin is looking for is "a fresh voice, something that is different in a good way. Most of the manuscripts I get really aren't bad. There's got to be something outstanding about the book, something that will make me want to continue reading it. This is not necessarily some violent happening in the prologue. It's what the author has done that's personal, different and interesting. It's the voice and the way the author handles things."

In order for a mystery to have a large audience it's necessary to have a great deal of suspense. Yet, she says, "if you have good writing, believable characters with some depth and reality, and a real sense of atmosphere, a problem with the plot can be fixed; but it can't work the other way around. Plot gimmicks and cardboard characters, no real sense of place or clunky writing are harder to get away with."

Cavin, who also writes a mystery newsletter each month for St. Martin's, says that she isn't seeking particular professions or locales, but that she is trying to publish books that a range of people will want to read. "The mystery audience is so wide and varied; all sorts of people read mysteries—from truck drivers to presidents (and Clinton is not the first one), from Ph.D.s to people who have barely made it through high school."

Cavin is suspect of the talk of trends within the genre. She says that the expansion of the cozy into quieter and more sophisticated mysteries is more popular now than it has been in the past, but she warns that these things come and go. "For the past ten years people have spoken of the female private eye as new. But of course it's not a trend anymore; it's an established fact." She does admit, though, that people still seem to be clamoring for books about women by women. "There have always been women mystery writers, but they haven't had hard-boiled private eyes; they've had little old ladies. So there is a desire for more hard-boiled women, but that doesn't influence my buying. If I like a book, I'll buy it; I don't care if the author or protagonist is male or female."

Because the press is always on the lookout for new writers, it holds two contests every year—one for the best private eye mystery and one for the best malice domestic or traditional

*mystery. With regard to regular submissions, Cavin prefers an outline or synopsis in addition to two to three chapters. "The proposal will let me know whether I want to see more or not," she says. Just as it did with Mary Anne Kelly.*
—Lauri Miller

# Scholastic Inc.

► **Considers:** novels
► **Categories:** juvenile
young adult

**Address:** Scholastic Corp., 730 Broadway, New York NY 10003, (212) 505-3000 Fax: (212) 505-3377
**Contact:** Regina Griffin, Senior Editor
**Profile:** Scholastic is a large, commercial, juvenile publisher. Established 1920. Publishes 300 books/year. Publishes "very few" mystery hardcovers; 10 mystery paperbacks/year.
**How to Contact:** Does not accept unsolicited mss. Submit through agent only. SASE required for query and ms response. Reports on queries in 1 month; mss in 3 months.
**Terms:** Pays advance and royalties. Publishes ms 12-18 months after acceptance.

# Scribner Crime Novels

► **Considers:** novels

► **Categories:** hard-boiled detective
private eye
police procedurals
cozy
amateur sleuth
malice domestic

**Address:** Charles Scribner's Sons, Macmillan, Inc., 866 3rd Ave., New York NY 10022, (212) 702-2000 Fax: (212) 605-3099

**Contact:** Susanne Kirk, Executive Editor

**Profile:** Scribner Crime Novels is a mystery imprint of Charles Scribner's Sons, a part of Macmillan, one of the largest commercial publishers. Established 1846. Publishes 24-25 mystery hardcovers/year. Publishes 5 first novels/year.

**How to Contact:** Submit through agent only. SASE required for query and ms response. Fax queries and simultaneous submissions are OK. Disk submissions acceptable. 98% of accepted mss are agented.

**Terms:** Pays standard royalty percentage. Average advance varies. Usually buys North American rights. Publishes ms 1 year after acceptance. Average time to write book after contract signing is 1 year. Author reviews galleys, copyedited ms and jacket copy. Author receives bio note.

**Tips:** "The writing and the depth of the characterization make a manuscript stand out. I look for something stylish and fresh and original, whatever the type of mystery." Taboos and tired topics: "Drugs. Not much interested in international thrillers."

**Titles/Authors of Note:** *All That Remains*, by Patricia D. Cornwell; and *The Hangman's Beautiful Daughter*, by Sharyn McCrumb.

## *Interview*

*Susanne Kirk, Executive Editor*
Charles Scribner's Sons

*Susanne Kirk, executive editor at Charles Scribner's Sons, has been editing mystery books for about fifteen years now. "It started with just the occasional mystery, and then it became my specialty," she said. Kirk is a graduate of the Columbia School of Journalism and began her publishing career in Tokyo in the early seventies. She joined Scribner's Sons in 1975 as editor for co-editions and imports.*

*Kirk said she "definitely" reads mysteries just for fun and her favorite authors are her own, "of course." Her list reflects her own taste. "Other favorites include Reginald Hill, Colin Dexter, Elizabeth Peters, Lindsey Davis, P.D. James, Sara Paretsky, and Sue Grafton."*

*While Scribner's has one of the bigger mystery lists, with twenty-four books published per year, Kirk finds that the two available slots open each month are never enough for all the books she would like to do. Kirk does mostly police procedurals and amateur detectives, with a few private eyes. "But there are no absolute guidelines. I like to have a good mix. The list has reflected my personal taste for quite some time, but I am also guided by what sells. The tough private eyes have not sold well for us recently.*

*"Most first mysteries don't turn a profit," according to Kirk, who views taking on a new writer as a long-term investment. "You're building. You're hoping that by the time you have two or three or four [books] this author will have received some wonderful reviews and word-of-mouth. At that point, if not earlier, you will make a paperback sale." Furthermore, to gain one of the open slots, the beginner must beat out other talented writers trying to break in and, perhaps, dislodge an established author. Kirk confesses to us that she hates to lose one of her writers. "That, of course, is a terribly difficult decision. It's a business decision, but it's also emotional . . . it's difficult."*

*The most memorable book of Kirk's career is Postmortem, by Patricia D. Cornwell. "It started as a 'small' book and went on to win just about every prize, including the Edgar for best first book. The author is now a best-selling author in both hardcover and paperback."*

*Good writing, as well as the ability to convey characters and pace, are essential manuscript ingredients that interest Kirk. "I want to be entertained. I look for a story that I literally can't put down." She tells of taking a promising manuscript to the beach to read, which is, after all, what a lot of readers do. Unfortunately, even though the work was from a successful,* published writer, she found she could all too easily put it down. She never finished it.

"Drug-related plots tend to be boring. I like an interesting motive. I'm less favorably inclined toward manuscripts that rely on action and dialogue to the exclusion of texture, mood, character, etc." There are no absolute taboos for Kirk, but she is not interested in gratuitous violence and sex. "I want what's right and necessary for the book," she says.

This is an exciting time for mystery publishing according to Kirk. "We have thrown out our old notions and are open to new ideas. We're looking for fresh locations and interesting new characters. The world is beginning to recognize that fine mysteries are fine novels."

Among the clues Kirk offers aspiring mystery writers are: study the form, write and rewrite, and think of character as well as plot. One more clue—"It may be a personal preference, but I do like humor." She also suggests attending mystery conventions—especially the regional ones. And, finally, "don't give up hope."

—Donna Collingwood with Hal Blythe and Charlie Sweet

---

# Simon & Schuster

▶ **Considers:** novels
▶ **Categories:** considers all
categories

**Address:** 1230 Avenue of the Americas, New York NY 10020

**Profile:** This large commercial publisher includes many divisions and imprints. Mystery and suspense are included in their adult trade lines.

**How to Contact:** Does not accept unsolicited submissions. Submit through agent only. 100% of accepted mss agented.

**Terms:** Pays advance and royalty.

# Soho Press, Inc.

▶ **Considers:** novels
▶ **Categories:** hard-boiled detective
private eye
police procedural
amateur sleuth

**Address:** 853 Broadway, New York NY 10003, (212) 260-1900 Fax: (212) 260-1902
**Contact:** Juris Jurjevics, Editor-in-Chief
**Profile:** Soho is a "small, fiercely independent press." Established 1986. Publishes 25 books/year. Publishes 1 mystery hardcover/year. Publishes 5-8 first novels/year.
**How to Contact:** Submit complete ms. SASE required for ms response. Simultaneous submissions are OK. Receives 300 unsolicited mss/month. 50% of accepted mss are agented. Reports on mss in 2 months. Rarely comments on mss. Guidelines available for SASE. Catalog available for $1.21 postage.
**Terms:** Average royalty 10-12-15%. Author receives 20 copies of printed book; additional copies at 50% discount. Buys world rights, all languages. Publishes ms 1 year after acceptance. Author reviews galleys, copyedited ms. Author receives bio note. Sometimes conducts author tours.

# Viking Children's Books

▶ **Considers:** novels
▶ **Categories:** young adult
juvenile

**Address:** Penguin USA, 375 Hudson St., New York NY 10014, (212) 366-2000 Fax: (212) 366-2666

**Contact:** Elizabeth Law, Mystery Editor
**Profile:** Viking Children's Books is "a prestigious trade publisher of children's books for all age groups, from very young to young adult. Publishes a whole spectrum from 'standard' to avant garde slant." Established 1933. Publishes 20-110 books/year. Publishes 1-2 mystery hardcovers/year; 5 mystery trade paperbacks/year.
**How to Contact:** Submit complete ms with cover letter. SASE required for ms response. Receives 400 unsolicited mss/month. 50% of accepted mss are agented. Reports on mss in 8-12 weeks. Sometimes comments on mss.
**Terms:** Pays advance and royalty. Author receives 20 copies of printed book; additional copies at 40% discount. Buys world rights, all languages. Author reviews galleys and jacket copy. Author receives bio note.
**Tips:** Looks for "good writing, original stories, and characters that are authentic. I'd love to find a good children's mystery or mystery series, but they are rarer than hen's teeth." Taboos and tired topics: "Don't try to be politically correct or write about the environment—just write the book you want to."

---

# Walker & Company

▶ **Considers:** novels
▶ **Categories:** hard-boiled detective
private eye
police procedural
cozy
amateur sleuth
malice domestic

**Address:** Walker Publishing Co., Inc., 720 5th Ave., New York NY 10019, (212) 265-3632 Fax: (212) 307-1764
**Contact:** Michael Seidman, Mystery Editor
**Profile:** Walker is a "small, privately owned, privately

held company publishing commercial, traditional books. Also publishes for the book trade industry." The publisher does not have a separate mystery imprint. Established 1959. Publishes about 100 books/year. Publishes 24-26 mystery hardcovers/year. Average print run in hardcover 2,500. Publishes 9-12 first novels/year.

**How to Contact:** Submit outline and 3 preliminary chapters. SASE required for query responses. Simultaneous submissions are OK. Receives 100 unsolicited mss/month. 50% of accepted mss are agented. Reports on queries in 1-2 months; mss in 4-5 months. Sometimes comments on mss. Guidelines available for SASE. Catalog available for 2 first-class stamps.

**Terms:** Average royalty 12½%. Average advance $2,000-4,000. Author receives 10 copies of printed book; additional copies at 40% discount. Rights are negotiated. Publishes ms 1 year after acceptance. Average time to write book after contract signing is 9-12 months. Author reviews galleys, copyedited ms. Author receives bio note. Conducts author tours.

**Tips:** "The writing, first and foremost, followed by an interesting (read: different) story line" makes a ms standout. "I look for writers who are aware of the traditions and know how to play with them and, also important, for people who are writing what they want to write, not what they think will sell." Will be concentrating on "the traditional mystery (i.e., one in which there is a crime and a puzzle and a 'game' between detective and reader to get to the answer first) is our mainstay. Beyond that, however, I hope to find writers who will save the genre by making it breathe again, rather than repeat the hackneyed tales of yesterday." Taboos and tired topics: "I am sick unto death of politically correct novels. I believe that if you have a message, you use Western Union. If I see one more book about a one-eyed, ethnic minority with other sexual preferences, I'm just gonna burn the damn thing. No more drug dealers, drug cartels or dirty, incompetent cops."

**Titles/Authors of Note:** *Suffer Little Children, The January Corpse* and *Dead on the Island,* all nominees for best private eye novel, PWA Shamus Award; *Murder of Frau Schutz,* nominee for Edgar Award.

# *Interview*

Michael Seidman, Editor
Walker & Company

Michael Seidman sees the trend toward more female private eyes and sleuths in mysteries as little more than a cosmetic change. "The character's sensibility is not all that different," he says. "A female character might not be as given to physical action, or might be less cynical perhaps, but when you get down to the mystery, it's still the same.

"You take Miss Marple, make her younger, tougher, and give her a license," continues the mystery editor from Walker Books, "Now whether a literary or sociological sensibility is changed—that I don't know. I'd have to have four or five bourbons before I'd agree with that."

Although he admits to preferring the hard-boiled mystery himself, he says Walker's mainstay today is the same as it was in 1959—"the vast majority of the mysteries we publish are pure puzzles, procedural P.I.s or amateur sleuths. Every once in a while I'll look for suspense—not a whodunit but a howcatchem."

Seidman traces the beginnings of his thirty-year career as mystery editor to little more than happenstance. "Category books are given over to the new editor—sometimes a young kid. My boss saw me carrying a Richard Prather novel and he said 'Oh, you like mysteries. You're going to be our mystery editor.' " Had his boss seen him the next day, Seidman would've become the science fiction editor. "My own reading is still wildly varied," he says, pointing to recent readings in horror, historical and science fiction genres.

What does he look for in a mystery? "Sheer writing ability," he says without hesitation. "I don't like the opening sentence to be three paragraphs long. I look for the use of language, a sense of rhythm and poetry." After a pause, "I don't always find that so I start sacrificing my ideals. Next I look for a hook—do I care about the characters? Is there any reason to turn the page?"

For those interested in breaking into the field, he has succinct advice. "Don't say in your cover letter that your novel 'is in the tradition of . . .' " He urges writers to follow the KISS principle: "Keep It Simple, Stupid. Look around at what's being done, know what you are doing."

That means authenticity. "If a character screws a silencer onto a revolver, I reject it right then and there. Make sure the plot works, make the characters memorable. Make the writer, and simultaneously the characters, someone I want to spend time with once or twice a year."

And, please, he begs, don't make the mistake of trying to be pointedly politically correct. "If you want to send a message, use Western Union."

What about content? "Well, other editors say, 'No gratuitous sex or violence.' I'm grateful for whatever sex and violence I can get."

One of the most memorable books he's been associated with is Triangle, by Teri White, a first novel that won the Edgar Award. "It's one of the single best novels I've ever been associated with. It's very tough writing that concentrates more on characters and relationships than on mystery."

Seidman dislikes writer's guidelines. "I prefer to let writers write. Writers are supposed to write what they see, what is born out of their experience or their passion," he says. When a writer focuses more on what will sell, Seidman says it's all too obvious. "When they've gerry-rigged a book rather than writing it, it's missing the necessary passion."
—Carol Lloyd

---

# Albert Whitman & Co.

► **Considers:** novels
► **Categories:** juvenile

**Address:** 6340 Oakton Street, Morton Grove IL 60053-2723, (708) 581-0033 Fax: (708) 581-0039
**Contact:** Kathleen Tucker, Editor
**Profile:** Albert Whitman & Co. is a "medium-size, independent publisher with a growing market." Established 1919. Publishes 30 books/year. Publishes 1-2 mysteries/year. Publishes 1 first novel/year.

**How to Contact:** Send outline and sample chapters. SASE required for query and ms response. E-mail and fax queries and simultaneous submissions are OK. Receives 200 unsolicited mss/month. Reports on queries in 2-3 months; mss in 2-3 months. Sometimes comments on mss.

**Terms:** Pays advance and royalties. Buys North American rights. Publishes ms 18 months after acceptance. Average time to write book after contract signing is 1 year.

**Tips:** Looks for "good plot—good characters." Will be concentrating on "picture books."

---

# Zebra Books

► **Considers:**  novels
► **Categories:**  young adult
cozy
amateur sleuth (female)
romantic suspense

**Address:** Kensington Publishing Corp., 475 Park Ave. South, New York NY 10016, (212) 889-2299 Fax: (212) 779-8073

**Contact:** Ann LaFarge, Executive Editor

**Profile:** Zebra is a large commercial publisher of hardcover reprints and paperback originals. Mysteries are an integral part of the publisher's line. Publishes 400 books/ year. Established 1975. Zebra books will start Partners in Crime, a paperback imprint, in October 1993.

**How to Contact:** Query with 3-5 page outline/synopsis and sample chapters, or send complete ms. SASE required for query and ms response. Simultaneous submissions are OK. 50% of accepted mss are agented. Reporting time varies. Guidelines available for SASE. Catalog available.

**Terms:** Pays advance and royalty. Author receives 25 copies of printed book; additional copies at 40% discount. Buys world rights. Publishes ms 1 year after acceptance. Author reviews galleys. Author receives bio note.

---

∞

# Mark V. Ziesing

> ▶ **Considers:** novels
> ▶ **Categories:** dark mystery

**Address:** P.O. Box 76, Shingletown CA 96088, (916) 474-1580
**Contact:** Mark Ziesing
**Profile:** This small press is interested in dark mystery. Established 1975. Publishes 6 books/year. Publishes 1 mystery hardcover/year.
**How to Contact:** Query first. SASE required for query and ms response. Fax queries and simultaneous submissions are OK. Receives 10 unsolicited mss/month. 70% of accepted mss are agented. Reports in 2 months. Sometimes comments on rejected mss. Catalog available for 4 first-class stamps.
**Terms:** Average advance $3,000. Average royalty 10%. Author receives 10-20 copies of printed bok. Rights bought varies. Author reviews copyedited ms. Author receives bio note.

## Mystery Writers Talk About Their Favorite Editors

### Sara Paretsky

Jackie Farber at Delacorte is a writer's editor. Most editors today are too harassed by the accounting demands of the industry to pay attention to writing. Farber is a great exception to this: She reads with an eye for the story the writer is trying to tell. Her criticisms deal with whether that story is working or not, not whether the book will sell more or less with certain changes, nor even what she would do with this book if she were writing it. In addition, Delacorte makes a personal response to their writers. In that way they remind me of the old Dial Press, which published my first book and made me feel like a person of value to them, even though they didn't sell many copies of it.

### Ed Gorman

I've been blessed with good editors. I've only ever worked with one I'd call bad, and that was more a matter of personality than competence. Indeed, in her snotty way she taught me a number of things about my craft. Over the last year-and-a-half I worked on a very long suspense novel called *The Marilyn Tapes*, which is about J. Edgar Hoover trying to lay hands on secret recordings that could link Marilyn Monroe to John Kennedy. Hoover means to blackmail Kennedy with the tapes. However the book is received, it grew me up as a writer. Or rather, my editor, Bob Gleason of TOR, grew me up as a writer. I'd send in a draft and he'd say, "Pretty nice but it could be better." And then he'd show me how to make it better. This went on long after the first draft. By the time the book is published, it will have had five complete drafts and then a "final polish" as Bob calls it. He pushed, but gently; and he taught me things, but never imperiously. He was careful to give me my dignity while he was showing me what he wanted done. Bob's a writer, too, and a very good one, and I think that helped the process. One day we were talking about the final polish, and he said, "When you're packing it in, I want you to look up at your bookshelf and have at least one book that you know took the best of everything you had." I knew just what he meant, and it made that final polish a lot of fun to do. I've never had an editor expend that much time, thought, care, patience and enthusiasm on me before and I was really flattered by the way he helped me write the book. All writers need and deserve a Bob Gleason at least once in their careers.

### Max Byrd

Kate Miciak of Bantam Books is without question the best in the business.

### George C. Chesbro

Joan Sanger at Simon & Schuster — she taught me how to write.

Neil Nyron — while at Atheneum he resurrected my character Mongo, buying *The Beasts of Valhalla* when it looked as though nobody else would be interested.

Otto Penzler — publishes mysteries well, and with love and respect.

William Malloy, editor-in-chief, Mysterious Press—Bill is a truly gifted editor with a very deep knowledge of mysteries, and very respectful of writers and their work.

### Loren Estleman

I've been blessed with a number of genial geniuses with whom I've often done battle—and never without results complimentary to the work at hand. These include Yvonne MacManus at the now-defunct Major Books; her associate, the late Gaye Tardy; Doubleday's Pat Lo-Brutto; Bantam's Greg Tobin; Dale L. Walker, late of Texas Western Press; Cathleen Jordan, formerly of Doubleday and now editor-in-chief of *Alfred Hitchcock's Mystery Magazine*; Fawcett's Louisa Rudeen; and Bill Malloy and Sara Ann Freed of the Mysterious Press. All are solid professionals with a deep love of books and understanding of the craft of writing.

### Anne Wingate

My first really good editor was Hope Dellon, with St. Martin's Press . . . Hope asks for a lot of changes, and I'm able to see how each one improves the book.

### Charlie Sweet & Hal Blythe

Bill Brohaugh at Writer's Digest Books. We like him because he's professional—he does what he says. He's personable like Richard Cory, "he was always human when he talked."

Fred Davvey at *Ellery Queen's Mystery Magazine* because of his willingness to read our stories and write out individual critiques.

Susanne Kirk at Scribner's because of her willingness to talk to us individually.

### Dick Lochte

My publisher was Eden Collinsworth, at Arbor House, who accepted my debut novel, *Sleeping Dog*, just a week after it was submitted. She was never less than helpful and encouraging. And she made me feel that she cared about my book and my career as an author. Eden spoiled me. *Sleeping Dog* was the best publicized of any of my books and went into three printings, winning the Nero Wolfe Award and being nominated for the Mystery Writers of America and the Private Eye Writers Awards. By the time my second novel, *Laughing Dog*, was published, Eden and the helpful and pleasant Arbor House gang had been dismissed and the imprint had become a part of William Morrow, not really for the better. As for editors, I'm very happy with my two present ones—Susanne Jaffee at Simon & Schuster and Daniel Zitin at Fawcett. Neither of them will hesitate to tell you what they like about a manuscript and what they don't like. It's refreshing to deal with people who can articulate their feelings. Both provide pages of notes. Authors and editors are able to discuss (or even argue over) specifics and come to some definite conclusions. There's nothing worse than having an editor give you feedback that is too broad to be of any practical use. I once had an editor inform me "The book is too cold." Too cold how? Out of the mainstream? Sexually? Metaphysically? Emotionally? Weather-wise? I never bothered to find out.

### John Lutz

Michael Seidman, now of Walker. He cares a great deal about the fiction he edits, the most important qualification for any editor.

### Marilyn Wallace

All the people I've worked with at Doubleday/Bantam—editors, publishers, publicists, art designers, sales and marketing people—have been savvy, enthusiastic, dedicated professionals who obviously care a great deal about the books with which they're connected . . . and they're fun, too!

### Stephanie Kay Bendel

Cathleen Jordan at *Alfred Hitchcock's Mystery Magazine*. What I like about Cathleen is that she appreciates stories that stretch the boundaries of the mystery genre.

### Tony Hillerman

Joan Kahn at (then) Harper & Row—she did a superb job editing my copy, making me write better books than I intended.

### Foreign Markets

---

# Allison & Busby Crime

▶ **Considers:** novels

▶ **Categories:** hard-boiled detective
private eye
police procedural
malice domestic

**Address:** The Lodge, Richmond Way, London W12 8LW
England, (081) 749-9441/3254 Fax: (081) 749-9496
**Contact:** Peter Day, Publisher
**Profile:** Allison & Busby is a newly independent publisher. Established 1968. Publishes 30 books/year. About 7/year are mystery. Publishes 3 first novels/year. Average print run in hardcover: 2,000; trade paperback: 3,000; mass market paperback: 6,000.
**How to Contact:** Submit outline and sample chapters. SASE required for query and ms response. Fax queries and simultaneous submissions are OK. Receives 100 unsolicited mss/month. 80% of accepted mss are agented. Reports in 1 week. Guidelines available. Free catalog available.
**Terms:** Average advance £1,500. Average royalty 10% hardcover; 1½% paper. Author receives 12 hardcover, 20 paper copies of printed book. Buys world rights if possible; always buys U.S. and United Kingdom rights. Publishes ms 1 year after acceptance. Average time to write book after contract signing is 1 year. Author receives galleys and copyedited ms and reviews jacket copy. Author gets bio note.
**Tips:** "Writing makes a manuscript stand out." Will be concentrating on "literary fiction, literary nonfiction, biography, crime, writer's guides." Taboos and tired topics: science fiction, romantic fiction.
**Titles/Authors of Note:** *Lives of the Saints*, by Nina Ricci; *The Marquis de Sade*, by Donald Thomas; *A Scandalous Woman*, by Alan Chedzon.

## Interview
*Peter Day, Publisher*
Allison & Busby Crime

    *Peter Day, publisher at Allison & Busby Crime, has been editing mystery books for twenty-five years and has been in his present position since 1989. Day worked as a lawyer for four* years before starting a career in writing and journalism. More recently, Day has served for many years as a judge of fiction and short story contests and as a lecturer to writers' groups. As editor of Pen International, Day works with many new writers.

Classic American crime novels and new English crime writers are of special interest to Allison & Busby Crime. Day himself is most interested in hard-boiled mysteries. In his spare time, he enjoys reading the works of Ross Macdonald, Margaret Millar, Ed McBain, P.D. James, Ted Lewis, Jo Bannister and Denise Danks.

Allison & Busby publishes thirty books per year, seven of which are mystery. During his career, Day first identified such popular and successful novelists as Tom Sharpe, Jennifer Johnston, James Herriot and Peter Benson, as well as the crime writers June Thompson and Dorothy Simpson.

Day recalls Ted Lewis's Jack's Return Home *as the most memorable project he's ever worked on. It was made into a cult movie titled* Get Carter, *which featured Michael Caine. "It was memorable because it was so raw and fresh," says Day. "A complete break from the cozy British tradition. It was the first time I had come across a mystery novel in such an uncompromising vein."*

When asked about trends, Day replied, "In the U.K. the hard-boiled crime novel is gaining ground against the traditional British 'cozy' crime novel, particularly if it can be adapted for the television screen. Because the market in classic American crime has fallen off in the U.K., we are fast developing our new British crime list."

Day advises aspiring mystery writers to "concentrate on atmosphere, pace, plot and characterization. Ensure it can be read at a sitting and remember it is escapist literature, bookstall stuff."

As a publisher, Day has no particular taboos, but there are subjects he just does not like or "emote with," such as science fiction. Generally, acceptance depends on the novel and how it is written. "Too much explanation and too little action" are turn-offs for Day.

—Donna Collingwood

# Century Books

▶ **Considers:** novels
▶ **Categories:** hard-boiled detective
private eye
police procedural
historical

**Address:** Random Century Group, 20 Vauxhall Bridge Rd., London SW1V 2SA England, (071) 973-9000 Fax: (071) 233 6115
**Contact:** Oliver Johnson
**Profile:** Established 1982. Publishes hardcovers, trade paperbacks and mass market paperbacks. Publishes 2-3 first novels/year.
**How to Contact:** Submit through agent only. Fax queries and simultaneous submissions are OK. Receives 20 unsolicited mss/month. 99% of accepted mss are agented. Reports on queries in 1-2 weeks; mss in 1-2 months.
**Terms:** Average royalty 10% minimum. Author receives 6 copies of printed book. Buys English language world rights. Publishes ms 1 year after acceptance. Average time to write book after contract signing is 1 year. Author receives galleys and copyedited ms and reviews jacket copy. Author receives bio note.

# Constable & Co., Ltd.

▶ **Considers:** novels
▶ **Categories:** hard-boiled detective
private eye
police procedural
cozy
malice domestic

**Address:** 3, The Lanchesters, 162 Fulham Palace Rd., London W6 9ER England, (081) 741-3663 Fax: (081) 748-7562

**Contact:** Mystery Editor

**Profile:** Established 1790. Publishes 75 books/year. Average print run in hardcover 1,750. Publishes 4 first novels/year.

**How to Contact:** Submit outline and sample chapters. Reports in 1 month. E-mail and fax queries are OK. Receives 30 unsolicited mss/month. 90% of accepted mss are agented. Sometimes comments on mss. Catalog available for adequate return postage in IRCs.

**Terms:** Average advance £1,500. Average royalty 10%. Author receives 10 copies of printed book. Buys United Kingdom and commonwealth rights. Publishes ms 9 months after acceptance. Average time to write book after contract signing is 3 months. Author receives galleys and copyedited ms and reviews jacket copy. Author gets bio note.

**Titles/Authors of Note:** *Night Frost*, by R.D. Wingfield; *Death's Bright Angel*, by Janet Neel.

---

# The Crime Club

► **Considers:** novels
► **Categories:** private eye
police procedural
cozy
amateur sleuth
malice domestic

**Address:** HarperCollins Publishers Ltd., 77-85 Fulham Palace Rd., Hammersmith, London W6 8JB England, (081) 741-7070 Fax: (081) 307-4440

**Contact:** Elizabeth Walter

**Profile:** The Crime Club is the mystery imprint of the large publisher, HarperCollins. Established 1930. Publishes 1-6 first novels/year.

**How to Contact:** Query with outline and sample chapters. SASE required for ms response. 65% of accepted mss are agented. Reports on queries in 2 weeks; mss in

2 months. Sometimes comments on mss.
**Terms:** Pays advance and royalty. Author receives 10 copies of book. Buys world rights, all languages. Publishes ms 9-10 months after acceptance. Author receives galleys and reviews jacket copy. Author gets bio notes.
**Tips:** "We look for good writing, which means pace, good characterization, and a sense of place or period around the essential hardcore of a sound and credible plot." Taboo: "torture." Tired topic: "everlasting four-letter words."

---

# Victor Gollancz, Ltd.

► **Considers:** graphic novels
novels
► **Categories:** young adult
juvenile
hard-boiled detective
private eye
police procedural
cozy
amateur sleuth
malice domestic
romantic suspense

**Address:** 14 Henrietta St., Covent Garden, London WC2E 8QJ England, (071) 836-2006 Fax: (071) 379-0934
**Contact:** Mystery Editor
**Profile:** Established 1928. Publishes 200 books/year. Publishes 1-2 first novels/year.
**How to Contact:** Submit outline and sample chapters. SASE required for query and ms response. Fax queries are OK. Receives 20 unsolicited mss/month. 95% of accepted mss are agented. Reports on queries in 1-2 months; mss in 2 months. Sometimes comments on mss. Catalog available.
**Terms:** Payment terms not disclosed. Author receives galleys and copyedited ms. Author gets bio notes.

# Headline Book Publishing PLC

► **Considers:** novels
► **Categories:** private eye
police procedural
cozy
amateur sleuth
malice domestic

**Address:** 79 Great Titchfield St., London W1P 7FN England, (071) 631-1687 Fax: (071) 436-4220
**Contact:** Susan J. Fletcher
**Profile:** A mainstream publisher of popular fiction and nonfiction. Established 1986. Publishes 300-400 titles/year. Publishes hardcovers, trade paperbacks and mass market paperbacks. Publishes 3 first novels/year.
**How to Contact:** Submit outline and first 100 pages. SASE required for query and ms response. E-mail and fax queries and simultaneous submissions are OK. Receives 300 unsolicited mss/month. 98% of accepted mss are agented. Reports in 1 month. Comments on mss. Catalog available for adequate return postage in IRCs.
**Terms:** Average advance and royalty varies. Author receives 6 hardcover; 10 paper copies of printed book. Rights purchased vary. Publishes ms 9 months after acceptance. Average time to write book after contract signing: 6-12 months. Author receives galleys and copyedited ms and reviews jacket copy. Author gets bio notes.
**Titles/Authors of Note:** Dean Koontz, Dan Simmons, David Morreu, Martha Grunies and Ellis Peters.

# Hodder & Stoughton, Ltd.

► **Considers:** novels
► **Categories:** hard-boiled detective
private eye
police procedural
malice domestic

**Address:** Mill Road, Dunton Green, Sevenoaks, Kent TN13 2YA England, (071) 636-9851 Fax: (071) 631-5248
**Contact:** Mrs. Ormsby
**Profile:** Large commercial publisher. Mystery imprint is Coronet (which also covers romance, humor, historical). Other imprints include NEL (horror, science fiction, fantasy, humor, serious nonfiction) and Sceptre (literary fiction and nonfiction). Established 1868. Publishes over 1,000 books/year. Publishes 10 mystery hardcovers and 15-20 mystery mass market paperbacks/year. Publishes "a few" first novels/year.
**How to Contact:** Submit query letter only. SASE required for query and ms response. No simultaneous submissions. Receives "many" unsolicited mss/month. "Nearly all" accepted mss are agented. Reports in 3 months. Sometimes comments on mss.
**Terms:** Pays advance and royalties. Author receives 12 hardcover copies of printed book. Buys world rights. Publishes ms about 9 months after acceptance (varies). Author reviews galleys, copyedited ms and jacket copy. Author usually gets bio notes.
**Tips:** Looks for "originality, skill and presentation (in that order)."
**Titles/Authors of Note:** Lawrence Sanders, Ed McBain, Dorothy L. Sayers, Linda Banes, Elizabeth (E.X.) Ferrars.

# MacMillan Crime Case

▶ **Considers:** collections
novels
▶ **Categories:** hard-boiled detective
private eye
police procedural
cozy
amateur sleuth
malice domestic
romantic suspense
psychological suspense

**Address:** Pan MacMillan Ltd., 18-21 Cavaye Pl., London SW10 9PG England, (071) 373-6070 Fax: 071 370-0746
**Contact:** Maria Rejt
**Profile:** MacMillan Crime Case is an imprint of the large international publishing group, Pan MacMillan. Established early 1970s. Publishes hardback books. Publishes 2-4 first novels/year.
**How to Contact:** Query first, then submit sample material. "It is not necessary to acquire an agent before contacting editor." Fax queries and simultaneous submissions are OK. Receives 10-20 unsolicited mss/month. 90% of accepted mss are agented. Reports on queries in 2 weeks; mss in 6 weeks. Sometimes comments on mss. Catalog available for large, self-addressed envelope and IRC's.
**Terms:** Average advance varies. Average royalty 10%/12½%/15%. Author receives 6 copies of printed book. Buys all rights. Publishes ms 9-12 months after acceptance. Average time to write book after contract signing is 1 year. Author receives galleys and copyedited ms and reviews jacket copy. Author gets bio notes.
**Tips:** "A fresh, original voice stands out to us as a publisher. Use original, yet believable, characters and an ingenious plot. Specifically interested in medical/hospital whodunits and forensic backgrounds. Everybody wants to discover the new Thomas Harris or P.D. James! I am willing to publish in every category that comes under the broad umbrella of crime fiction, but do have a preference for contemporary whodunits and psychological suspense (a la Barbara Vine) and strong series characters." Taboo: "Violence that is excessive for the dynamics of the plot, especially when involving children." Tired topic: "Private eyes with drinking problems (i.e. wise-cracking, cynical P.I.'s pounding the mean streets)."
**Titles/Authors of Note:** Colin Dexter (Inspector Morse series) and Sue Grafton.

# Severn House Publishers, Ltd.

▶ **Considers:** novels
▶ **Categories:** hard-boiled detective
private eye
police procedural
amateur sleuth
malice domestic
romantic suspense

**Address:** 9-15 High St., Sutton, Surrey England, (081) 770-3830 Fax: (081) 770-3850
**Profile:** "Small publisher specializing in new hardcover fiction (including reprints) for the library market." Established 1974. Publishes about 120 books/year. Publishes 40-50 mystery hardcovers/year. Average print run in hardcover: 1,500.
**How to Contact:** Submit through agent only. Reports on queries in 2-3 weeks; mss in 2 months. Sometimes comments on mss. Catalog for self-addressed envelope with 1 U.K. or 3 U.S. first-class stamps.
**Terms:** Average royalty 10-15%. Author receives 6 hardcover copies of printed book. Buys world rights, if possible. Publishes ms 6-7 months after acceptance. Author receives copyedited ms. Author gets bio note.
**Tips:** "A well-thought-out plot, essential characters, and a good twist in the end" make a manuscript stand out. Will be concentrating on "trade paperbacks of good crime writing" in the future.
**Titles/Authors of Note:** Ruth Rendel, Patricia Highsmith, Patricia Wentworth.

# Virago Press, Ltd.

> ► **Considers:** novels
> ► **Categories:** private eye
> amateur sleuth
> psychological thriller

**Address:** Centro House, 20-23 Mandela St., London NW1 0HQ England, (071) 383-5150 Fax: (071) 383-4892
**Contact:** Melanie Silgardo
**Profile:** Established 1973. Publishes about 110-120 books/year. Publishes 2 first novels/year. Average print run in hardcover 1,000-2,000; trade paperback 5,000-7,000; mass market paperback 7,000.
**How to Contact:** Submit outline and sample chapters. SASE required for query and ms response. E-mail and fax queries and simultaneous submissions are OK. Receives 10-12 unsolicited mss/month. 90% of accepted mss are agented. Reports in 2 months. Comments on mss. Catalog available.
**Terms:** Average advance is confidential. Average royalty 10% hardcover; 7.5% paper. Author receives 6 copies of printed book. Buys worlds rights, all languages. Publishes ms 12-18 months after acceptance. Average time to write book after contract signing is 1 year. Author receives galleys and copyedited ms and reviews jacket copy.
**Tips:** "We look for manuscript with intelligent, lively writing and well-researched subject matter, a sleuth who is quirky, engaging and well-thought-out as a personality and, obviously, a plot with plenty of suspense and psychological twists. We are looking for good British crime and mystery fiction, which there seems to be a dearth of. Our crime competition, we hope, will elicit a positive response. We welcome American submissions."
**Titles/Authors of Note:** *Gandi Afternoon*, by Barbara Wilson (won the Crime Writers' Association Award 1992 for best crime novel set in Europe).

## Markets for Reviews and Articles

The following are brief listings of publications that publish mystery book reviews, interviews with mystery authors and articles about mysteries or mystery writing. We've included some comment, but it is best to read several issues of the magazines that interest you to determine if their interests and style match yours. For more about magazines that cover mystery see Magazines About Mysteries, on page 205. For more markets for reviews, interviews and articles see *Writer's Market* (published by Writer's Digest Books).

## The Armchair Detective

**Address:** 129 W. 56 St., New York NY 10019, (212) 765-0902

**Contact:** Kate Stine, Editor

**Profile:** Established 1967. Magazine: 8½ × 11; 128 pages. Published quarterly. Circulation: 4,500.

**Comments:** *The Armchair Detective* maintains a list of people who are interested in the genre and in reviewing; the editors send books to the people on this list. A couple of sample reviews and a request to be added to the list would be the way to go here. Let them know the kind of mystery you like—P.I., cozy, espionage, etc. Familiarize yourself with the kinds of reviews *The Armchair Detective* runs and make certain that you don't, in your critique of a book, give away any of the clues. (If you are submitting an article that reveals the kinds of information a reader wouldn't want to know before picking up a book, be sure to offer a warning above the text.) *The Armchair Detective* pays $10 per printed page for articles and interviews; they do not pay for reviews. The page count includes photographs or other art, but does not include ad space.

While inquiries are not required, it makes sense to query them. The editors receive hundreds of pieces every year, have a long lead time (remember, they publish quarterly), and the article you're working on may parallel something awaiting publication. (I'd guess that if you interview someone, that person would have the

good sense to tell you that something is scheduled. I've been known to guess wrong.)
—*M. Seidman*

# Clues
**Address:** Popular Culture Center, Bowling Green State University Center, Bowling Green OH 43403, (419) 372-7867 Fax: (419) 372-8095
**Contact:** Pat Browne, Editor
**Profile:** Established 1980. Magazine: 5 × 7½; 156 pages. Published biannually. Circulation: 500. *Clues* publishes scholarly criticism of the mystery field. Many articles are by academics and there is no payment. Send a query first with an SASE. The magazine receives 5-10 unsolicited mss/month and publishes about 12 per issue. Reports on queries in 1-2 weeks; on mss in 2-3 months.

# Drood Review of Mystery
**Address:** 5047 W. Main, #110, Kalamazoo MI 49009, (616) 349-3006
**Contact:** Jim Huang, Editor/Publisher
**Profile:** Established 1982. Magazine: 8½ × 11; 12-24 pages. Published monthly. Circulation: 1,700. *Drood* does not accept individual articles or reviews. Those interested in doing reviews and other articles for the magazine may inquire about joining the staff. Send a brief query letter about your interests, experience along with a writing sample.
**Comments:** *Drood*'s reviews are among the finest in the country. In addition to the reviews—and extensive listings of new releases in hardcover and paperback—Jim Huang, the editor and publisher, is looking for interviews and commentary on current mystery writing.

There is no interest here in the past — in terms of articles — nor is the magazine looking for stories.
—*M. Seidman*

## Mystery Notebook

**Address:** Box 1341, FDR Station, New York NY 10150,
**Contact:** Stephen Wright
**Profile:** Established 1984. Magazine: 8½ × 11; 10-16 pages. Published irregularly. Circulation: 1,000. This magazine features reviews, essays, information and news about the mystery field. Query first with an SASE. Reports on queries in 3 weeks; on mss in 1 month. There is no payment, but regular contributors may receive a free subscription. This publication also includes "Ashenden," a special section of articles on the work of W. Somerset Maugham. A sample copy is available for $7.50.

## The Mystery Review

**Address:** P.O. Box 233, Colborne Ontario KOK 150 Canada, (613) 475-4440
**Contact:** Barbara Davey, Editor
**Profile:** Established 1993. Magazine. Published quarterly. Accepts submissions and is seeking material in the following categories: word games and puzzles; interviews with authors (or others involved in mystery writing); real-life unsolved mysteries. Guidelines available on request.

## Mystery Scene

**Address:** Mystery Enterprises, 3840 Clark Rd., SE, Cedar Rapids IA 52403
**Profile:** Established 1986. Magazine: 8½ × 11; about 70 pages. Published bimonthly. Circulation: 6,700.

**Comments:** As a market, *Mystery Scene* presents some difficulties for newcomers. There is an enormous backlog of material on submission, and the editors prefer to be queried because many articles and interviews are solicited. The editors *do not* publish fiction, although they experimented with it briefly a few years ago. Payment rates aren't fixed; if your material is accepted, the editors will negotiate a fee with you. Again, they prefer queries, and they prefer that you've read several issues before you try to write for them, and they accept no responsibility for unsolicited manuscripts.
—*M. Seidman*

## Scarlet Street

**Address:** R.H. Enterprises, P.O. Box 604, Glen Rock NJ 07452, (201) 836-1113
**Contact:** Richard Valley, Editor-in-Chief
**Profile:** Established 1991. Magazine: 8½ × 11. Published quarterly. Circulation: 2,000. *Scarlet Street* covers mystery and horror entertainment in all genres, including but not limited to literature, movies, television, theatre, comics and radio. It focuses on Sherlock Holmes, classic horror films, fictional detectives, and interviews with celebrity and supporting actors. Foreign media are also covered, from Italian horror films to British mystery television. Regular columns include "Mystery!" (PBS TV), "Baker Street Regular," "Bat Beat," "Poirot Investigates," "Better Holmes and Watson," "Book Ends" and "The News Hound."

## Writer's Digest Magazine

**Address:** 1507 Dana Ave., Cincinnati OH 45207
**Contact:** Angela Terez
**Profile:** Established 1921. Magazine: 8½ × 11. Published monthly. Circulation: 225,000. This publication for writers is interested in how-to articles, personal

experience with how-to, profiles and interviews. Buys 90-100 manuscripts per year plus an additional 200 short pieces for various departments including "Writing Life" and "Tip Sheet." Does not accept reviews. Has published articles on mystery writing and marketing, and interviews and profiles with top-name mystery authors (with a focus on their writing). It's best to query them first, but complete manuscript with SASE is okay. For an extensive listing of this publication, see *Writer's Market*. Single copy $2.75, subscription $21.

**Fanzines**

The following are a few fan magazines open to mystery reviews and articles. Write to them for more information. There are many more such publications, many devoted to particular mystery authors or characters. To find more, one of the best sources is the publication, *Factsheet Five* (c/o William Dockery and Andrew Roller, 5960 S. Land Park Dr., #253, Sacramento CA 95822). For even more on zines, see *The World of Zines: A Guide to the Independent Magazine Revolution*, a well-received book by Cari G. Janice and Mike Gunderloy, the founder of *Factsheet Five*.

# Mystery and Detective Monthly

**Address:** % Cap' Bob Napier, 5601 N. 40th St., Tacoma WA 98407

**Profile:** A "letterzine," which consists entirely of arguments, debates, comments, snide remarks and reactions thereto from a group of dedicated fans, readers and some professional writers.

# The Mystery FANcier

**Address:** % Guy Townsend, 2024 Clifty Dr., Madison IN 47250-1632

**Profile:** Like all fanzines, this is a non-paying market.

# Tower Books Mystery Newsletter

**Address:** 211 Main St., Chico CA 95928

**Profile:** *Tower Books Mystery Newsletter* carries reviews of a couple of current titles and lists of upcoming releases. They welcome short reviews and comments; there's no payment.

## Clues to the Literary Agent

*by Gary Provost*

**QUESTION:** *What exactly is a literary agent?*

**ANSWER:** A literary agent receives written material from writers . . . usually books or book proposals . . . and assesses the material for literary merit and marketability. That is, he asks the single most important question in publishing: Will people pay money to read this? If the answer is yes, the agent sends the material to those publishers he thinks would be most interested in buying the right to publish it.

The agent does not have to be a writer, but he should understand writing well enough to carry on an intelligent conversation with the writer. He does not have to be an editor, but he should have enough editorial wisdom to point out weaknesses in a manuscript and suggest improvements. He does not have to be a lawyer, but he should be able to recognize a devious clause when he sees one, and he should be able to read a publisher's contract as well as he reads English. A literary agent does not have to be a publisher, but he should know who reads, what they read, why they read, and what they will want to read next year.

The good agent is informed by material that any writer can get his hands on, such as *Publishers Weekly*, *Writer's Digest* or the *New York Times* best-seller list. And he is further informed through his own special channels of information, such as industry newsletters, cocktail party conversations, phone calls from editor friends, and his cousin Nate, who's a mail clerk at Simon & Schuster.

**Q:** *Who can become a literary agent?*

**A:** Anyone with a paintbrush can paint "Literary Agent" on a shingle and hang it outside his door, and he's an agent. Simply "being an agent" does not make one a good agent. No license is required, no university bestows a Masters of Literary Agenting, and there is no way to prove that a person is not a literary agent.

**Q:** *Who needs a literary agent?*

**A:** Almost any person who wants to make the best possible deal for the publishing rights to his book or other major literary property. The exception would be a writer who has as much time and agenting skills as a very good literary agent, and can apply both objectively to his own work.

**Q:** *Who does not need a literary agent?*

**A:** Plumbers, druggists, trained seals, neurologists and writers who are writing only short stories, articles or poems. And anybody else who has neither a book nor a book proposal in good enough shape to be seen by an editor. I am often disturbed by people who ask my advice about getting an agent: When I ask what they have written, the answer is nothing. "But I've got this terrific idea for a book," they say. If your book is still in the idea stage, terrific or otherwise, you are not ready for an agent. Would you go to a real estate agent and say "I've got this terrific idea for a house?"

**Q:** *What specifically can an agent do for me?*

**A:** He can give you a professional opinion of your manuscript. He can send that manuscript to the editors most likely to want it, and keep it out of the hands of editors who wouldn't want it or shouldn't get it. He can negotiate for the most favorable split on reprint rights, serial rights, movie rights, etc. Often he will keep for you rights that you might have shared with the publisher.

**Q:** *What would be a good example of that?*

**A:** Robert Cormier, author of *The Bumblebee Flies Anyway*, is one of the most successful writers for young adults in the country. Cormier has had the same agent for twenty-five years, and he gives this example. "Three of my books are on records that are sold to schools all over the country. I make money from this because my agent looked into the future and held on to 'stereophonic rights' in my book contracts. If I had negotiated the contracts myself, I probably would have given the rights away without even thinking about it.

**Q:** *What can an agent not do for me?*

**A:** Most of all, he cannot get a buyer for a lousy book, or for a book that's good but would be too expensive to produce. He also cannot save your marriage, lend you lots of money, teach you to write, make airline reservations for your trip to Germany, or spend any more of his professional time on you than is necessary to serve you well. Also, he generally cannot handle your short stories, articles or poems, unless he is also selling books for you.

**Q:** *What can an agent do for me after a book contract is signed?*

**A:** He can harass the editor to see that your advance check is sent out. He can talk to you briefly once in a while about the book in progress.

He can hound the publisher to spend more money on promoting your book, and he can just generally be the troubleshooter when one is needed so that you don't have to get in the ring with your editor.

**Q:** *What else can an agent do for me?*

**A:** Act as insulation between you and editorial opinions of your work. In *On Becoming a Novelist,* John Gardner put it this way: "Whereas after a certain number of rejections the writer is likely to give up on a story or novel, the agency goes on, impartial as a pulsar, sending out the fiction, getting it back, sending it out again. And whereas the writer is likely to be humbled or enraged by letters of rejection, with all their perhaps foolish advice on how to fix the book, agents tend to be unimpressed. At the writer's instruction, the agent will tell him nothing of what editors advise, except if some editor comes up with a suggestion that seems to the agent important."

**Q:** *What are the chances of my selling a book without an agent?*

**A:** If we're assuming the book could have been sold with an agent, your chances are pretty good, though not as good. You will probably send it to more publishers before you sell it, and you will probably sell it for a lot less money. "The beginning writer does not have to have an agent," says Bob Cormier, "but I think any established writer should have one." Cormier also says, "I think there's an inevitability about a good book. I don't believe there are many good book manuscripts sitting in drawers because they couldn't be sold."

**Q:** *When can I get an agent?*

**A:** One popular myth about agents is that they are like bank loans; you can't get one until you don't need one. The fact is you can't get a literary agent until you do need one. That is, when you have a publishable book to sell. Anybody can get unacceptable work rejected without an agent. It requires no professional expertise at all to send a bad manuscript to an editor who doesn't want it. The time to start looking for an agent is when you have finished a book or written a professional book proposal that you are convinced is salable.

**Q:** *Why should I use an agent on my first book?*

**A:** Because I don't have a word processor yet.

Let me explain. Like many beginning writers, I once cloaked the literary agent in an aura of magic, of mystery, as if he were engaged in some exotic practice light years beyond the realm of my ordinary experience. I put agents on a pedestal, and until I was well-established, I was shy about approaching them. I figured they were too busy with big-name, big-bucks authors to bother with me. So, like most writers, I used no agent on my first book and, also like most writers, I signed the first contract that came within my reach, and I didn't even consider asking for changes. I estimate that not using an agent on that contract has cost me about $7,000 so far. If I had that $7,000 now, I'd buy a word processor and a few other goodies. So you should use an agent on your first book for the same reason you'd use him on your second book or your fifteenth book: to get the best possible deal.

**Q:** *Why would an agent handle me?*

**A:** Why would a real estate agent handle your house? An agent catalyzes a transaction between a buyer and a seller. If there's no product, there's no transaction and if there's no transaction, there's no commission. The agent needs your product.

**Q:** *Why would an agent take on a client without a track record?*

**A:** Usually he wouldn't, but he might. Certainly good agents look for a solid track record when considering potential clients. If you've published articles, short stories and books, you perhaps have a following. It will be easier for the agent to sell you to the publisher. But the real value of that track record is that it serves as a body of evidence that you can write well, stick with a project, adjust to an editor's needs, and just generally conduct yourself in a professional manner. If you don't have a lot of credits, you must find other ways to convince the agent that these things are true. The most obvious way is to give him a carefully prepared, well-written book or proposal, and a résumé of your professional credits, even if they are not writing credits. If he believes he can sell your book, and if he is accepting new clients, he will probably take you on, and it doesn't much matter whether it's your first book or your tenth.

**Q:** *How much will the agent charge?*

**A:** The traditional agent's fee has been 10 percent of whatever is due as a result of the contracts the agent negotiated. In other words, 10 percent of your royalties, movie rights money, and whatever you get for licensing somebody to print T-shirts with your book's title on them. In recent years, many agents have lifted their rates to 15 percent and predicted that everybody else will do the same. Perhaps. Certainly a good agent is worth 15 percent, but it's hard for me to understand why most agents can survive on 10 percent and some need 15 percent and why the increase must be 50 percent. Where are the 11 percent, 12 percent and 13 percent agents? It makes me wonder if agents have difficulty dealing with numbers that don't end with a zero or a five. Anyhow, the 15 percent agent is probably the agent of the future, but for now the price difference does not separate the good agents from the bad agents, and there is no sense in encouraging higher costs for writers by going to a 15 percent agent when you can get the same quality of service for 10 percent.

**Q:** *How much should I pay to have my manuscript read by an agent?*

**A:** The question isn't, "How much?"; the question is, "Should I pay a reading fee at all?" It's a controversial question. Some people say that reading new manuscripts from new writers is a normal part of an agent's business and he must do it to find product, just as an oil company must drill holes in the ground, hoping to find product. Others insist that working with newcomers takes too much of the agent's professional time and that if he can't charge for it he can't do it. It's not a moral issue; it's just a difference in opinion.

There are so-called agents who are primarily in the business of reading manuscripts and sending bills to writers. Obviously, if an agent makes more money from reading manuscripts than he does from commissions, he's not a very good agent, and he should be avoided. But the fact of a reading fee, per se, or the lack of one, does not give you any information on which to evaluate an agent's competence and integrity. You need more information for that, and we'll discuss it. As for how much to pay for a reading, the answer is: as little as possible.

**Q:** *How can I get an agent interested in me?*

**A:** Some agents will not read work from anybody who has not been referred to them by another publishing professional. Some agents will not read complete manuscripts from newcomers. Some agents will not read book proposals from newcomers. But there is one thing that every agent will read: a short, well-written, neatly prepared letter. So write a letter first. Tell the agent who you are, what your book is about, and what stage it is in (complete manuscript, proposal, etc.). Tell the agent your credits and any special ideas you have for selling the book. Now it is his move.

The agent will write back to you. He will tell you: (A) He's not taking on any new clients; (B) He's not interested in your project; or (C) Send your material along, because he would like to read it.

If the answer is A or B, writer to another agent. If the answer is C, send the best possible manuscript presented in the most professional manner. (Never send the same material to two agents at the same time.)

**Q:** *How do I know he's the right agent for me?*

**A:** You don't. If an agent wants to take you on as a client, ask to see a client list. Find out what kind of material he's been selling and to whom. Meet him if possible; certainly you should talk on the phone at length. Find out what kind of material he handles and if it fits your publishing plans. Most agents are pretty broad in what they will market, but many won't handle juvenile fiction, for example, or material that they think is in bad taste. Find out what his commission is and if he charges additional fees for expenses such as photocopying. Some agents do. Learn his definition of the agent-client relationship. Will he handle your short fiction? Will he market a book that he doesn't like but that you feel strongly about?

I think an agent and a writer should always begin on a trial basis. A good reputable agent and a good professional writer are not automatically compatible, and if the personal chemistry between them is not good, the professional relationship will suffer. In other words, get an agent you like.

**Q:** *How can I help my agent help me?*

**A:** Give him the names of all your connections in publishing, such as editors who have bought, or at least praised, your work in the past. Give him any ammunition you can that will help him sell your book.

**Q:** *Any final advice?*

**A:** Remember that the agent-writer relationship is much like a marriage. You get into it hoping it will last forever, but divorces do occur. Many writers have one or two brief, unsatisfactory relationships with agents before they find the one who is right for them. But also accept the fact that there can be disagreements in any good marriage and you and your agent can work them out.

When I met my agent for the first time, we had lunch. He told me what he expected from a client, and I told him what I expected from an agent. By the time lunch was over we had committed ourselves to an agent-client relationship. As we went out the door of the restaurant, I said to him, "What if I send you a book and you think it's awful and just cannot be marketed and you don't want to send it out, and I think it's wonderful and salable and I want it seen by as many editors as possible?"

"Well," he said, "if that happens, you and I will have to have lunch again."

# Agents Interested in Mystery/Suspense

A.M.C. Literary Agency
234 5th Ave.
New York NY 10001
(212) 673-9551

Acton, Dystel, Leone & Jaffe, Inc.
928 Broadway
New York NY 10010
(212) 473-1700

Lee Allan Agency
P.O. Box 18617
Milwaukee WI 53218
(414) 357-7708

James Allen, Literary Agency
P.O. Box 278
Milford PA 18337

Marcia Amsterdam Agency
41 W. 82nd St.
New York NY 10024
(212) 873-4945

Appleseeds Management
Suite 302, 300 E. 30th St.
San Bernardino CA 92404
(909) 882-1667

The Axelrod Agency
66 Church St.
Lenox MA 01240
(413) 637-2000

Helen Barrett Literary Agency
175 W. 13th St.
New York NY 10011
(212) 645-7430

Reid Boates Literary Agency
P.O. Box 328
274 Cooks Crossroad
Pittstown NJ 08867
(908) 730-8523

Barbara Bova Literary Agency
207 Sedgwick Rd.
West Hartford CT 06107
(203) 521-5915

Joan Brandt Agency
52 S. Prado N.E.
Atlanta GA 30309
(404) 881-0023

Brandt & Brandt Literary Agents,
Inc.
1501 Broadway
New York NY 10036

Jane Butler, Art and Literary
Agent
P.O. Box 33
Metamoras PA 18336

Cantrell-Colas, Inc., Literary
Agency
229 E. 79th St.
New York NY 10021
(212) 737-8503

Maria Carvainis Agency, Inc.
Suite 15F, 235 West End Ave.
New York NY 10023
(212) 580-1559

SJ Clark Literary Agency
56 Glenwood
Hercules CA 94547

Diane Cleaver, Inc.
55 5th Ave.
New York NY 10003
(212) 206-5606

Ruth Cohen, Inc., Literary
Agency
P.O. Box 7626
Menlo Park CA 94025
(415) 854-2054

Frances Collin Literary Agent
Suite 1403, 110 W. 40th St.
New York NY 10018
(212) 840-8664

Columbia Literary Associates,
Inc.
7902 Nottingham Way
Ellicott City MD 21043
(410) 465-1595

Richard Curtis Associates, Inc.
171 E. 74th St.
New York NY 10021
(212) 772-7363

Elaine Davie Literary Agency
Village Gate Square
274 N. Goodman St.
Rochester NY 14607
(716) 442-0830

The Lois de la Haba Agency, Inc.
142 Bank St.
New York NY 10014
(212) 929-4838

Anita Diamant, The Writer's
Workshop, Inc.
310 Madison Ave.
New York NY 10017
(212) 687-1122

Diamond Literary Agency, Inc.
3063 S. Kearney St.
Denver CO 80222
(303) 759-0291

Sandra Dijkstra Literary Agency
#515, 1155 Camino del Mar
Del Mar CA 92014
(619) 755-3115

Doyen Literary Services, Inc.
19005 660th St.
Newell IA 50568-7613
(712) 272-3300

Robert Ducas
350 Hudson St.
New York NY 10014
(212) 924-8120

Dupree/Miller and Associates,
Inc., Literary Agency
Suite 3, 5518 Dyer St.
Dallas TX 75206
(214) 692-1388

Vicki Eisenberg Literary Agency
929 Fernwood
Richardson TX 75080
(214) 918-9593

Ethan Ellenberg Literary Agency
#5-E, 548 Broadway
New York NY 10012
(212) 431-4554

Embers Literary Agency
R.R. 3, Box 173
Spencer IN 47460

The Fallon Literary Agency
Suite 13B, 301 W. 53rd St.
New York NY 10019
(212) 399-1369

Marje Fields-Rita Scott, Inc.
Suite 1205, 165 W. 46th
New York NY 10036
(212) 764-5740

Jay Garon-Brooke Assoc., Inc.
Suite 80, 101 W. 55th St.
New York NY 10019
(212) 581-8300

Max Gartenberg, Literary Agent
Suite 1700, 521 5th Ave.
New York NY 10175
(212) 860-8451

Irene Goodman Literary Agency
17th Floor, 521 5th Ave.
New York NY 10175
(212) 682-1978

Joe Gotler Metropolitan Talent
Agency
9320 Wilshire Boulevard
Beverly Hills CA 90212
(310) 247-5580

Stanford J. Greenburger
Associates
55 Fifth Ave.
New York NY 10003
(212) 206-5600

John Hawkins & Associates, Inc.
71 W. 23rd St.
New York NY 10010
(212) 807-7040

Susan Herner Rights Agency
P.O. Box 303
Scarsdale NY 10583
(914) 725-8967

Hull House Literary Agency
240 E. 82nd St.
New York NY 10028
(212) 988-0725

J De S Associates, Inc.
9 Shagbark Road, Wilson Point
South Norwalk CT 06854
(203) 838-7571

Sharon Jarvis & Co., Inc.
260 Willard Ave.
Staten Island NY 10314
(718) 720-2120

KC Communications
Suite 201, 11512 N. Poema Place
Chatsworth CA 91311
(818) 998-7265

Kidde, Hoyt & Picard
335 E. 51st St.
New York NY 10022
(212) 755-9461

Harvey Klinger, Inc.
301 W. 53 St.
New York NY 10019
(212) 581-7068

Barbara S. Kouts, Literary Agent
P.O. Box 558
Bellport NY 11713
(516) 286-1278

Edite Kroll Literary Agency
12 Grayhurst Park
Portland, ME 04102
(207) 773-4922

Peter Lampack Agency, Inc.
Suite 2015, 551 5th Ave.
New York NY 10017
(212) 687-9106

The Robert Lantz-Joy Harris
Literary Agency
888 7th Ave.
New York NY 10106
(212) 262-8177

M. Sue Lasbury Literary Agency
4861 Ocean Blvd.
San Diego CA 92109
(619) 483-7170

Ray Lincoln Literary Agency
Suite 107-B, Elkins Park House
7900 Old York Rd.
Elins Park PA 19117
(215) 635-0827

Wendy Lipkind Agency
165 E. 66th St.
New York NY 10021
(212) 628-9653

Literary Bridge
Box 250 Alamo C.C.
Alamo TX 78516
(512) 702-4873

Literary Group
#7A, 153 E. 32nd St.
New York NY 10016
(212) 779-9214

Nancy Love Literary Agency
250 E. 65th St.
New York NY 10021
(212) 980-3499

Lyceum Creative Properties, Inc.
P.O. Box 12370
San Antonio TX 78212
(210) 732-0200

Gina Maccoby Literary Agency
Suite 1010, 1123 Broadway
New York NY 10010
(212) 627-9210

Helen McGrath
1406 Idaho Court
Concord CA 94521
(415) 672-6211

Mildred Marmur Associates, Ltd.
Suite 607, 310 Madison Ave.
New York NY 10017
(212) 949-6055

Greg Merhige-Merdon
Marketing/Promo Co., Inc.
Suite 203, 1080 E. Indiantown Rd.
Jupiter FL 33477
(404) 747-9951

MGA Agency, Inc.
Suite 510, 10 St. Mary St.
Toronto Ontario M4Y 1P9 Canada
(416) 964-3302

Multimedia Product
Development, Inc.
Suite 724, 410 S. Michigan Ave.
Chicago IL 60605
(312) 922-3063

Jean V. Naggar Literary Agency
1E, 216 E. 75th St.
New York NY 10021
(212) 794-1082

Regual Noetzli Literary Agency
444 E. 85th St.
New York NY 10028
(212) 628-1537

Richard Parks Agency
5th Floor, 138 E. 16th St.
New York NY 10003
(212) 254-9067

Rodney Pelter
129 E. 61st St.
New York NY 10021
(212) 838-3432

L. Perkins Associates
5800 Arlington Ave.
Riverdale NY 10471
(212) 543-5344

Alison J. Picard Literary Agent
P.O. Box 2000
Cotuit MA 02635
(508) 420-6163

Helen Rees Literary Agency
308 Commonwealth Ave.
Boston MA 02116
(617) 262-2401

Riverside Literary Agency
Suite 123, 2673 Broadway
New York NY 10025
(212) 666-0622

Jean Rosenthal Literary Agency
28 E. 11th St.
New York NY 10013
(212) 677-4248

Roth Literary Agency
No. 2, 106 Rockview St.
Boston MA 02130
(617) 522-3213

Pesha Rubinstein, Literary
Agency, Inc.
#1D, 37 Overlook Terrace
New York NY 10033
(212) 781-7845

Harold Schmidt Literary Agency
Suite 1005, 668 Greenwich St.
New York NY 10014
(212) 727-7473

Lynn Seligman, Literary Agent
400 Highland Ave.
Upper Montclair NH 07043
(201) 783-3631

Bobbe Siegel Literary Agency
41 W. 83rd St.
New York NY 10024
(212) 877-4985

Evelyn Singer Literary Agency,
Inc.
P.O. Box 594
White Plains NY 10602
(914) 631-5160/1167

Michael Snell Literary Agency
Box 655
Truro MA 02666
(508) 349-3718

Philip G. Spitzer Literary Agency
788 9th Ave.
New York NY 10019
(212) 265-6003

Lyle Steele & Co., Ltd.
Suite 6, 511 E. 73rd St.
New York NY 10021
(212) 288-2981

Gloria Stern Literary Agency
15E, 1230 Park Ave.
New York NY 10128
(212) 289-7698

Patricia Teal Literary Agency
2036 Vista Del Rosa
Fullerton CA 92631
(714) 738-8333

Mary Jack Wald Associates, Inc.
111 E. 14th St.
New York NY 10003
(212) 254-7842

John A. Ware Literary Agency
392 Central Park W.
New York NY 10025
(212) 866-4733

Watkins Loomis Agency, Inc.
Suite 530, 150 E. 35th St.
New York NY 10016
(212) 532-0080

Cherry Weiner Literary Agency
28 Kipling Way
Manalapan NJ 07726
(908) 446-2096

Weingel-Fidel Agency
#21E, 310 E. 46th St.
New York NY 10017
(212) 599-2959

Westchester Literary Agency,
Inc.
Suite 4-I, 50 E. Hartsdale Ave.
Hartsdale NY 10530
(914) 428-8897

Wieser & Wieser, Inc.
118 E. 25th St., 7th Floor
New York NY 10010
(212) 260-0860

Gary S. Wohl Literary Agency
1 5th Ave.
New York NY 10003
(212) 254-9126

Ruth Wreschner, Authors'
Representative
10 W. 74th St.
New York NY 10023
(212) 877-2605

Susan Zeckendorf Assoc., Inc.
171 W. 57th St.
New York NY 10019
(212) 245-2928

# *The Sources*

## Magazines About Mysteries:
## The Documents in the Case
*by Michael Seidman*

Doctors and other professionals are expected to "keep up with the literature"; to read the journals and other printed media that keep them informed about new developments, new procedures, rulings, and everything else that allows them to perform in the manner we expect of them.

Writers are professionals and they, too, have to keep up with the literature. And while the phrase "publish or perish" has entirely different connotations for us, our literature — our media — often pays us for submissions. Appearing in the pages of the magazines read by other writers and by our fans serves to keep our names in front of our audience between books. Reading these media help us keep in touch with what's going on. The combination has a certain charm, doesn't it? At the top of any recommended reading list for writers is *Publishers Weekly*, the bible of the book trade. The magazine is aimed at booksellers, but the reviews, surveys (which consist of interviews with editors) and general information appearing every week are indispensable. The subscription price is generally prohibitive for individuals, but the magazine is available at every library and, if you've become chummy with a bookseller (something else you should seriously consider doing), you might be able to borrow the store's copy or at least leaf through it. Further information is available from R.R. Bowker, 249 West 17th St., New York NY 10011.

Also a must, because of the articles and market reports, are magazines like *Writer's Digest*. Don't think that just because you've started selling your work — stories, articles or novels — that you've outgrown your need for magazines of this kind. There's always something to be discovered. Write to the magazine at 1507 Dana Ave., Cincinnati OH 45207.

You might also look through *Writer's Market*, not with an eye toward places that might be worth submissions, but to discover a wealth of other magazines and journals whose subject matter will be useful to you. True crime magazines offer extensive information about procedure; media aimed at the legal profession may give you an insight into something that can be turned into a mystery story; medical journals contain articles that could help you build a case against your criminal through the use of advances in forensic medicine.

When we think in terms of crime fiction specifically, however, there are three magazines that virtually everyone reads: *The Armchair Detective*, *Mystery Scene* and *The Drood Review of Mystery*. They all began as fanzines, magazines published by fans, for fans — a way of sharing information about a genre, expressing feelings, likes and dislikes, comments about books — in short, a bull session in print. Fanzines continue to be a staple of the category (just as they are found in science fiction, horror and romance), and their value to you, as a writer, is something you have to discover and decide. It would be impossible to even begin listing them all; however, a good mystery specialty bookstore will be able to lead you to the bulk of them and there may be copies available for you to examine.

They are usually inexpensively produced (*TAD* — as *The Armchair Detective* is called — began twenty-five years ago as ten mimeographed pages with a circulation numbered in the tens; there are others today that still reach less than fifty readers), do not offer payment (except, maybe, in copies), and while they'll let you know what certain fans are thinking, their overall value is questionable. Fanzines, by their very nature, preach to the already converted, and while arguments and discussions abound, the view is often limited. The three magazines we've chosen to discuss, however, have expanded far beyond the fanzine definition (although *Drood* still defines itself as a fanzine and the publisher, Jim Huang, has made it clear that he doesn't want to go beyond that).

*The Armchair Detective* is the oldest of the three. The winner of an

Edgar Allan Poe Award, *TAD* is a quarterly, critical journal devoted to all aspects of crime fiction. It contains reviews; essays; historical perspectives; interviews; columns about everything from collecting mysteries to theater, movie and television reviews; lists of recently released titles; and Walter Albert's catalog of secondary sources: a guide to the readers of where they might find other articles of interest to them (given the shared interest in criminous fiction). A staple of the magazine—as it is with all genre magazines, reflective of the needs of fans to be able to get in touch with each other—is the letters column. (I turn to them first; my second choice is two-time Edgar winner Bill DeAndrea's "J'Accuse!"—a freewheeling, free-spirited discussion of anything and everything, from politics to writers to a meal he may have enjoyed. The column was started when I was the editor; it is one of the very few holdovers from that era. Is it any wonder that it is one of my favorites?)

The Winter 1993 issue (Vol. 26, #1) contains an interview with Jonathan Kellerman, an examination of the novels of Thomas Harris, Robert Bloch and Bret Easton Ellis, an article about mystery writers who've spent time behind bars, and a piece about the *Columbo* series focusing on the fact that in all the years the series has been produced, all the bad guys are "evil capitalists receiving their richly deserved comeuppance. All those crimes in all those years and not one proletarian bad guy. . . ."

Of the regular features, first among equals being DeAndrea, are "Detour: The Column," a new column by critic and anthologist Michele Slung, Otto Penzler's "Collecting Mystery Fiction," Janet Rudolph's "Murderous Affairs," a column about conventions, conclaves, meetings, publications, and other matters of like interest (and an excellent way to find other material), and "Report from Baker St.," which deals with matters Sherlockian, as well as all the reviews.

The magazine's readership is very sophisticated and knowledgeable (and to my mind, just more than a bit stodgy, overall), and many of the articles have an academic tone. The piece on Block, Harris and Easton, for example, has eighteen footnotes of the kind that read: "Lovecraft to August Derleth, 6 November 1931 (*MS*, State Historical Society of Wisconsin)."

The reviews are received in two ways: certain writers—Al Hubin, the founder of *The Armchair Detective*, and Jon Breen, an author and critic of the category—both offer regular columns. Hubin's is general: Breen contributes two columns: One deals with novels that have courtroom settings, the other with books about the genre. Marvin Lachman reviews first novels, often in retrospective commentaries. The bulk of current reviews, however, come in from the readership. The magazine maintains a list of people who are interested in the genre and in reviewing; the editors send books to the people on this list. A couple of sample reviews and a request to be added to the list would be the way to go here. Let them know the kind of mystery you like—P.I., cozy, espionage, etc. Again, familiarize yourself with the kinds of reviews *The Armchair Detective* runs and make certain that you don't, in your critique of a book, give away any of the clues. (If you are submitting an article that reveals the kinds of information a reader wouldn't want to know before picking up a book, be sure to offer a warning above the text.)

The page count includes photographs or other art; it does not include ad space. While inquiries are not required, it makes sense to query them. The editors receive hundreds of pieces every year, have a long lead time (remember, they publish quarterly), and the article you're working on may parallel something awaiting publication. (I'd guess that if you interview someone, that person would have the good sense to tell you that something is scheduled. I've been known to guess wrong.)

Without question the most professionally produced and slickest of the three magazines discussed here, *The Armchair Detective* is edited by Kate Stine (and published by Otto Penzler); their address is 129 W. 56th St., New York NY 10019. Subscriptions are $26 annually in the United States, $30 elsewhere. Individual issues are $7.50. The magazine should be available at mystery bookstores and at some of the chains.

*Mystery Scene* was begun by two mystery writers, Ed Gorman and Robert J. Randisi, in 1985, and was designed to fill a gap between the traditional fanzine and *TAD*. It has, since its beginning, undergone a number of changes, and it is still transforming itself; the one thing that hasn't changed is the excitement.

Virtually all the writers appearing in *Mystery Scene* are professionals, people who are writing for a living (or trying to); people for whom the mystery goes beyond the passion of the reading. While that doesn't guarantee the quality of the writing will be any better, it does mean that the concerns addressed, the points of view, are directly applicable to your life as a writer. At one time, in talking about the magazine, I described it as a pro fanzine—a magazine written by professionals for professionals, a sort of *Journal of American Medical Association* for mystery writers, with information that was accessible to anyone who wanted to read it. No matter what changes *Mystery Scene* has undergone, that aspect of it remains.

The letters column is, not surprisingly, quite lively and, on occasion, downright acrimonious. Debates about first-amendment rights — especially as they are affected by issues of political correctness — have gone on for months, several writers and one reviewer "discussed" quality of writing versus the fulfillment of the readers' needs, an open debate between Stephen King and an antiquarian bookseller about the prices being quoted for some of King's work that appeared in a "questionable" edition, and some heated comments about the validity of theme anthologies by women. On the lighter side, every now and then a letter will show up from someone like Brian Garfield, just saying "hello" and letting some folks know he was still alive.

Regular columns in the magazine include market reports (featured there is a column by New York agent, Sharon Jarvis) and reports on the activities of writers in various parts of the country (who's doing what, just sold a new book, going on a sell tour). Furthering the image of a kaffee-klatch for professionals, these columns sorta kinda parallel the same kinds of reports you'd find in the newsletter of your local writer's group . . . and for a brief time, *Mystery Scene* was called a newsletter. There are also overseas reports, reports from Canada, reports from Sisters in Crime, regular commentary about things happening on Broadway and in the movies and television; in short, the magazine offers a way to keep up with what's goin' down.

But there's more than news and markets, much more. Hugh Holton, a commander with the Chicago police department, contributes a column that discusses police procedure and points out the errors that appear all too often in crime fiction and offers ways around them. Several writers — Carole Nelson Douglas, Joan Hess, Bob Randisi, Max Allan Collins and me, to name a few, appear regularly (or as regularly as their schedules allow). Columns tend to be about whatever it is that interests them at the moment, sometimes contentious, sometimes loving, and always — well, almost always — engaging.

*Mystery Scene*, as might be expected, also runs reviews and general articles — a recent issue, for example, had an in-depth piece about mystery magazines by one of the leading fan commentators, Bob Napier, an interview with John Lutz (a well-respected private eye writer who's recent novel, *SWF, Seeks Same*, became the hit movie, *Single White Female*), as well as other interviews and more general commentary, including the first portion of Richard Wheeler's study of the contributions of Dale Walker to the field of Western writing. Because writers write for *Mystery Scene*, and because so many writers work in different genres, the magazine has always had room to discuss other categories of popular fiction. This breadth is part of its appeal.

Current subscription rates are $35 annually (for seven issues) in the United States; foreign subscriptions are $63.50, U.S. funds. Single copies are $4.75. The address is *Mystery Scene Magazine*, P.O. Box 669, Cedar Rapids IA 52406-0669, (815) 397-3146.

*The Drood Review of Mystery* is an old-fashioned, straightforward fanzine: written by fans, read by fans, and while they are open to submissions (as a fanzine must be), they do not pay for contributions. The writers here are very much the readers, and many professionals read the magazine regularly to keep up with the work of their peers and, in a very real sense, to discover what they may want to read themselves; it is generally thought that *Drood*'s reviews are among the finest in the country.

In addition to the reviews — and extensive listings of new releases in hardcover and paperback — Jim Huang, the editor and publisher, is looking for interviews and commentary on current mystery writing. There is no interest here in the past — in terms of articles — nor is the magazine looking for stories.

*Drood Review* is, then, a solid informational source, with cogent reviews that reveal the tastes and mindsets of some of the most knowledgeable mystery readers around, and the popularity of the magazine is revealed in the way it dominates voting for best fanzine. Published monthly, when they're on schedule (there were some problems in 1992 because the magazine moved from its base in Boston to Kalamazoo, Michigan), *The Drood Review of Mystery* costs $20 for a one-year subscription; $36 for two years. For further information, write to Jim Huang, *The Drood Review of Mystery*, Suite 110, 5047 W. Main St., Kalamazoo MI 49009.

There are lots of smaller publications that serve to inform the readers about the mystery: Tower Books in Chico, California, issues a newsletter called, cleverly enough, *Tower Books Mystery Newsletter* (211 Main St., Chico CA 95928) with reviews of a couple of current titles and lists of upcoming releases. They welcome short reviews and comments; there's no payment.

Two popular fanzines are *The Mystery FANcier*, % Guy Townsend, 2024 Clifty Dr., Madison IN 47250-1632, which has fascinating letters and reviews and interesting articles; and *Mystery and Detective Monthly*, a "letterzine," which consists entirely of arguments, debates, comments, snide remarks and reactions thereto from a group of dedicated fans, readers and some professional writers. It sometimes takes a while to understand what's going on in this publication's pages because whenever you pick it up you're stepping into the middle of a family argument that may have been going on for years. The love of mysteries—and some of the pettiness that evolves in any family—is apparent on almost every page, and the members of this family gather at almost every convention to carry on in person what was started on the printed page. Subscription information, etc., is available from the perps % Cap'n Bob Napier, 5601 N. 40th St., Tacoma WA 98407.

As you begin reading any of these publications you will be led to others; writing to the editors and buying a copy will allow you to decide whether you want to subscribe to—and consider as markets, free or fee—such magazines as *The Mystery Caucus of the Popular Culture Association* or *Mystery Readers International* or the newsletter of the *Maltese Falcon Society*. If you start reading them all, you'll never have any time to write, so pick and choose accordingly.

Finally, membership in Mystery Writers of America, Private Eye Writers of America, Sisters in Crime, or any peer group organization, will put you on the mailing list for their newsletters. (See the section on organizations for contact information.) Market reports and other articles of interest to you as a writing business professional—from the finer points of contracts to payment problems to updates on what people are doing—all help you to be a more professional, and thus more successful, writer. And that's what it's all about.

## Mystery and Crime Writer's Organizations

---

# American Crime Writers League
**Address:** 12 St. Ann Dr., Santa Barbara CA 93109
**Contact:** Barbara Mertz, President
**Profile:** National organization. Approximately 150 members. Membership open only to published mystery and crime writers. (Applicants must have had a novel, three short stories or a work of nonfiction published.) "The only mystery organization open *only* to published authors." Benefits of membership include bimonthly newsletter that provides a forum for discussion of issues of interest to mystery writers. The organization

acts to support and advocate improvements in matters relating to writers of mysteries. Fee: $35/year.

## Crime Writer's Assoc.

**Address:** P.O. Box 172, Tring, Herts HP23 5LP England
**Contact:** Anthea Fraser, Secretary
**Profile:** International organization. Established 1953. 450 members. Levels of Membership: full, country, overseas, associate. Publishes *Red Herrings* monthly newsletter for members only. Dues £30 (Sterling). Monthly meetings held in London and local chapters. Annual conference. Benefits of membership include ability to increase technical knowledge and social contacts. Complete list of award winners available for IPC.
**Awards:** CWA/Cartier Diamond Dagger Award, Gold Dagger, Silver Dagger, Gold Dagger for nonfiction, John Creasey Memorial Award, and Last Laugh Award.

## International Association of Crime Writers (North American Branch)

**Address:** JAF Box 1500, New York NY 10116, (212) 757-3915
**Contact:** Mary Frisque, Executive Director
**Profile:** International organization. Established 1987. 225 members. Open to "published authors of crime fiction, nonfiction, screenplays, and professionals in the mystery field (agents, editors, booksellers)." Benefits include information about crime writing world-wide and publishing opportunities in other countries. Sponsors annual members' receptions during Edgar Award week in New York, hosts a reception at Bouchercon in Spring. Holds occasional receptions for visiting authors/publishers. Presents the North American Hammett Prize annually for the best work (fiction or nonfiction) of literary excellence in the crime-writing field.

Publishes a quarterly newsletter, *Border Patrol*, for members. Fee: $50/year.

## Mystery Writers of America
**Address:** 236 W. 27th St., New York NY 10001
**Contact:** Priscilla Ridgway, Executive Director
**Profile:** Established 1945. 2,500 members. Types of membership: active (professional, published writers of fiction or nonfiction crime/mystery/suspense), associate (professionals in allied fields: editors, publishers, writers, critics, reporters, publicists, librarians, booksellers), corresponding (writers qualified for active membership who live outside the U.S.) and affiliate (unpublished writers, students and mystery fans). Benefits include counsel and advice on contracts, courses and workshops, a national office with an extensive library, an annual conference featuring the Edgar Allan Poe Awards, the *MWA Mystery Writer's Handbook*, the *MWA Anthology*, a national newsletter, regional conferences, meetings and newsletters. Newsletter, the *Third Degree*, is published 10 times/year for members. Annual dues: $65 for U.S. members; $32.50 for corresponding members.

## Private Eye Writer's of America
**Address:** 330 Surrey Rd., Cherry Hill NJ 08002, (609) 482-1018
**Contact:** David Masterton, Membership Chairman
**Profile:** Private Eye Writer's of America was founded in 1982 by Robert J. Randisi to "promote and recognize private eye writers." Levels of membership: active, associate and international. Newsletter, *Reflections in a Private Eye*, edited and published by Jan Grape (11804 Oak Trail, Austin TX 78753, (512) 339-1615). Fees: active members $30/year; associate $24/year; international $30/year.

## Sisters in Crime

**Address:** P.O. Box 442124, Lawrence KS 66044-8933
**Contact:** M. Beth Wasson, Executive Secretary
**Profile:** Open to all interested in promoting women in the mystery field (writers, fans, publishers, editors, men, women, etc.). The "purpose is to combat discrimination against women in the mystery field, to educate publishers and the general public as to the inequality in treatment of female authors and to raise the level of awareness of their contributions to the field." Fee: $25.

## Mystery Conventions

*by Michael Seidman*

### Round Up All the Usual Suspects

We all know the value of networking, of keeping in touch with the people who in one way or another have impact on our lives. As writers, as mystery writers, those people are the booksellers, editors and fans—especially the fans, the people who read what we're writing if an editor buys it and a bookseller stocks it. (Some mighty big "ifs" in there, but hey, that's what it's all about.)

How do you manage to meet all those folks? It's easy: Just go to one of the mystery conventions. All the usual suspects are there, and they're all more than happy to meet and greet and even offer a word of encouragement and advice. (Well, most of them are—as with anything, there are a couple of people who are a bit more impressed with themselves than they should be, even if they are selling well . . .

Perhaps the best way to illustrate this for you is to relate a tale about something that happened at Bouchercon XXIII in Toronto, in October 1992. I was talking to one of my authors, a first novelist who'd just received an award. He saw Lawrence Block standing across the room, and asked me whether I'd introduce him.

"Sure. Although if you just went up to him, it would be fine."

"Yeah, well . . ."

It wasn't until the next morning that an opportunity presented itself, and I brought the author over to Larry, who held out his hand, said hello first and congratulated the writer on his honor. At that point, I just walked away.

Want to meet Larry Block? Or maybe Mary Higgins Clark? Or Julie Smith or Bob Randisi or Marcia Muller or Walter Mosely or . . . ? At one convention or another, at one time or another, the opportunity will present itself. You will also have the chance to meet some of the leading mystery specialty booksellers in the country, folks like Otto Penzler or Steve Stilwell or Bruce Taylor or Tom and Enid Schantz or Barbara Peters. You might wind up having drinks with Ruth Cavin of St. Martin's Press, or Janet Hutchings, the editor of *Ellery Queen's Mystery Magazine*, or Bill Malloy of Mysterious Press, or even me.

You will also be able to sit in on some of the most interesting (or deadly dull) panels and discussions about virtually every aspect of crime fiction. Very few — almost none — of these panels are about writing, per se, or about craft or any of the other things one attends a writer's conference to learn or accomplish. The mystery conventions are fan-organized, fan-run and fan-oriented — and most of the people you'll meet are, like you, fans of the genre. (Writers who aren't fans tend not to be quite as successful; if you can't understand that, go directly to jail, do not pass GO, do not collect a contract.)

The granddaddy of mystery conventions is the Bouchercon. It's traditionally held over the Columbus Day weekend, and number XXIV is scheduled for Omaha, Nebraska, on October 1, 1993; XXV will be in Seattle, Washington, the following year, and the year after that the convention is going to Nottingham, England. You have stumbled onto the fact that this gathering moves around a little. The idea was to make it accessible to people all over the country (and now, obviously, the world). The formal name of the convention is Bouchercon, the World Mystery Fan Convention, and it is based on the principles of the World Science Fiction Convention, at which the Hugo Award is presented. Several years ago, the Bouchercon began presenting the Anthony Award, voted on by the fans registered to attend.

A word about those names: Anthony Boucher was one of the leading critics in the field of crime fiction; the convention is named after him, as is the award. While the Hugo is the same trophy every year, each Bouchercon steering committee creates its own Anthony. At least so far.

Clearly, this is an informal operation. When you attend one convention you get to vote on the location for the convention three years down the road, and then you're in the hands of the people who've won. Some years are better than others. In Pasadena a few years ago, we wound up meeting in the lobby for several panels because the hotel gave our rooms to some local football team (I think it was UCLA; do they play football?). For those of us sitting in the bar, watching the World Series and the Hill/Thomas hearings (there were a couple of TV sets), having the panel going on right outside was a terrible distraction. They felt the same way about us. The panel was on the business of publishing; none of the editors or agents attending the convention were invited to be on the panel. As I said, some conventions are better than others.

This is a convention that's gotten a bit unwieldy over the last few years. Up until the early 1980s attendance hovered between 350 and 500 people, and many of us, and certainly those of us who'd attended science fiction conventions, looked askance. Now, however, the numbers are beginning to nudge the 2,000 mark and that means the hotels don't handle the crowds quite as well, meeting rooms are crowded and uncomfortable, and there may be as many as five panels going on at the same time. This isn't to everyone's taste, nor are the trips overseas (London hosted the Bouchercon a few years ago), and as a result of that several regional conventions have evolved.

The first of these was the Midwest Mystery Convention which has been held in Omaha for three years and which will be renamed the Southwest Mystery Convention in 1993, when it moves to Austin, Texas. At this time none of us are certain as to whether or not it will be held at all in 1994. Much smaller than Bouchercon, and usually held around Memorial Day, this convention offers an opportunity to writers and readers in America's heartland to meet and talk, without facing the often prohibitive expense of travel away from there. The regional conventions are not as well attended by publishers and agents, but they are just as valuable to you. Consider: If an editor is willing to travel to ostensibly the middle of nowhere, his or her interest and commitment must be pretty intense.

Left Coast Crime began in San Francisco. In February 1993, it will begin to alternate between northern and southern California. The organizers are attempting to keep it on schedule as a President's Day weekend event. Again, the idea was to give people on the West Coast the opportunity to attend a convention if they couldn't get to the east for Bouchercon.

The last of the regional conferences is Mid-Atlantic Mystery, which is held in Philadelphia in November. Celebrating its third anniversary in 1993, this conference is the smallest of the regional meetings, which allows for the most intimacy.

Choosing between these meetings is as much a matter of economics as anything else: Where can you afford to go? In terms of what they offer you, they are pretty much the same. The differences—with one exception which we'll look at in a minute—lie in the dynamics of the people attending. The same discussion, let's say Social Responsibility in the Mystery, might be held at all of the conventions, and in the same yea. But the people on the panel, their willingness to mix it up (the panel runs because it offers so much opportunity of bloodletting as the politically correct tangle with folks with different priorities – like writing or reality), and their insights can make one exciting and another a failure.

I don't think that the panels themselves are all that important. Oh, sure, they draw crowds, and sometimes offer marvelous insights of one kind or another, but the real reason for the convention is that it allows like-minded people to gather and celebrate their passion. If you don't like a panel (and there are generally at least two or three to choose from at any given time), you'll find mystery readers and writers mingling in the halls, in the bar, in the lobby, just talking. Everyone is welcome to join in. (I've seen some of the most obnoxious people it's been my misfortune to meet treated with the utmost courtesy. Of course, those were readers; obnoxious writers seem to get cut out of things.) As always, the most interesting information seems to get exchanged during these informal periods.

Each convention, except Philadelphia, holds a banquet, generally on Saturday night. The food is what you'd expect at a hotel but the entertainment varies. At Bouchercon, the banquet is used to present the guest of honor (or guests – sometimes fans or booksellers or editors receive accolades), is hosted by a toastmaster who is usually quite funny, and there might be other entertainment as well: Parnell Hall, a private eye writer from New York, has been known to pick up a guitar and sing for his supper, and others have exposed themselves in the same way. The highlight of the banquet is the presentation of the Anthony Award, which the attendees have been voting on since their arrival. As we said earlier, this is a fan award, as opposed to the Edgar Allan Poe Award, which is voted by the membership of the Mystery Writers of America (MWA). So the Anthony is more of a popularity contest than a comment on writing ability. As an aspiring writer, however, paying attention to who is popular with the fans may give you an indication of things you might or might not want to do in your own work.

The banquets at the other conventions also provide guests of honor life achievement awards and entertainment: Mid-Atlantic had a band (led by Shamus Award-winning author Max Allan Collins) provide music for dancing, and Southwest is planning Texas two-step lessons and an old-fashioned barbecue. If you don't like banquets, though, you're not alone, and you'll find other people willing to join you for dinner at Burger King or the hotel dining room.

Bouchercon is also the site for the presentation of the Private Eye Writers of America's (PWA) Shamus Awards. Usually held as the last panel event on Saturday afternoon, it offers something most award functions lack: brevity and some great humor. (When Bouchercon goes overseas, another convention is chosen as the site of the PWA Award program. There's been some discussion of creating another convention around the theme of the P.I., but nothing has been firmed up.) The PWA also has a luncheon during the course of the convention — at which the winner of the Best First Private Eye Novel competition, jointly sponsored by PWA and St. Martin's Press, is announced — and nonmembers do seem to find a way to join in the fun, even though it's supposed to be a "professional" meeting.

Another special interest group, Sisters in Crime (SinC), has a breakfast at Bouchercon; many fans attend and it is a worthwhile meeting for any writer who wants to get a career on track, regardless of gender. SinC has done more to raise the publicity and promotion consciousness of mystery writers than any other group I can think of and while they're still politicized, it seems that now that they've corrected some of the more outrageous problems women in crime fiction faced, they're getting on with the business of writing and selling books. Their meetings are informative and useful.

On the lighter side, there are some panels that have taken the public's fancy and are requested at every convention. One of them is Bob Randisi's Gat Heat, named after his occasional column in *Mystery Scene*. Formatted like a late-night talk show, the panel is a mix of comedy and interviews. Bob usually finds a compatible group of guests, brings them on and lets things happen. The panel has been visited by the Ghost of Bimbos Past (who wanted to know where all the bimbos are going to go now that they can't be portrayed comfortably, and wound up slugging the host over the head with a bottle of water and taking over the show), a couple of divorced (from each other) writers who made a far more entertaining combo than Mia and Woody ever could, a magician . . . well, you get the idea. Of course, all of these people are mystery writers, touting their books, and talking about writing in answer to questions from another writer. Hidden in all the fluff is a kernel of truth about this business that is always worth discovering. (Like all talk show guests, however, every now and then a dud shows up.)

Another panel deteriorated into a pie-tossing contest; they began by discussing violence.

Randisi is also the evil mind behind a traveling game show: sometimes based on "Jeopardy," "Family Feud" or "Wheel of Fortune," these panels provide entertainment value, bring the fans and readers together, and offer prizes—usually books.

And the dealer's room is another feature of every convention. One of the things fans are looking for is autographs and after every panel, the published authors sit down for an hour or so, and sign their most recent (or most available, or only) book. That's a particular drawing card for the writers: The organizers try to get as many writers as possible onto panels; the booksellers make certain they have books in stock (and there can be fifty dealers displaying current and collectible books) and sometimes bring signed books home with them or bring books to be signed for people who couldn't attend the convention. Those signed books aren't going back to your publisher's warehouse. (Okay, there's a downside: An unknown first novelist signing and sitting next to one of the superstars is going to begin to feel very lonely. One collector, carrying a huge pile of books for someone, put the rest of his stuff in front of someone who didn't have quite the same following. "You wouldn't mind watching these for me, would you?" The hapless author just nodded. After having all the books signed, the person returned, picked up his stuff, said thanks, and walked off. At least he said thanks.)

There's something else you're going to be hearing about at the conventions, and that's "The Poker Game." It exists. It moves from convention to convention (and has become such an important aspect of the convention for some players that organizers are now providing a room for it). It is not open to the general public. What started out as five people killing time has become a something more than a habit. I hate words like "bonding," but that's part of what's going on, and it is an outgrowth of the convention experience, of people having an opportunity to share their interests and talents with others. The game is made up of writers, agents, editors and booksellers and it is by invitation only. At some conventions, there are so many players that there may be three or four tables! At other events, the house may be looking for you. Imagine sitting down across the table from some of the biggest names in the field . . . and taking part of their last six-figure advance. Business isn't discussed at the game, no deals are done, no writer offers an editor a look at a manuscript. But for some it is the reason to attend.

There are two other annual gatherings you should be aware of: The Edgar Award dinner (and the couple of days of discussion and parties that accompany it), and Malice Domestic, another convention much like the others but very specific in outlook and intent.

The Mystery Writers of America produce the Edgar Allan Poe Awards, always in New York City (though there have been cries heard around the country asking that it become a moveable feast), usually at the end of April or beginning of May and, for some reason the board of directors of MWA thinks highly of, always on Thursday night. Literally thousands of people attend, the speeches are long, the room is hot and the waiters surly. For the last several years, there's been a band to entertain and a very nice cocktail hour prior to the dinner. (The last time I looked, the banquet cost about $70 per person.) In a crowd that size it is a bit difficult to have a meaningful conversation—or even one in which both speakers can hear each other—but there are signings at the major New York mystery bookstores such as The Mysterious Bookshop, an afternoon of panels on the campus of John Jay School of Criminal Justice, and other special events: a trip to the morgue is just the thing to get you ready for the dinner that evening.

All members of MWA receive invitations and since the organization welcomes associates (people who are trying to get their first mystery sold), the opportunity to attend and meet, however briefly, with writers, editors and agents is an added bonus to membership.

Malice Domestic is held in suburban Washington, D.C., again usually in May. (They try to schedule it so that it doesn't conflict with the Edgars, but still allow people to attend both without undue financial hardship.) As the name suggests, this conference is dedicated to the cozy and traditional—amateur—sleuths and their creators also offer an award, The Agatha. St. Martin's Press sponsors a Best First contest (for traditional mysteries, naturally) in conjunction with Malice Domestic. The panels and meetings are focused in terms of subject matter and if you are considering tilling those cozy fields, attending at least one or two of these gatherings is mandatory. While there is no Cozy Writers of America as a peer group, Malice Domestic provides the closest thing to it; the fans are welcoming and warm, and the writers charming and criminally devious.

We've included information about the conventions below. Dates, costs and sometimes lists of people who have registered (which means writers who have registered; they are the drawing card) also appear in mystery magazines (*The Armchair Detective*, *Mystery Scene*). Mystery booksellers will also have information, if not registration forms, available. If you attend any of the conventions, there'll be flyers around for some—if not all—of the others, and once you get on the mailing list, you're set.

There may be more conventions on the horizon—some of them

are turning into money makers — and other special interest groups have seen the advantages to these annual comings together of the clan. As a way of meeting the people whose interest can help further your career, and as a way of learning what other writers are thinking, what editors are looking for, and what the readers expect of you, there's nothing that can beat them.

And for me, now, I hear someone shuffling a deck of cards. . . .

## Conventions, Conferences and Workshops of Interest to Mystery Writers

The following are contact addresses for a variety of conventions and conferences of interest to mystery writers. Some are general writing conferences open to, but not excusive to, mystery writing. Others are mystery writing conferences or "fan" conferences devoted to both the reading and the writing of mystery. For exact dates, costs and locations, write for details or check mystery magazines. For an extensive list of fiction conferences, see *Novel and Short Story Writer's Market* or the *Guide to Writer's Conferences* (Shaw Associates, Suite 1406, 625 Biltmore Way, Coral Gables FL 33134). *Writer's Digest* includes hundreds of writers' conferences and workshops in its May issue.

---

## Boucheron

**Address:** P.O. Box 59345, Philadelphia PA 19102-9345

**Profile:** Named for famed critic Anthony Boucher, this is the largest fan convention and site of the Anthony Awards presentations. Although the location changes every year, the convention always is held over the Columbus Day weekend. Watch mystery magazines for information, location and contact addresses for upcoming conventions.

---

## Cape Cod Writers Conference, Inc.

**Address:** Marion Vuilleumier, Executive Director, % Cape Cod Conservatory, Route 132, West Barnstable MA 02668

**Profile:** The Cape Cod Writers Conference is held at

the beautiful Craigville Conference Center every August. The conference lasts one week and includes a series of workshops and panels. Although the conference tries to have something for everyone—a poetry, fiction writing, nonfiction writing and children's writing workshop—they also set aside a slot for a special subject each year. This varies each year, but mystery has been included as a special topic at past conferences.

## Iowa Summer Writing Program Festival

**Address:** Iowa Summer Writing Festival, Division of
**Profile:** Continuing Education, 116 International Center, University of Iowa, Iowa City IA 52242
**Profile:** The Iowa Summer Writing Program Festival is held every year at the end of June to the beginning of July. The festival includes a series of workshops lasting from a weekend to two weeks. Fiction writing is always included, sometimes with a focus on mystery.

## Left Coast Crime

**Address:** alternates between southern and northern California
**Profile:** This regional mystery convention is held over Presidents' Day weekend each year. Check mystery magazines for time, location and contact information.

## Maine Writers Workshops

**Address:** Rockport ME 04856
**Profile:** The Maine Writers Workshops are held from June to October, each lasting one or two weeks. Includes a mystery writers workshop.

# Malice Domestic
**Address:** P.O. Box 701, Herndon VA 22070
**Profile:** This annual conference, celebrating the tradi-
tonal (or cozy) mystery is held each year in May near
Washington, D.C. The Agatha Awards are presented at
this conference.

# Mid-Atlantic Mystery Book Fair
**Address:** Deen and Jay Kogan, % Detecto Mysterioso
Books at Society Hill Playhouse, 507 S. 8th St., Phila-
delphia PA 19147
**Profile:** This is a regional mystery fan convention and
book fair held each November in Philadelphia.

# Mystery Cruise
**Address:** Omni Group Cruises, Inc., 6513 Hollywood
Blvd. #205, Hollywood CA 90028
**Profile:** This is a week-long annual cruise to the Carib-
bean Islands featuring an on-board mystery to be
solved by participants, as well as lectures and workshops by mystery authors.

# Mystery Writers of America Annual Conference and Edgar Awards Banquet
**Address:** 17 E. 47th St., 6th Floor, New York NY 10017
**Profile:** Sponsored by the Mystery Writers of America,
this annual event includes guest speakers and panels
on a wide variety of mystery-related topics and culmi-
nates with the Edgar Awards Banquet. It is held in New
York City each year in late April or early May.

# Of Dark and Stormy Nights

**Address:** MWA Midwest, P.O. Box 8, Techny IL 60082
**Profile:** Sponsored by the Midwest branch of the Mystery Writers of America, this annual one-day workshop is held each year on a Saturday in June in the Chicago area. Includes mystery writing workshops, manuscript critiques, panels and guest speakers.

# Southwest Mystery Convention

**Address:** Austin TX
**Profile:** This is an annual regional mystery fan convention. Check mystery magazines for date and location announcements.

# Split Rock Arts Program

**Address:** University of Minnesota, 306 Wesbrook Hall, 77 Pleasant St., SE, Minneapolis MN 55455
**Profile:** This is an annual series of more than 45 one-week workshops held on the University of Minnesota's Duluth campus in July and August each year. Workshops cover all types of fiction and nonfiction writing.

# Writers Connection Seminars

**Address:** 1601 Saratoga-Sunnyvale Rd., Suite 180, Cupertino CA 95014
**Profile:** Writers Connection sponsors several writing seminars and weekend conferences throughout the year that focus on all types of writing. Of particular note is the group's Selling to Hollywood conference held annually in August. This conference includes script and screen writing and novel adaptations. Writers Connection is a service organization for writers.

# Writers at Work

**Address:** 2100 Emigration Canyon Rd., Salt Lake City
UT 84108
**Profile:** This is a large, week-long conference for writers held annually in June. Includes workshops, panels, readings and seminars on all types of fiction and nonfiction. Holds special sessions on mystery writing.

## Mystery-Related Book Clubs

The following book clubs specialize in mystery and crime fiction.

Mystery Guild
(Doubleday Book & Music Clubs)
245 Park Ave.
New York NY 10167
(212) 984-7561
Mary Ann Eckles

Detective Book Club
Division of Walter J. Black, Inc.
99 Seaview Blvd.
Port Washington NY 11050
Director: Walter J. Black, II
(516) 484-4445
Fax: (516) 484-4709

Mystery and Thriller Guild
Book Club Association
87 Newman St.
London W1P 4EN England
(071) 323-5665

Mysterious Book Club
Book-of-the-Month-Club, Inc.
Time & Life Bldg.
1271 Ave. of the Americas
New York, NY 10020
(212) 522-4200
(212) 522-7127
Director: Juanita James

The Crime Club
77-85 Fulham Palace Rd.
Hammersmith London W6 8JB
England
(081) 307-4656

Some general clubs that carry mystery fiction or books on how to write are listed here:

Book-of-the-Month Club
Subsidiary of Time, Inc.
Time & Life Building
1271 Ave. of the Americas
New York NY 10020-2686

Writer's Digest Book Club
1507 Dana Ave.
Cincinnati OH 45207
Contact: Julia Groh

Quality Paperback Book Club
(see Book-of-the-Month Club)
Linda Lowenthal, Senior Editor

## Mystery and Crime Bookstores

Listings with an (*) indicate a catalog only service.

### Arizona

---

## Footprints of a Gigantic Hound, Ltd.

**Address:** 123 S. Eastbourne, Tuscon AZ 85716, (602) 326-8533
**Owner/Contact person:** Elaine Livermore
**Established:** 1986
**Profile:** Mystery and detective fiction.
**Services:** Carries 3 mystery magazines. Catalog available — write to request. Conducts author book signings.

---

## Janus Books, Ltd.

**Address:** P.O. Box 40787, Tuscon AZ 85717, (602) 881-8192
**Owner/Contact person:** Michael S. Greenbaum
**Established:** 1979
**Services:** Buys and sells used books. 95% of books are old or rare. Catalog available — write or call to request.
**Profile:** First editions of detective, mystery and sus-

pense fiction, related bibliography and criticism, Sher-lockiana.

## The Poisoned Pen

**Address:** 7100 E. Main St., Scottsdale AZ 85251, (602) 947-2974, Fax: (602) 945-1023
**Owner/Contact person:** Barbara Peters
**Profile:** Large selection of British imports; bookshopping services, mail, phone and fax orders; mystery discussion club (monthly). Focus is southwestern mystery, British mystery and historical mystery.
**Services:** Selectively buys used books; sells used books. Carries 6 mystery magazines. 10% of books are old or rare. Catalog available — write or call to request. Frequently conducts author book signings, some readings.

### California

## Acorn Books

**Address:** 740 Polk St., San Francisco CA 94109, (415) 563-1736
**Owner/Contact person:** Joel M. Chapman
**Established:** 1980
**Profile:** "Noted for our large quality, well-organized stock."
**Services:** Buys, trades and sells used books. Carries some mystery magazines. 75% of books are old or rare. Sells memorabilia. Catalog available for $2. Sells only old/rare self-published books.

## Book Carnival

**Address:** 348 S. Tustin, Orange CA 92666, (714) 538-3210
**Owner/Contact person:** Ed and Pat Thomas
**Established:** 1981

**Profile:** "We cater to the reader and the collector. We have had over 60 author signings so far this year. 20% of our stock is new mystery and new dark suspense (horror). We specialize only in mystery, science fiction and horror."

**Services:** Buys, trades and sells used books. Carries 3 mystery magazines. 80% of books are old or rare. Conducts author book signings.

---

# Book'em Mysteries

**Address:** 1118 Mission St., Pasadena CA 91030, (818) 799-9600
**Owner/Contact person:** Barry Martin
**Established:** 1990
**Profile:** Contemporary mystery fiction and in-print vintage mysteries. Also, stock thrillers, true crime, horror gothic, juvenile and young adult mysteries, mystery writers reference books, how-to, audiotapes, mystery games and puzzles, and mystery/horror/true crime anthologies.
**Services:** Carries 3 mystery magazines. Conducts author book signings and readings.

---

# Fantasy Etc.

**Address:** 808 Larkin, San Francisco CA 94109, (415) 441-7617
**Owner/Contact person:** Charlie Cockery
**Established:** 1976
**Profile:** "Fantasy Etc. defies physics. There is no way a space so small can hold either so many books or so many titles. Our focus is both fantastic literature (including SF, fantasy, old Gothic, weird, horror and supernatural) and mystery literature (including hardboiled, British, spy, thriller) and adventure."
**Services:** Buys, trades and sells used books. Small

selection of books are old or rare. Conducts author
book signings.

## Gallery Bookshop
**Address:** P.O. Box 270, 319 Kasten St., Mendocino
CA 95460, (707) 937-2665
**Contact person:** Tony Miksak, Owner; Linda Pack,
Manager
**Profile:** "We have an astonishingly deep and large selection of mysteries, thrillers, true crime, books on
tape, and solve-it-yourself's arranged in a nook between a cozy fireplace and a creaky, wooden-bolted
door. Our black cat frequently sleeps on the bench
there."

"We are a small, intensely stocked general trade
bookstore, known throughout the northern coast of
California for the quality and breadth of our stock."
**Services:** Sells self-published books. Conducts author
book signings.

## Green Door Mystery Bookstore
**Address:** 31781 Camino Capistrano, San Juan Capis-
trano CA 92675, (714) 248-8404
**Owner/Contact person:** Richard Hart
**Established:** 1990
**Profile:** "We make mysteries fun."
**Services:** Buys and sells used books; sells memora-
bilia. Catalog available—write or call to request. Con-
ducts author book signings and readings.

## Grounds for Murder, A Mystery Book Store
**Address:** 3287 Adams Ave., San Diego CA 92116,
(619) 284-4436
**Owner/Contact person:** Phyllis Brown
**Established:** 1981

**Profile:** "Ours is one of the largest mystery book stores (3,000 square feet), and we have more backlist titles than any other mystery book store I know of. We carry all subgenres of mystery. Our clientele largely favors the gentler, funny mysteries and those by and about women, so we are careful to carry all of those. We also try to carry most of the private eye novels."

**Services:** Buys, trades and sells used books. Carries 6 mystery magazines. 5 to 10% of books are old or rare. Sells memorabilia; newsletter lists and reviews new and coming books. $8.50 for subscription to newsletter; $10 for first-class mailing of it. Conducts author book signings and readings.

## Mitchell Books

**Address:** 1395 E. Washington Blvd., Pasadena CA 91104, (818) 798-4438

**Owner/Contact person:** John Mitchell

**Established:** 1980

**Profile:** "We have a stock of 40,000 to 50,000 hardbacks and 1,000 to 2,000 paperbacks. We carry first editions as well as readers' copies. We reply to want lists internationally."

**Services:** Buys and sells used books. Carries 3 mystery magazines. 100% of books are old or rare. Sells memorabilia.

## *Mysteries by Mail

**Address:** Box 679, Boonville CA 95415-0679, (800) 722-0726

**Owner/Contact person:** Lucinda May and Tom Segar

**Established:** 1989

**Profile:** "We publish a quarterly catalog of in-print mysteries (also classic videos and some audios, a few games). Each catalog has about 700 titles."

**Services:** Catalog available. "We are a mail-order company—write or phone or fax." Sells some self-published books. Carries some autographed bookplates for specific titles.

---

## Mysterious Book Shop West Inc.
**Address:** 8763 Beverly Blvd., Los Angeles CA 90048, (310) 659-2959 or (800) 821-9017
**Owner/Contact person:** Sheldon McArthur or Jeffory Hart
**Established:** 1983
**Profile:** Weekly author signings, monthly author readings (in collaboration with the Sweet Art Cafe). "Large autographed book section, large rare and out-of-print section, and largest Sherlock Holmes and Sherlockian/Doyle section on the West Coast." Complete in-print stock of mysteries, crime, detective fiction. Some horror and dark fantasy.
**Services:** Buys and sells used books. Carries 10 mystery magazines. 33% of books are old or rare. Sells memorabilia: T-shirts, mugs, tote bags, etc. Catalog available—write or call to request. Conducts author book signings and readings.

---

## The Mystery Annex
**Address:** 1407 Ocean Front Walk, Venice CA 90291, (310) 399-2360
**Owner/Contact person:** Terry L. Baker
**Established:** 1987
**Profile:** Mystery and vampire literature.
**Services:** Carries 3 mystery magazines. Conducts author book signings and readings.

## Richard Kyle, Books

**Address:** 242 E. 3rd St., Long Beach CA 90802, (310) 432-1192
**Owner/Contact person:** Richard Kyle
**Established:** 1972
**Profile:** "We publish *Argosy Magazine,* which has featured many mystery stories, including *A Study in Fear,* Ellery Queen's Sherlock Holmes novel (with a classic steranko cover painting of Holmes), Jack Boyle's "Boston Blackie's Mary" and others. We are an in-print book store, specializing in science fiction, comics and mysteries. Our small mystery section will be substantially enlarged in 1993."
**Services:** Carries 6 mystery magazines. Sells limited amounts of memorabilia and self-published books. Conducts author book signings.

## The San Francisco Mystery Bookstore

**Address:** 746 Diamond St., San Francisco CA 94114
**Owner/Contact person:** Bruce Taylor
**Established:** 1975
**Services:** Buys, trades and sells used books. Carries 5 mystery magazines. 50% of books are old or rare. Conducts author book signings.

## Sherlock's Home

**Address:** 5624 E. 2nd St., Long Beach CA 90803, (213) 433-6071
**Owner/Contact person:** Elizabeth Caswell
**Profile:** Store fashioned in a Victorian parlor. Sherlock Holmes mail order catalog. "Wonderful readings/signings." Signed editions. Will ship any title.

Services: Buys, trades and sells used books. Carries 2 mystery magazines. 10% of books are old or rare. Sells memorabilia. Catalog available — SASE. Sells self-published books. Conducts author book signings and readings.

# The Silver Door
Address: P.O. Box 3208, Redondo Beach CA 90277, (310) 379-6025
Owner/Contact person: Karen LaPorte
Established: 1977
Profile: "Over 12,000 hardcover and paperback books. Free search service without obligation or fee. We carry only mystery and detective fiction and related items. The public is always welcome by appointment only."
Services: Buys and sells used books. 90% of books are old or rare. Catalog available — write or call to request.

# Vagabond Books
Address: 2076 Westwood Blvd., Los Angeles CA 90025, (310) 475-2700
Established: 1977
Profile: Bookstore also operates a press: Blood & Guts Press. Specializes in first editions.
Services: Buys, trades and sells used books. 50% of books are old or rare. Sells graphic novels. Catalog available — write to request. Conducts author book signings and readings.

## Colorado

# Book Sleuth
Address: 2513 W. Colorado, Colorado Springs CO 80904, (719) 632-2727
Owner/Contact person: Mrs. Helen C. Randal
Established: 1984

**Profile:** Publishes a newsletter. Carries mystery books, games, puzzles and tapes.
**Services:** Trades books; sells used books. Carries some Sherlock Holmes memorabilia. Conducts author book signings.

## Murder by the Book

**Address:** 1574 S. Pearl St., Denver CO 80210, (303) 871-9401
**Owner/Contact person:** Shirley Beaird
**Profile:** Mail and/or phone orders accepted.
**Services:** Buys and sells used books. Carries 3 mystery magazines. 30% of books are old or rare. Sells memorabilia. Conducts author book signings.

## The Rue Morgue

**Address:** 946 Pearl St., Boulder CO 80302, (303) 443-8346 or (800) 356-5586 (orders)
**Owner/Contact person:** Tom or Enid Schantz
**Established:** 1970
**Profile:** "We have a very large mail-order business in both new and used books and are the oldest mystery bookstore in business today. Our newsletter, *The Purloined Letter*, reviews most new mysteries. We also sell books at most major mystery conventions. We carry a large stock of signed books."
**Services:** Buys (hardcover), sells and trades books. Carries 3 mystery magazines. Over 33% of books are old or rare. Sells memorabilia; T-shirts, bookbags, and mugs. Catalog of used and rare books available; monthly newsletter lists new arrivals. Introductory issues free. Conducts author book signings and readings. "In 1992 we had over 50 signings. We can seat 50 + people."

## Connecticut

# Dunn & Powell Books

**Address:** P.O. Box 2544, Baldwin Ave., Meriden CT
06450, (203) 235-0480
**Owner/Contact person:** William Dunn
**Profile:** Store's focus is used and collectible mysteries.
"15,000 titles in stock. We catalog 9,000 books per
year."
**Services:** Buys, trades and sells used books. 90% of
books are rare or old. Sells memorabilia. Catalog available — write or call to request.

## Florida

# Snoop Sisters Mystery Bookshoppe and Boutique

**Address:** 566 N. Indian Rocks Rd., Belleair Bluffs FL
34640, (813) 584-4370
**Owner/Contact person:** Susan Rose
**Established:** 1991
**Profile:** "We are located in an 'alley' of antique shops.
Our shop is furnished with antiques and collectibles
that are for sale. The focus is mystery fiction, specialized orders, personalized service and search service.
We have 2 mystery book clubs and will be teaching a
course in detective fiction this fall."
**Services:** Buys only rare or out-of-print books. 15%
of books are old or rare. Sells memorabilia. Conducts
author book signings and readings.

## Georgia

# The Science Fiction and Mystery Bookshop, Ltd.

**Address:** 752½ N. Highland Ave. NE, Atlanta GA
30306, (404) 875-7326
**Owner/Contact person:** Mark Stevens
**Established:** 1983
**Profile:** Open 7 days a week. New, in-print science

fiction, mystery, true crime thrillers, horror and associated reference.

**Services:** Sells graphic novels. Conducts author book signings.

## Illinois

---

# Women & Children First
**Address:** 5233 N. Clark St.
Chicago IL 60640, (312) 769-9209
**Owner/Contact person:** Linda Bubon
**Established:** 1979
**Profile:** Feminist literature. "Sara Paretsky is a frequent visitor to our store and had her first reading here. You can find women's mysteries here that you might not find elsewhere."
**Services:** Sells self-published books. Conducts author book signings and readings.

## Indiana

---

# The Corner Shop
**Address:** 116 East Water, Portland IN 47371, (219) 726-4090
**Owner/Contact person:** Miss E.M. Cheeseman
**Profile:** Special orders and shipping, search service. Catalog is being reformatted and system changed — date for availability not set at this time. Store's focus is, "mystery and adventure books. Books priced for readers though I carry some collectible volumes."
**Services:** Buys and sells used books. Carries some old issues of mystery magazines. 1% of books are old or rare. Sells very little memorabilia; sells self-published books. Conducts author book signings, "about one a year."

## Murder and Mayhem
**Address:** 6412 Carrollton Ave., Indianapolis IN 46220, (317) 254-8273
**Owner/Contact person:** Jane Ellen Syrk
**Established:** 1991
**Profile:** Mystery, suspense, horror, also children's mysteries and horror.
**Services:** Buys and sells used books. Carries 9 mystery magazines. 5% of books are old or rare. Sells memorabilia; considers self-published books. Conducts author book signings and readings.

### Kansas

## The Raven Bookstore
**Address:** 8 E. 7th St., Lawrence KS 66044, (913) 749-3300
**Owner/Contact person:** Pat Kehde and Mary Lou Wright
**Established:** 1987
**Profile:** Occasional mystery participation events including monthly book discussions. Mysteries, good fiction and regional and travel books.
**Services:** Buys and sells used books. 10% of books are old or rare. Sells memorabilia, sells graphic novels. Newsletter available — $5. Conducts author book signings and readings.

### Maine

## Dunn & Powell Books
**Address:** The Hideaway, Bar Harbor ME 04609, (207) 288-4665
**Owner/Contact person:** Steve Powell
**Established:** 1991
**Profile:** Store's focus is used and collectible mysteries. "15,000 titles in stock. We catalog 9,000 books per year."

**Services:** Buys, trades and sells used books. 90% of books are old or rare. Sells memorabilia. Catalog available — write or call to request.

## Maryland

# Mystery Bookshop Bethesda
# Home of Masterpiece Murder and Collectible Crime

**Address:** 7700 Georgetown Rd., Bethesda MD 20814, (301) 657-2665 or (800) 572-8533

**Owner/Contact person:** Jean and Ron McMillen

**Established:** 1989

**Profile:** "We are the complete mystery bookstore with 18,000 titles, the largest selection in our area. We will special order any title, but we work hard to have every mystery title in stock. We ship worldwide, provide free gift wrap, sell tickets to mystery events, publish a newsletter and provide the best service this side of heaven. We sponsor the Chesapeake-Potomac chapter of Mystery Readers International. We sell hard- and soft-boiled, British, suspense, spy fiction and reference, but we specialize in malice domestic, which is the modernization and Americanization of the classic English mystery."

**Services:** Buys, trades and sells used books. Carries 7 mystery magazines. 10% of books are old or rare. Sells memorabilia. Catalog available — write or call to request. Conducts author book signings and readings.

## Massachusetts

# Kate's Mystery Books

**Address:** 2211 Massachusetts Ave., Cambridge MA 02140, (617) 491-2660

**Owner/Contact person:** Kate Mattes

**Established:** 1983

**Services:** Buys, trades and sells used books. Carries 6 mystery magazines. 40% of books are old or rare. Sells memorabilia and games. Bimonthly newsletter available for $6/year subscription or, from the store, for $1 per issue. Newsletters by subscription (mailed newsletters) contain a $1 coupon that may be redeemed with the purchase of a book. Sells a few self-published books. Conducts author book signings and readings.

**Profile:** "The store is very cozy and has easy chairs. It's located in the first floor of a Victorian house. I have an extensive black cat collection. I have a Christmas tree decorated entirely with skeletons and black cats. And the front yard has a beautiful garden. I have special sections on New England, strong women, gay and lesbian, British and malice domestic."

## Spenser's Mystery Bookshop

**Address:** 314 Newbury St., Boston MA 02115, (617) 262-0880
**Owner/Contact person:** Andrew Thurnauer
**Established:** 1983
**Profile:** "A large stock of vintage paperbacks from the 1940s and 1950s.

Low prices — new hardcovers are discounted; thousands of used paperbacks at half price or less. Used hardcovers (including first editions) priced modestly."
**Services:** Buys, trades and sells used books. Carries 6 mystery magazines. 50% of books are old or rare. Occasionally conducts author book signings.

### Michigan

## Deadly Passions Bookshop

**Address:** 157 S. Kalamazoo Mall, Kalamazoo MI 49007, (616) 383-4402
**Owner/Contact person:** Jim Huang and Jennie Jacobson
**Established:** 1992
**Profile:** "We have a frequent buyers club offering discounts." Store's focus is mystery, romance and science

fiction only. Large, well-organized section of used books, in addition to comprehensive stock of new books.

**Services:** Buys, trades and sells used books. Carries 3 mystery magazines. 20% of books are old or rare. Newsletter available. Will consider self-published books. Conducts author book signings and readings.

## Else Fine Books

**Address:** P.O. Box 43, Dearborn MI 48121, (313) 834-3255

**Owner/Contact person:** Louise Oberschmidt and Allen M. Hemlock

**Profile:** "By appointment only. Friendly, efficient service." Store's focus is fine first editions: modern literature, mystery/detective/thriller, science fiction, fantasy, horror.

**Services:** Buys and sells first-edition used books. 100% of books are old or rare. Catalog available; call or write.

### Minnesota

## Green Lion Books

**Address:** Suite 409, 2402 University Ave. W., St. Paul MN 55114, (612) 644-9070

**Owner/Contact person:** Mark D. Goodman

**Established:** 1977

**Profile:** Accepts Visa/MasterCard; foreign orders, want lists and searches performed at no charge. "Focus is hard-boiled crime fiction, mystery/crime and some true crime. Also other genre fiction: SF, horror, Western, literature. Specializes in TV and movie tie-ins/editions and vintage paperbacks."

**Services:** Buys, trades and sells used books. Carries most older digest magazines—some pulps also. 90-95% of books are old or rare.

# Once Upon a Crime

**Address:** 604 W. 26th St., Minneapolis MN 55405, (612) 870-3785
**Owner/Contact person:** Steven Stilwell
**Established:** 1987
**Profile:** Quarterly newsletter, used and rare catalog, and a wide stock of mystery reference books. A reading club meets in the store.
**Services:** Buys and sells used books. Carries 4 mystery magazines. 10% of books are old or rare. Sells memorabilia. Catalog available — write or call to request. Conducts author book signings and readings.

# Uncle Edgar's Mystery Bookstore

**Address:** 2864 Chicago Ave. S., Minneapolis MN 55407, (612) 824-9984
**Owner/Contact person:** Don Blyly
**Established:** 1980
**Profile:** "We share a building with Uncle Hugo's Science Fiction Bookstore — the newsletter is for both stores." Store's focus is mystery books.
**Services:** Buys, trades and sells used books. Carries 4 mystery magazines. 50% of books are old or rare. Catalog available by mail. Sells self-published books. Conducts author book signings.

## Missouri

# Big Sleep Books

**Address:** 239 N. Euclid, St. Louis MO 63108, (314) 361-6100
**Owner/Contact person:** Chris King, Helen Simpson
**Established:** 1988
**Profile:** Mystery, espionage, detection, true crime, suspense and thriller fiction.
**Services:** Trades books; sells used books. Conducts author book signings.

**New Hampshire**

# Mystery Lovers Ink
**Address:** 8 Stiles Rd., Salem NH 03079
**Owner/Contact person:** Joanne L. Romano
**Established:** 1986
**Services:** Carries 4 mystery magazines. Sells self-published books. Catalog available — write or call to request. Conducts author book signings (on occasion).

**New Mexico**

# Murder Unlimited — A Mystery Store
**Address:** 2510 San Mateo Pl. NE, Albuquerque NM 87110, (505) 884-5491
**Owner/Contact person:** Tasha Mackler
**Established:** 1977
**Profile:** Mystery book and audiotape lending library. Supports New Mexican authors and mysteries set in New Mexico. "I have a bimonthly newsletter featuring forthcoming books for customers who purchase books from me on a regular basis."
**Services:** Trades and sells used books. Carries several mystery magazines. 25% of books are old or rare. Conducts author book signings and readings.

**New York**

# Bengta Woo Books
**Address:** One Sorgi Ct., Plainview NY 11803-1822, (516) 692-4426
**Profile:** "I see clients by appointment, conduct searches and accept want lists. I specialize in mystery and detective fiction, romance and some science fiction/fantasy."
**Services:** Buys, trades and sells used books. 100% of books are old or rare.

## Foul Play: Books of Mystery and Suspense
**Address:** 1465 2nd Ave., New York NY 10021, (212) 517-3222
**Owner/Contact person:** Bonnie Claeson

## Foul Play: Books of Mystery and Suspense
**Address:** 13 8th Ave., New York NY 10014, (212) 675-5115
**Contact person:** John Douglas
**Established:** 1986
**Profile:** Stores' focus is mystery.
**Services:** Buys used books, softcover mostly; sells used books. 5% of books are old or rare. Conducts author book signings.

## Haven't Got a Clue
**Address:** 1823 Western Ave., Albany NY 12203, (518) 464-1135
**Owner/Contact person:** Betsy Blaustein
**Established:** 1989
**Services:** Buys, trades and sells used books.

## Mysterious Bookshop
**Address:** 129 W. 56th St., New York NY 10019, (212) 765-0900 or (800) 352-2840
**Owner/Contact person:** Otto Penzler
**Established:** 1979
**Profile:** "We have a strong reference section (genre info, author bios and how to write) and a Sherlock Holmes section. Autographed books are a specialty." Store's focus is mystery fiction.
**Services:** Buys and sells used books. Carries mystery magazines. 50% of books are old or rare. Sells memora-

bilia. Catalog available—call or write to request. Conducts author book signings.

## *Interview*

Otto Penzler, Owner
Mysterious Bookshop

Otto Penzler opened the Mysterious Bookshop in New York City fourteen years ago. The best thing about owning a mystery book store, according to Penzler, is "dealing with customers, building collections and introducing favorite authors to new readers."

Penzler is a mystery enthusiast who started reading Sherlock Holmes novels at the age of ten. His favorite deceased authors are Arthur Conan Doyle, Wilkie Collins, E.W. Hornung and Raymond Chandler; among active writers he likes Ross Thomas, James Crumley and Ruth Rendell.

The Mysterious Bookshop "carries every new book and most everything in print. We try to find what others are looking for. We carry a lot and search for the rest. We can answer most reasonable questions—and a lot of unreasonable ones."

The store hosts readings and signings by many authors every year. Among those who have visited, Penzler remembers Eric Ambler as "the most distinguished author I've met." Stephen King, Robert Parker and Dick Francis drew crowds that lined up outside of the store.

Penzler started the Mysterious Press (see interview with Sara Ann Freed, page 145) eighteen years ago, with The Adventures of Sherlock Holmes the first book published. "The Mysterious Press is a house devoted to the publication of mystery, crime, suspense and espionage fiction of the highest quality—both in terms of literary content and production values." He sold the press to Time-Warner three years ago. His new company, Otto Penzler Books, was launched in February 1993, concentrating primarily on mysteries, crime and suspense novels. Each month, the press publishes two hardcover originals, one trade paperback, one Armchair Detective Library edition and one facsimile of a rare first edition collectible volume (see listing page 144).

As for trends developing in the mystery field, Penzler expects to see more books from non-English speaking countries and more with environmental themes. To new mystery writers

*hoping to break in, he advises, "Write brilliantly but keep your day job. Also, work harder on pure, old-fashioned plotting than you think you have to."*
— Donna Collingwood

## Oceanside Books, Inc., dba The Mystery Bookstore of L.I.

**Address:** 173a Woodfield Rd., W. Hempstead NY 11552, (516) 565-4710
**Owner/Contact person:** Adrienne Williams, President
**Established:** 1973
**Profile:** "Our catalogs are informative. Deal only in quality — do not overstate condition of books or dust jackets. We specialize in the vintage. Build customer collections and maintain search service only in mystery genre."
**Services:** Buys and sells used books. Carries 2 mystery magazines. 95% of books are old or rare. Sells memorabilia (Sherlockiana). Catalog available — $2. Conducts author book signings and readings.

## Saratoga Science Fiction & Mystery Bookshop

**Address:** 454 Broadway, Saratoga Springs NY 12866, (518) 583-3743
**Owner/Contact person:** Karl Olsen
**Established:** 1989
**Profile:** Over 20,000 paperbacks. Focus is science fiction and mystery.
**Services:** Buys, trades and sells used books. Carries 4 mystery magazines. 5% of books are old or rare. Catalog available. Conducts author book signings.

## North Carolina

# Murder for Fun Books

**Address:** 2006 Fairview Rd., Raleigh NC 27608, (919) 755-0013
**Owner/Contact person:** Pat O'Keefe
**Established:** 1990
**Profile:** Offers a country-wide search service for out-of-print titles. "We carry mysteries from many small presses not available elsewhere." Store's focus is mystery and detective fiction only.
**Services:** Buys, trades and sells used books. Carries 2 mystery magazines. 50% of books are old or rare. Occasionally sells memorabilia. Catalog available soon. Sells self-published books. Conducts author book signings.

## Ohio

# Fickes Crime Fiction

**Address:** 1471 Burkhardt Ave., Akron OH 44301, (216) 773-4223
**Owner/Contact person:** Patricia A. Fickes
**Established:** 1983
**Profile:** "Recycled hardbound mystery, adventure, suspense fiction running the gamut from uncommon to current, classic to new. Closed shop—open by appointment only. Free catalogs. Want cards for specific titles welcomed."
**Services:** Buys and sells used books. 90% of books are old or rare. Catalog available—write or call to request.

# *Grave Matters—Mysteries by Mail

**Address:** P.O. Box 32192, Cincinnati OH 45232, (513) 242-7527 (phone or fax)
**Owner/Contact person:** Alice Ann Carpenter and John Leininger

**Established:** 1986

**Profile:** "We have a nice selection of Sherlockiana. We can generate an in-stock list of everything we have by a given author that is not included in our current catalog. Our main focus is good, used mystery fiction. We also carry new books and first editions of older books. We publish a monthly catalog and do antiquarian book fairs in the Midwest."

**Services:** Buys and sells used books. Carries 1,400 used mystery magazines. 50% or more of books are old or rare. Sells memorabilia, particularly Sherlockiana; Catalog available — write to request.

# Mysteries From the Yard

**Address:** 253B Xenia Ave., Yellow Springs OH 45387, (513) 767-2111

**Owner/Contact person:** Mary Frost-Pierson

**Established:** 1979

**Profile:** "Recently expanded to four rooms, including a book room for children, this is the Midwest's first full-service mystery bookshop. Hosts an annual A.C. Doyle/Sherlock Holmes symposium now in its twelfth year."

**Services:** Buys, trades and sells used books. 25% of books are old or rare. Sells memorabilia. Catalog available "intermittently" — write to request. Conducts author book signings and readings.

## Oregon

# Escape Books

**Address:** 488 Willamette, Eugene OR 97401, (503) 484-9500

**Owner/Contact person:** Bill Trojan

**Established:** 1984

**Profile:** "Located in a historic old building that used to be an old hotel." Have both mystery and science fiction, fantasy, horror, with a special focus on P.I. novels.

**Services:** Buys, trades and sells used books. Carries 7 mystery magazines. Small selection of books are old or rare. Sells memorabilia. Catalog available — call to obtain. Conducts author book signings.

## Murder by the Book

**Address:** 3210 S.E. Hawthorne Blvd., Portland OR 97214, (503) 232-9995

## Murder by the Book

**Address:** 7828 S.W. Capitol Highway, Portland OR 97219, (503) 293-6507

**Owner/Contact person:** Carolyn Lane or Jill Hinckley

**Established:** 1983

**Profile:** "More or less monthly newsletter *Murder by the Bye* $1/year subscription. Murder by-line (weekly telephone survey of new releases), reading and discussion conference — usually annually, search service, mail order, gift certificates, bonus purchase plan (murder by the dozen) and hardcover rentals. Focus is mysteries, thrillers, spy fiction."

**Services:** Buys, trades and sells used books. Carries 3 mystery magazines. 65% of books are old or rare. Sells memorabilia. Catalog available — write or call to request. Sells self-published books. Conducts author book signings and readings.

## Wrigley-Cross Books

**Address:** 8001A S.E. Powell, Portland OR 97206, (503) 775-4943

**Owner/Contact person:** Debbie Cross and Paul M. Wrigley

Established: 1990
Profile: "Large selection of small press and British imports (many signed) in our area of specialization: mystery, science fiction and fantasy, horror."
Services: Buys, trades and sells used books. 90% of books are old or rare. Catalog available — write or call to request. Conducts author book signings and readings.

### Pennsylvania

# Whodunit?
Address: 1931 Chestnut St., Philadelphia PA 19103, (215) 567-1478
Owner/Contact person: Art Bourgeau
Established: 1977
Services: Buys, trades and sells used books. 90% of books are old or rare.

### Rhode Island

# Murder by the Book
Address: 1281 N. Main St., Providence RI 02904, (401) 331-9140
Owner/Contact person: Kevin Barbero
Established: 1978
Services: Buys, trades and sells used books. Carries 8-9 mystery magazines, both current and back issues. 80% of books are old or rare. Catalog available — write to request. Conducts author book signings.
Profile: "We share space with a science fiction store called Other Worlds that does the same thing."

### Texas

# Limestone Hills Books
Address: P.O. Box 1125 Paloxy River Estates, Glen Rose TX 76043, (817) 897-4991
Owner/Contact person: Aubyn Kendall
Established: 1975

**Profile:** English and American literature, mystery and detective fiction, P.G. Wodehouse, first editions.
**Services:** Buys and sells used books. 75% of books are old or rare. Catalog available upon request.

---

# Mordida Books
**Address:** P.O. Box 79322, Houston TX 77279, (713) 467-4280
**Owner/Contact person:** Richard D. Wilson
**Established:** 1987
**Profile:** First editions of mystery and detective fiction.
**Services:** Buys, trades and sells used books. 100% of books are old or rare. Rarely sells memorabilia. Catalog available — write to request.

---

# Murder by the Book
**Address:** 2342 Bissonnet, Houston TX 77005, (713) 524-8597
**Owner/Contact person:** Martha Farrington
**Established:** 1980
**Profile:** Mysteries, crime fiction, espionage and true crime books.
**Services:** Buys and sells used books. 20% of books are old or rare. Sells memorabilia. Catalog available — write to request. Conducts author book signings and readings.

---

# Mysteries and More
**Address:** 11139 N. IH35 #176, Austin TX 78753-3242, (512) 837-6768
**Owner/Contact person:** Elmer or Jan Grape
**Profile:** "Semi-private browsing areas with chairs and excellent lighting."
**Services:** Buys, trades and sells used books. Carries

2 mystery magazines. 20% of books are old or rare. Catalog available — write to request. Conducts author book signings.

## Virginia

# Magna Mysteries
**Address:** P.O. Box 5732, Virginia Beach VA 23455, (804) 464-5861
**Owner/Contact person:** Gordon A. Magnuson
**Established:** 1987
**Profile:** "I sell by mail order only."
**Services:** Buys and sells used books. 100% of books are old or rare. Catalog available — write to request.

# *TLC Books
**Address:** 9 North College Ave., Salem VA 24153, (703) 389-3555
**Owner/Contact person:** Thomas L. Coffman
**Established:** 1990
**Profile:** "I do not have an open shop for mysteries now (though perhaps in time). Sell only by mail and telephone through catalogs and response to customers' requests. I also respond to customers' want lists for used, rare and out-of-print mysteries, as well as issuing catalog offerings. I specialize somewhat in author's first mystery books."
**Services:** Buys and sells used books. Approximately 90% of stock is old or rare. Catalog available, write or phone, no charge.

## Washington

# Becks Bookstore
**Address:** 1301 5th Ave., Seattle WA 98101, (206) 624-1328
**Owner/Contact person:** Maureen P. Bekemeyer
**Established:** 1979

**Profile:** "We are a general bookstore selling new books. We have an excellent paperback mystery section."

**Services:** Carries 1 mystery magazine. Occasionally sells self-published books. Conducts author book signings.

## Elliott Bay Book Co.

**Address:** 101 S. Main St., Seattle WA 98115, (206) 624-6600

Toll free from Washington and Alaska: (800) 962-5311

**Established:** 1973

**Profile:** "We accept special orders, carry a strong backlist, and have a large mystery section."

**Services:** Carries 3 mystery magazines. Sells self-published books. Conducts author book signings and readings.

### Wisconsin

## Booked for Murder, Ltd.

**Address:** 2701 University Ave., Madison WI 53705, (608) 238-2701

**Owner/Contact person:** Mary Helen Becker

**Established:** 1988

**Profile:** The best in mystery past and present and outstanding customer service. Store's focus is mystery, suspense, espionage and medieval period items. "We write our own book reviews (in newsletter) announce author visits, list new titles." Specializes in mystery-related book baskets; can be made to order for customers, or choose theme basket in stock.

**Services:** Carries 12 mystery magazines. 5% of books are old or rare. Sells memorabilia; sells graphic novels. Newsletter available on request. Conducts author book signings and readings.

## Canada

## Almark & Co. — Booksellers
**Address:** P.O. Box 7, Thornhill, Ontario L3T 3N1 Canada, (416) 764-BOOK
**Owner/Contact person:** Al Navis
**Established:** 1974
**Profile:** "We have a mail/phone order service. We're a 'by appointment only' store of almost 6,500 square feet and more than 30,000 titles. We specialize in modern first-edition fiction: literature and general fiction; crime, mystery and detective fiction, science fiction/fantasy; dark fantasy/horror; historical and military fiction; Kennedy assassinations; true crime; espionage; Churchilliana; and U.S. Civil War history."
**Services:** Buys, trades and sells used books. 90-95% of books are old or rare. Catalog available by request. Conducts author book signings.

## Ann's Books and Mostly Mysteries
**Address:** 225 Carlton St., Toronto, Ontario M5A 2L2 Canada, (416) 962-7947
**Owner/Contact person:** David Srene-Melvin
**Profile:** By appointment only. Canadian military history and Canadian crime fiction *only*.
**Services:** Buys and sells used books. 100% of books are old or rare. Catalog available occasionally; request. Sells self-published books.

## Comic World
**Address:** 374 Donald St., Winnipeg, Manitoba R3B 2J2 Canada, (204) 943-1968
**Owner/Contact person:** Doug Sulipa
**Profile:** Buy, sell and trade.
**Services:** Trades books; sells used books. Carries

many mystery magazines. 35% of books are old or rare; sells memorabilia; sells self-published books.

## *Michel Lanteigne — Bookseller

**Address:** 5468 St. Urbain #4, Montreal, Quebec H2T 2X1 Canada, (514) 273-4963
**Owner/Contact person:** Michel Lanteigne
**Established:** 1979
**Profile:** Bimonthly vintage paperback (1939-1968) auction catalog fully illustrated with photocopies of covers. Out-of-print/collectible first editions. "Mail order only — no open shop as such at this time. A mystery bookstore might be in the works for a future date."
**Services:** Buys, trades and sells used books. Over 95% old and collectible editions. Sells memorabilia, including Sherlockiana. Write to request the catalog.

## Prime Crime Books

**Address:** 891 Bank St., Ottawa Ontario K1S 3W4 Canada, (613) 238-2583
**Owner/Contact person:** James Reicker
**Profile:** Detective and mystery fiction.
**Services:** Buys, trades and sells used books. 5% of books are old or rare. Conducts author book signings and readings.

## Sleuth of Baker Street

**Address:** 1595 Bayview Ave., Toronto, Ontario M4G 3B5 Canada, (416) 483-3111
**Owner/Contact person:** J.D. Singh
**Established:** 1979
**Profile:** Knowledgeable staff and owners, search service offered and mail order. "Best selection of crime/

detective fiction in North America. Or so our customers tell us."

**Services:** Buys and sells used books. 25% of books are old or rare. Catalog available — write to request. Conducts author book signings and readings.

### Australia

# Abbey's Bookshop

**Address:** 131 York St., Sydney NSW 2000 Australia, (02) 264-3111, Fax: (02) 264-8993
**Owner/Contact person:** Peter Milne
**Established:** 1968
**Profile:** "In addition to over 6,000 titles carried in crime fiction and nonfiction, we also have extensive sections on philosophy, history, classics, literature, music, science, writing and publishing. We have a separate shop devoted to science fiction and fantasy: Galaxy Bookshop, 222 Clarence St., Sydney."
**Services:** Carries new mystery titles only. Carries a number of mystery magazines. Catalog available, plus monthly *Crime Chronicle* newsletter free on application. Conducts author book signings and readings.

### United Kingdom

# A1 Crime Fiction

**Address:** Westridge House, 3 Horsecastles Lane, Sherborne, Dorset DT9 6DW England, (093) 581-4989
**Owner/Contact person:** D.C. Ireland
**Established:** 1966
**Profile:** Lists issued every three weeks. 25,000 books in stock. "Open every day of the year, but telephone call advised in case I'm book buying." Store's focus is entirely crime, detective and spy fiction.
**Services:** Buys, trades and sells used books. 95% of books are old or rare. Catalog available; apply to above address.

# Ergo Books

**Address:** 46 Lisburne Rd., London NW3 2NR England, (071) 482-4431 Fax: (071) 485-2510
**Owner/Contact person:** Elliott Greenfield
**Established:** 1976
**Services:** Buys, trades and sells used books. 98% of books are old or rare. Many magazines available. Sells memorabilia—"ephemera (especially Sherlockiana) is big with us." Catalog available.
**Profile:** "I see people by appointment at any time. I've made appointments for 2 A.M.! Operate from home where 2 book rooms contain a great deal."

# Mainly Murder Bookstore

**Address:** 2a Paul St., Cork Ireland, (021) 272413
**Owner/Contact person:** Patricia Barry
**Profile:** "Only bookshop in Ireland specializing in crime and detection."
**Services:** Buys and sells used books. 10% of books are old or rare. Catalog available—write to request.

# Murder One

**Address:** 71-73 Charing Cross Rd., London WC2H 0AA England, (071) 734-3483
**Owner/Contact person:** M. Jakubowski
**Established:** 1988
**Profile:** "World's largest mystery bookshop. Also feature science fiction, fantasy and romance."
**Services:** Buys and sells used books. 10% of books are old or rare. Sells memorabilia. Catalog available upon request. Conducts author book signings.

The following bookstores were contacted, but didn't return our questionnaires. This could indicate there's a new location, so call before visiting at the addresses listed here.

# Bilipo, Bibliotheque des Litteratures Policieres
**Address:** 74/76 Rue Mouffetard, 75005 Paris France

# Clues Galore
**Address:** 36 Stonebridge, Clevedon, Avon BS21 England

# Post Mortem Books
**Address:** 58 Stanford Ave., Hassocks, Sussex BN6 England

# True Crime
**Address:** Geoffrey Cates Books, 1268 Cedar St., Oshawa L1J 3S2 Canada

## Awards Open to Mystery Writers

Contests and awards programs offer writers many opportunities. In addition to honors, recognition, publication or cash awards, they also give writers the opportunity to have their work judged on the basis of quality alone without some of the outside factors that sometimes influence publishing decisions. Often, award judges are a group of your writing peers or your readers.

Although mystery novels and short stories are eligible for a variety of general fiction awards, the following is a list of awards exclusively for mystery works. They include awards for novels and short stories, and they may go to either first-time or established authors. A few of these awards are intended specifically to recognize promising unpublished work.

Some magazines devoted to mystery sponsor awards for material published within their pages or to honor mysteries nominated by the magazine's readers. For these, check the magazines for announcements. For more awards open to fiction writers see *Novel and Short Story Writer's Market*, *Writer's Market* (both published by Writer's Digest Books) or *Grants and Awards Available to American Writers* (published by Pen American Center, 568 Broadway, New York NY 10012).

## Agatha Awards, sponsored by Malice Domestic

**Contact:** Malice Domestic, P.O. Box 701, Herndon VA 22070

**Profile:** Awards for Best Novel, Best First Novel and Best Short Story. Open to traditional mysteries published in year prior to award convention. Nominations are made by fans, voted on by members of the Malice Domestic Convention. Deadline is the December of the year prior to the convention. Awards presented at Malice Domestic Convention Banquet held annually in April. Award is an Agatha Teapot.

## Anthony Awards, sponsored by Bouchercon

**(address changes annually)**

**Profile:** Awards for Best Novel, Best First Novel, Best Paperback Original, Best Short Story and Best Critical Work; also movie and television presentations. Award selected by the membership of Bouchercon. Awards are presented at the Bouchercon Convention Banquet held annually in early October. Since location changes each year (convention has been held outside the United States), check mystery magazines or mystery organization newsletters for announcements. Award is either a plaque or sculpture.

## Best First Private Eye Novel, sponsored by St. Martin's Press, Macmillan — London, Private Eye Writers of America

**Contact:** St. Martin's Press, 175 5th Ave., New York NY 10010

**Profile:** Award for Best First Private Eye Novel. Open to unpublished private eye novels (authors may have been published in a different genre, but not in mystery). Deadline is August 31. Winner is announced at Bouchercon, held annually in early October. Award is publication, $10,000 plus standard royalties (all rights in hardcover go to St. Martin's in U.S. and Macmillan — London in U.K.).

## Crime Writers Association Awards

**Contact:** Crime Writers Association, P.O. Box 172, Tring, Herts HP23 5LP England

**Profile:** Awards include the Gold Dagger (Best Crime Novel published in year prior to the award); Silver Dagger (runner up to Gold Dagger); Gold Dagger for Nonfiction (Best Nonfiction Book); John Creasey Memorial Award (for an unpublished crime novel by an author who has never before published a full-length work of fiction); and the Last Laugh Award (for most amusing crime novel). Some categories open only to British authors; check first. Open to novels published in year prior to the award. Deadline is October 1. Also awards the Cartier Diamond Dagger Award (for an author who has made an outstanding contribution to the genre). Awards vary and may include jewelry, mementos (silver or gold-plated daggers) or checks. Write for additional details.

## Edgar Awards, sponsored by Mystery Writers of America

**Contact:** Mystery Writers of America, 17 E. 47th St., 6th Floor, New York NY 10017, (212) 888-8171

**Profile:** Awards for Best Mystery Novel, Best First Mystery Novel, Best Original Paperback, Best Fact Crime, Best Critical/Biographical, Best Short Story, Best Juvenile, Best Episode in Television Series, Best Television Feature and Best Motion Picture. Also awards the Robert L. Fish Memorial Award for Best

First Mystery Short Story. Open to mysteries published in year prior to the award. Nominations are usually made by the publisher, but authors and agents may submit. Deadline is December 1. Nominations are announced in February and awards are given out at the MWA annual conference and awards banquet in April. Award is statuette of Edgar Allan Poe.

# Malice Domestic Contest, sponsored by St. Martin's Press, Inc., and Macmillan London

**Contact:** Thomas Dunne Books/St. Martin's Press, 175 5th Ave., New York NY 10010

**Profile:** Award for Best First Traditional Novel. Open to unpublished traditional mystery novels (authors may have been published in a different genre, but not in mystery). Deadline is November 1. Winner announced at the Malice Domestic Convention, held annually in April. Award is publication, $10,000 plus standard royalties (all rights in hardcover go to St. Martin's in U.S. and Macmillan London in U.K.).

# North American Hammett Prize

**Contact:** International Association of Crime Writers, JAF Box 1500, New York NY 10116

**Profile:** Award for Literary Excellence in Crime Writing. Work can be either fiction or nonfiction published in the year prior to the award. Books are nominated by members of the publishing committee and members of the reading committee. Deadline for nominations is December 1. Awards are presented during the Edgars Week ceremonies held annually in April (in New York City). Award is a trophy.

# Shamus Awards, sponsored by Private Eye Writers of America

**Contact:** Max Allan Collins, General Awards Chair, 301 Fairview Ave., Muscatine IA 52761

**Profile:** Awards for Best Private Eye Novel, Best Private Eye Paperback Original, Best First Private Eye Novel and Best Private Eye Short Story. Awards chair sends list of committee members with submission information to publishers and media outlets each year. For more information contact above or Jan Grape, 11804 Oak Trail, Austin TX 78753. Open to mysteries published in year prior to award. For novels or short stories featuring a private investigator, by definition: any investigator who is not employed by a unit of government or paid by a unit of government for investigative services. Nominations are made by publishers. Deadline is mid-February. Awards presented at Boucheron Convention, held in a different location each year. Check with organization or mystery publications for next date and location. Award is a plaque.

### Additional awards

The following are other awards given to mystery writers from organizations whose function includes, but is not limited to, recognition of mystery:

# Lambda Literary Awards, sponsored by Lambda Book Report

**Contact:** Lambda Literary Awards, 1625 Connecticut Ave., NW, Washington DC 20009-1013

**Profile:** Awards for Best Gay Mystery Novel and Best Lesbian Mystery Novel. Open to gay and lesbian mysteries published in year prior to award. Deadline is early February. Books are nominated by readers of Lambda Book Report. Winners are announced at a black-tie banquet and gala held the night before the American Booksellers Association Convention held annually on Memorial Day weekend. Award is a Plexiglas book with medallion.

## Rita Awards and Golden Heart Awards

**Contact:** Romance Writers of America, 13700 Veterans Memorial Dr., #315, Houston TX 77014

**Profile:** Awards for Best Romantic Suspense Novel in both the Rita and Golden Heart categories. Open only to members of RWA. Open to romance novels that have suspense elements. The Rita Award is open to novels published in the year prior to the award. The Golden Heart Award is open to unpublished novels. Deadline is in January. Nominated by members of RWA. Awards presented at annual convention; locations vary.

# *For Your Reference*

## The Bookshelf

**M**ystery *Writer's Marketplace and Sourcebook* surveyed some of the top mystery writers working today about the books and writers that launched and shaped their writing careers. Two questions were posed: "What writer, book or short story most influenced your interest in becoming a mystery or suspense writer? Why?" and "What writer, book or short story taught you the most about mystery-writing technique? What lesson did it teach you?"

Their answers vary as widely as the styles of the writers who responded, though there seems to be one clear "winner": Raymond Chandler is mentioned several times, and appropriately so, as he is one of the founders of the American-style mystery.

This list is hardly meant to be exhaustive. Dashiell Hammett, for instance, is not mentioned. *Dozens* of superb writers past and present are not mentioned. But we suspected you'd enjoy sitting down with a few of today's masters to share thoughts about their influences.

## Some Successful Mystery Writers Reveal the Books That Influenced Them Most
### Stephanie Kay Bendel

*Making Crime Pay* (Spectrum/Prentice Hall); *A Scream Away* (Playboy Press)

*The Writing That Got Me Started:* I read Mary Roberts Rinehart in my teens — I responded to the feeling that normal, average people (of course, they usually happened to be rich) could get involved in a mystery. I liked the idea that present crimes were often the consequences of past relationships, a theme Rinehart used frequently.

*The Writing That Taught Me About Writing:* I read every mystery Agatha Christie ever wrote. The thing that impressed me about her stories is that Dame Agatha could always find more than one way (and sometimes a half dozen ways) to interpret events, clues, relationships and information. Is it any wonder that she so successfully "bamboozled" her readers?

### Max Byrd

*Target of Opportunity* (Bantam)

*The Writing That Got Me Started:* I think Raymond Chandler was a significant American novelist. His style is lyrical, while his subject matter is fiercely realistic in its vision of American life, especially American capitalism.

*The Writing That Taught Me About Writing:* Two or three of Dick Francis's novels showed me the importance of placing conflict at every level of a story, from plot to dialogue. *Whip Hand* is an outstanding novel, for this.

### George Chesbro

*An Incident at Bloodtide* (Mysterious Press)

*The Writing That Got Me Started:* All of Ross Macdonald's work: I have awesome admiration for his use of language in telling a story—mysteries, in this case—that interested me. Suspecting that mysteries might be my forté, I set about trying to emulate him.

*The Writing That Taught Me About Writing:* All of Ross Macdonald's work: See above—Macdonald was a master of the rich metaphor and simile—and simplicity at the same time. Very elegant, understated and "cool"—leading to maximum impact on the printed page. Again, a style I tried (and still try) to emulate.

### Loren Estleman

*Whiskey River* (Bantam); *People Who Kill* (Mystery Scene Press)

*The Writing That Got Me Started:* I realize that Sax Rohmer's exotic *The Insidious Doctor Fu-Manchu* lies pretty far afield from the kind of mystery I write now, but it, and the other Oriental adventures that followed it from his pen, were so packed with danger, diabolical schemes and cerebral acrobatics they made all other forms of fiction seem like watery gruel by comparison. How many other books first published in 1913 are still in print?

*The Writing That Taught Me About Writing:* Raymond Chandler's

*The Little Sister* taught me that there was romance even in squalor, and that the detective story need not deal with geriatric women and poison-tipped darts to hold its audience; it could, in fact, step up into the realm of social commentary without ever losing sight of its reason for existing, the need to entertain.

## Sue Grafton

*"J" Is for Judgment* (Henry Holt)

*The Writing That Got Me Started:* My father, C.W. Grafton, was a municipal bond attorney in Louisville, Kentucky, where I was born and raised. He was also a writer and published three mysteries in the course of his career ... *The Rat Began to Gnaw the Rope, The Rope Began to Hang the Butcher* and *Beyond a Reasonable Doubt.* His first mystery novel, *The Rat Began to Gnaw the Rope,* won the Mary Roberts Rinehart Award in 1943. Because of him, I not only became a writer, but I developed a real passion for the mystery genre.

*The Writing That Taught Me About Writing:* As for books on writing, I have several that I recommend. Three are by Lawrence Block: *Writing the Novel: From Plot to Print* and *Spider, Spin Me a Web* (Writer's Digest Books), and *Telling Lies for Fun and Profit* (Priam). I'm also impressed with the *The Mystery Writers Handbook* (Writer's Digest Books, currently out of print), *Writing Suspense and Mystery Fiction* (The Writer, Inc.) and Patricia Highsmith's *Plotting and Writing Suspense Fiction* (The Writer, Inc.). In 1992, I was asked to edit *Writing Mysteries* (Writer's Digest Books), a new anthology of essays on crime writing by some of the finest mystery writers working in the field today. The chapters are arranged so that the novice mystery writer can "walk through" the process of writing a mystery novel, from that first spark of an idea, to research, character development, plotting, outlining and story execution, culminating in suggestions for marketing once the book is completed. In my continuing self-education, I read other mystery writers first for pleasure and then, when a book impresses me, I read it again so that I can analyze how various effects have been achieved. I find that almost any how-to will yield up a nugget of information or inspiration, which is why I have such a selection on my shelves. When I'm stuck, I just go back to the experts and listen to their advice all over again.

## Tony Hillerman

*Talking God* (HarperCollins); *A Thief of Time* (HarperCollins); *Mudhead Kiva: A Novel* (HarperCollins)

*The Writing That Got Me Started:* Raymond Chandler, Eric Ambler,

Graham Greene—they showed what one can do with the genre.

*The Writing That Taught Me About Writing:* I'd say John LeCarre—he made me aware of the importance of mood and pacing.

### Dick Lochte
*Blue Bayou* (Fawcett); *The Neon Smile* (Simon & Schuster)

*The Writing That Got Me Started:* There were two books that influenced me greatly. *The Saint in New York* by Leslie Charteris was the first grown-up novel I ever got my hands on. I found it in the library of a school run by the Jesuits. Evidently the librarian had had some other sort of saint in mind. In any case, instead of selecting a book that I was supposed to review for class, I became addicted to mystery novels. It was (and is) a terrific novel—fast, funny, and very hard-boiled for Charteris. At twelve years old I may have missed a few of its subtleties, but I couldn't put it down. One of its enlightenments was that books didn't have to take themselves so seriously. I still feel that Charteris's phrasing and vocabulary, not to mention his sense of humor, are second to none. The other book, found a few years later on the paperback shelf of a friend's older brother, was Raymond Chandler's *The Big Sleep*. While Charteris made me a mystery reader, it was Chandler's style, his mixture of crisp prose, sharp dialogue and cynical humor, that made me want to write detective stories.

*The Writing That Taught Me About Writing:* Again, the answer would have to be Chandler. His first person narration pulled me into Philip Marlowe's world, let me look at it through Marlowe's eyes. Before that I'd never even thought about point of view, never understood why some books (even classics) seemed off—the point of view kept changing within a scene. It's impossible to make that mistake with first-person narration.

### John Lutz
*SWF Seeks Same* (St. Martin)

*The Writing That Taught Me About Writing:* A science fiction suspense story titled *The Sound of Thunder*, written by Ray Bradbury. It was the piece of fiction that first brought home to me the notion that words could be used for much more than simply conveying information and had true and awesome power.

### Sara Paretsky
*Guardian Angel* (Dell)

*The Writing That Got Me Started:* I've been reading crime fiction since my teens, starting with Nero Wolfe and Dorothy Sayers, but it was Raymond Chandler who made me want to try to write a mystery of my own. I read his books around 1970 and began imagining a woman private eye who could overturn some of the stereotypes about women that pervade Chandler, and other noir novelists' work. It was another decade before I actually wrote such a book.

*The Writing That Taught Me About Writing:* Since I was trying to write a P.I. novel, I did what Chandler himself did: analyzed in detail works by people writing in that form and tried to establish a rise and fall in action modeled on what they did.

### Charlie Sweet and Hal Blythe
*Private Eyes* (Writer's Digest Books)

*The Writing That Got Us Started:* Jacques Futrelle's "Thinking Machine" stories, Ellery Queen's puzzle stories, and Mike Shayne paperback novels.

*The Writing That Taught Us About Writing:* Robert B. Parker taught us the use of one scene per chapter, and the use of realistic dialogue.

### Ed Gorman
*Wolf Moon* (Fawcett); *Prisoners & Other Stories* (CD Publications)

*The Writing That Got Me Started:* While I had the mandatory Hardy Boys-Sherlock Holmes period, the Gold Medal line of suspense novels in the late fifties was my biggest early influence. After I started reading people such as John D. MacDonald, Charles Williams, Malcolm Braly and Vin Packer, I recognized the kind of material I wanted to work with. This was approximately ninth grade. By eleventh grade, I had discovered Chandler, James M. Cain and Chester Himes. I was thoroughly bedazzled.

*The Writing That Taught Me About Writing:* Raymond Chandler taught me more about writing than anybody except perhaps Hemingway or Fitzgerald, in his *Gatsby* period. Notice I didn't say "mystery writing." The mystery element of any book is usually so contrived that it doesn't interest me much. No mystery plot makes any realistic sense, so I don't often judge mysteries that way. Plots are just an excuse to write people and incident. From any book I want a tight story, interesting characters, and at least some sense of what the author holds sacred and profane. Chandler always did this. Most of his mystery plots were nonsense. He properly saw them as the least important part of his books. He taught me to value character and language, to use place and climate as part of character, and to imbue my work with myself. He wasn't in a strict sense an autobiographical writer, but read any of his books or stories and you soon have a vivid and unforgettable sense of the man telling the tale. The rest of it is all mechanics. I believe that most competent writers can learn how to plot mysteries by taking the Agatha Christie novel *The Body in the Library* and outlining it chapter by chapter, character by character. This is how I learned. Of course, I've outlined many books by many other authors as well, but for contriving a mystery there's nobody better than Christie. She was almost pure story, so she's useful to study. (I also think she was much better with character than she's ever been given credit for.)

### Marilyn Wallace

*The Seduction* (Doubleday); *So Shall You Reap* (Bantam)

*The Writing That Got Me Started:* The rich, atmospheric novels of Thomas Hardy and the Brontë sisters gave me my first taste of the dark delights of suspenseful storytelling, and the portraits of strong women in the work of Susan Dunlap, Sue Grafton, Marcia Muller, Sara Paretsky and Julie Smith convinced me that mysteries really were a vital, contemporary form of fiction.

*The Writing That Taught Me About Writing:* The truth is that I learn something important from every book I finish (the ones I put down teach me what not to do). I'm not an analytical reader, but I nonetheless absorb lessons about characterization, plot, voice, atmosphere, suspense and sense of place from all the mysteries I read—especially by contemporary writers who seem to have an exciting, genre-stretching view of mystery and suspense fiction.

### Anne Wingate

*Scene of the Crime* (Writer's Digest Books); *Yazuka, Go Home!* (Walker); *The Day That Dusty Died* (St. Martin's)

*The Writing That Got Me Started:* Probably Leslie Charteris was the most important early influence. I sent him a very early, highly half-baked idea, and he was most gracious and encouraging in his reply. Elizabeth Linington (who wrote also as Lesley Eagan and Dell Shannon) later became a close friend and was very helpful. Other major influences were William Colt MacDonald (who wrote Texas Ranger westerns), Edgar Rice Burroughs (who, of course, wrote Tarzan) and Emily Dickinson who, of course, wrote poetry. But all of these include strong elements of mystery/suspense. And like just about everybody, I read all of Nancy Drew and the Hardy Boys, as well as Agatha Christie, before I ever got to high school.

*The Writing That Taught Me About Writing:* Elizabeth Linington – "You aren't sending a telegram." Barnaby Conrad – "Conflict on every page! Where's the conflict?" Careful study of Edgar Allan Poe, Elizabeth Linington, Arthur Conan Doyle and Agatha Christie also was helpful.

## Books of Interest to Mystery Writers
### Marketing and Publishing Books

*Children's Writer's and Illustrator's Market* (Writer's Digest Books, 1507 Dana Ave., Cincinnati OH 45207). This annual directory features fiction and nonfiction markets for all types of writing for children from pre-school to young adult. Includes book publishers, magazines, script buyers, audiotape and audiovisual markets. Also includes contests and awards open to those who write for children and young adults.

*Guide to Literary Agents and Art/Photo Reps* (Writer's Digest Books, 1507 Dana Ave., Cincinnati OH 45207). This is an annual guide to literary agents, script agents and art representatives. The book features a handy subject and agent name directory and several articles on how to find, approach and work with literary agents.

*Insider's Guide to Book Editors, Publishers, and Literary Agents*, by Jeff Herman (St. Martin's Press, 175 5th Ave., New York NY 10010). This is truly an insider's guide to the top commercial publishing houses and the agents who work with them, updated regularly by literary agent Jeff Herman. Contains editors' names and their specialties.

*Manuscript Submissions*, by Scott Edelstein (Writer's Digest Books, 1507 Dana Ave., Cincinnati OH 45207). This book, a part of Writer's Digest Books' Elements of Fiction Writing series, covers the ins and outs of fiction manuscript submission both to agents and editors. Each book in this helpful series focuses on a different aspect of fiction writing. Other titles in the series include *Plot, Characters & Viewpoint, Theme & Strategy, Dialogue, Scene & Structure* and *Beginnings, Middles & Ends*.

*Novel and Short Story Writer's Market* (Writer's Digest Books, 1507 Dana Ave., Cincinnati OH 45207). This annual directory has almost 2,000 markets exclusively for fiction. Of particular interest to mystery writers is the Commercial Fiction Report. Includes articles on fiction marketing, writing techniques, publishing, and interviews with editors, writers and publishers. Mystery authors and editors interviewed in past editions have included Charles Raisch, Barbara Mertz (aka Elizabeth Peters and Barbara Michaels), Ira Levin and Sue Grafton.

*The Writer's Digest Guide to Manuscript Formats*, by Dian Dincin Buchman and Seli Groves (Writer's Digest Books, 1507 Dana Ave., Cincinnati OH 45207). This guide provides the basics of manuscript preparation and marketing formats from queries and cover letters to finished manuscript presentation for both nonfiction and fiction. Includes easy-to-follow instructions and format samples.

*Writer's Market* (Writer's Digest Books, 1507 Dana Ave., Cincinnati OH 45207). This annual directory features a wealth of how-to information for all types of writers and includes 4,000 markets for written work. Includes consumer and trade magazines, book publishers, script publishers and producers, and contest and award opportunities. The book also regularly features interviews with editors, writers and publishers.

*Writing and Selling Mystery and Suspense* (Writer's Digest Books, 1507 Dana Ave., Cincinnati OH 45207). From the editors of *Writer's Digest* magazine, this is a compilation of articles about mystery writing and publishing from top mystery and suspense writers, including Hillary Waugh, Mary Higgins Clark, P.D. James, Martha Grimes, Sue Grafton and Robert B. Parker.

### Mystery Writing Technique and Reference Books

*Armed and Dangerous*, by Michael Newton (Writer's Digest Books, 1507 Dana Ave., Cincinnati OH 45207). One of the Writer's Digest Books Howdunit series, this reference book explains types and uses of firearms and other weapons in detail.

*Cause of Death*, by Keith D. Wilson, M.D. (Writer's Digest Books, 1507 Dana Ave., Cincinnati OH 45207). Written by an expert in forensic medicine, this is another handy reference from the Writer's Digest Books Howdunit series. In easy-to-understand detail, this book enables writers to accurately "kill off" their characters.

*Deadly Doses*, by Serita Deborah Stevens with Anne Klarner (Writer's Digest Books, 1507 Dana Ave., Cincinnati OH 45207). One of the first titles in the Writer's Digest Books Howdunit series, this book describes the types, uses and effects of poisons in accurate detail.

*How to Write and Sell True Crime*, by Gary Provost (Writer's Digest Books, 1507 Dana Ave., Cincinnati OH 45207). For those mystery writers interested in venturing into the related world of suspense nonfiction this book provides how-tos on writing and selling true crime stories.

*How to Write Mysteries*, by Shannon OCork (Writer's Digest Books, 1507 Dana Ave., Cincinnati OH 45207). This book by leading mystery author Shannon OCork, is part of the Writer's Digest Books Genre Writing series. It offers no-nonsense advice on mystery writing with tips on marketing the finished product.

*Scene of the Crime*, by Anne Wingate, Ph.D. (Writer's Digest Books, 1507 Dana Ave., Cincinnati OH 45207). Another title in the Writer's Digest Books Howdunit series, this time-saving reference guide gives the details on the process of crime investigation and police work.

*Writing Mysteries*, edited by Sue Grafton (Writer's Digest Books, 1507 Dana Ave., Cincinnati OH 45207). This is an official handbook of the Mystery Writers of America. A collection of articles by the country's top mystery authors, it features a comprehensive how-to approach to writing mystery and piecing together the perfect mystery.

*Writing the Modern Mystery*, by Barbara Norville (Writer's Digest Books, 1507 Dana Ave., Cincinnati OH 45207). This step-by-step mystery writing guide by mystery author Norville takes writers through all phases of writing modern crime and detective stories from researching to plotting, pacing and characterization.

## Books and Bibliographies About the Mystery Field

*Crime and Mystery: 100 Best Books*, edited by H.R.F. Keating (Carroll & Graf, 260 5th Ave., New York NY 10001). One hundred best crime and mystery books selected by British crime writer H.R.F. Keating, a former crime fiction reviewer for the *Times* (London) and past chairman of the Crime Writers Association.

*Crime Fiction 1749 to 1980*, by Allen J. Hubin (Garland Publishing, Inc., 717 5th Ave., 25th Floor, New York NY 10022). Hubin has put together one of the most comprehensive bibliographies of crime fiction.

*Fifty Best Mysteries*, edited by Eleanor Sullivan (Carroll & Graf, 260 5th Ave., New York NY 10001). The fifty best short mystery stories from *Ellery Queen's Mystery Magazine*, selected by an acclaimed mystery author and former editor of the magazine.

*Hatchards Crime Companion*, edited by Susan Moody (Hatchards, 187 Piccadilly, London W1V 9DA England). This handy volume contains a list and description of one hundred top crime novels selected by members of the Crime Writers Association. Also includes articles and suggested reading lists from well-known English mystery authors.

*Hillary Waugh's Mysteries and Mystery Writing*, by Hillary Waugh (Writer's Digest Books, 1507 Dana Ave., Cincinnati OH 45207). This leading mystery author offers an entertaining study of the mystery and mystery writing, including an analysis of well-known mysteries and mystery characters.

*The Literature of Crime and Detection*, by Waltraud Woeller and Bruce Cassiday, (The Ungar Publishing Company, 370 Lexington Ave., New York NY 10017). The book chronicles the evolution of the modern detective story from the Middle Ages to the twentieth century, citing stories and authors of many different countries and in many ages. "Includes all levels as well—from classical dramatists like Aeschylus and Euripides to modern novelists and Nobel prize winners like William Faulkner and on to best-selling writers like Agatha Christie." (taken from flap copy)

*Murder Ink*, by Dilys Winn (Workman Publishing, 708 Broadway, New York NY 10003). This book appears to be out of print and somewhat hard to find, but well worth the search. Most libraries still stock a copy. This unusual, but fun, compendium for both mystery writer and reader was put together by the former owner of Murder Ink, the first bookstore devoted exclusively to mysteries. Contains articles about all aspects of the genre from great books and detectives to the ins and outs of crime investigation.

*Women of Mystery*, edited by Cynthia Manson (Carroll & Graf, 260 5th Ave., New York NY 10001). This book is a collection of the best short stories by women mystery writers from the pages of *Alfred Hitchcock Mystery Magazine* and *Ellery Queen's Mystery Magazine*. Manson has edited other themed anthologies of mystery fiction including *Mystery Cats* and *Future Crime*.

## Real-Life Private Eyes

At precisely 9:00 P.M. Landreth lept from his wife's Ford station wagon in time to catch the ringing pay phone at the edge of the parking lot. Then, following his latest instructions, he walked toward the back of the supermarket. In his hand was a gym bag containing the $5,000 in small bills—just as the thieves had demanded. Landreth had been in the business for over twenty years and had worked as a go-between before. Once, despite being a small-town, one-man operation, he had handed over the cash that had returned an only child to an aging movie star.

Even with his experience, Landreth was edgy. His first principle wasn't "If things can go wrong, they will," but rather "Things go wrong." Studying the recordings of the thieves' demands had convinced him the perps were amateurs. And those were the most dangerous kind. Pros, even sociopaths, form patterns of behavior. Amateurs adlib—and bungle, bungle, bungle. When something goes wrong, pros know how to react. Amateurs panic and are dangerous even if they only attempt to run away—they're liable to run over you.

The summer evening was warm, but not hot enough to cause all the sweat that saturated Landreth's white shirt. Landreth always wore a coat and tie—he was a professional. Two amateur burglars had gotten lucky. On a simple suburban B&E (breaking and entering), they had boosted some silverware and electronics gear. For some reason they had spotted the framed napkins on the wall and had taken them. Only when the perps had tried to fence their merchandise had they developed a sense of what they'd really stolen.

The napkins were from a French cafe, and Pablo Picasso, as he often did in his lean years, had doodled on them and signed them in lieu of paying for his meal. Of course, no low-rent fence in eastern Kentucky was really prepared to handle such artwork. So the thieves had decided to increase their profit margin by selling the *objets d'art* back to the victim. . . .

Sounds like a typical paperback mystery and Landreth, a hard-boiled P.I. in the mold of Spenser or Spade. And you have a pretty good idea how this plot would conclude in fiction. A few sharp quips, perhaps some quick uppercuts, maybe even a shootout. But in the end Landreth would get the Picasso art back, save the client's money, and cap off the evening with a bourbon, a blonde or both.

John Landreth, however, is not an urban gumshoe, a paperback P.I., a son of Sam (Spade). He is a very real, fortyish, licensed investigator, who operates out of the small town of Richmond, Kentucky. And here's how the Case of the Purloined Picasso really played out.

As John reached the back of the store, a nervous voice from the roof told him to toss the bag up. Arguing that he needed at least to see the stolen merchandise first, John glanced upward. The cold metal barrels of a shotgun pointed in his direction.

John was silent, inspired by fear rather than any professional consideration.

"Look in the boxes," commanded the still-shaky voice.

John began to rummage through discarded produce. "Which one?"

"Keep looking."

The tension was as powerful as the smell of rotting garbage. Suddenly the rear door to the supermarket opened. A skinny stockboy in a soiled apron came out and immediately noticed the kneeling detective. "Hey, you," he shouted, "what are you doing? Get away from those boxes!"

"Get lost, son," John said without looking up and not caring whether the kid thought him a thief or a well-dressed hobo. John knew the stockboy's life was in danger—and so was his. The amateurs on the roof might panic at this unforeseen event, and a 12-gauge makes no distinction between innocent intrusion and an orchestrated set-up.

In John's mind the three-way stand-off seemed to endure an eternity. The stockboy threatening John, John threatening the kid, and the agitated amateurs on the roof screaming for the money.

"If you don't go back inside," John threatened, "I'll turn your pimply face into something your mother won't recognize."

The stockboy immediately fled into the store, promising to call the cops. John finally found the art objects behind some moldy oranges, then tossed the Nike bag toward the roof—and missed, a perp nearly falling off while trying to reach it. On John's next try, he succeeded. The perps scampered away with the money. They have yet to be caught or the money recovered.

More often than not, real-life private investigators differ greatly from their fictional counterparts. Detectives are not all men, don't all utilize high-tech surveillance equipment, drive foreign sports cars, wear loud Hawaiian shirts, pull down $1,000 a day (plus expenses), attend AA meetings, and draw retirement from police departments. In fact, there is no single profile, no average P.I. They don't dress alike, look alike, get paid alike. There is one similarity, though. They're all businesspersons who've learned the majority of their trade from experience, not a textbook in Detection 101.

Some work for multimillion-dollar corporations where they do nothing but counter-terrorism or bank-takeover investigations. Still, the majority tend to be one-person operations. How many are out there? What's their average yearly income? What types of cases predominate? Unfortunately, no national clearinghouse for card-carrying P.I.s exists, no definitive studies have been done, and no agency has established national standards. In fact, in some states no license is required; the detective wannabe merely declares, "I am a P.I."

And those exciting cases that are the staple of mystery fiction—serial killings, daring night-time museum burglaries, breakneck-speed car chases? In truth, most real detective work is tedium. Countless hours in the country courthouse vault researching hard-to-read records, interviewing people who can't or won't provide needed information, sitting in parked cars swilling cold coffee while worrying that if you go to the bathroom, you'll miss that key moment you've waited three consecutive days and nights for. Frankly, most of what P.I.s really do would make for boring fiction.

So what does a true-life private instigator like John Landreth do? Whatever it takes.

Last January he got a call from a local attorney whose client was involved in a child custody suite. Divorced for seven years, the client wanted custody of his twelve-year-old daughter because he had recently become convinced his ex-spouse was an unfit parent. During a visitation, his daughter had talked about being left alone after school and on weekends in a pig-sty environment. A court-appointed psychiatrist had interviewed all parties and was about to recommend the father as custodial parent. However, the attorney explained to John, since judges are not bound by psychiatrists' decisions, the father wanted proof that his daughter's home environment was bad. John's job was to get that evidence.

On television a Mike-Hammer type could kick in the front door and videotape the premises ("The apartment smelled like the inside of a dying skunk"). Of course, in real life such information, being illegally obtained, would be inadmissible in court. A Rockfordesque detective could run elaborate scams to get inside the apartment. Suppose one night an air rifle shoots out the windows and the next day Happy the Glassman miraculously appears at the door to fix the windows, taking before and after candids for his "advertising brochure."

In real life, people check on repairpersons, and apartment managers seldom have workers appear the next day. Of course, procuring a glass truck costs money—lots of it. And most clients, like the father wanting custody, aren't independently wealthy. Then there are the problems of legal liability, getting caught by the local police with an air rifle in your hands, damaging private property, etc. Melodrama doesn't usually take these real-life concerns into consideration.

John considered several practical methods of accessing the apartment in question. Since human nature loves the free lunch, John had always had good luck with his free cable ploy. He played the role of the installer and a toolbox (cheap, but effective) was his sole prop. So the day after the attorney called, John drove the hour up to Georgetown for recon. Unfortunately, the apartment already had the tell-tale black wire running into its outside wall. John thought about the Orkin scam (free bug spray; all it takes is a garden sprayer filled with water), but while he was reconnoitering, he noticed something important, something more important than it being January when people never hire pest controllers.

The client had told his lawyer that his ex was nearly paranoid about her privacy. Thus, she kept all her shades and drapes tightly drawn. One of John's most basic rules is that *clients never tell the truth* — sometimes deliberately, sometimes inadvertently. In fact, John believes the most difficult phase of any case is separating the truth from the fiction in what the client reveals. An inspection of the front of the apartment, the only place the client had looked at, revealed the drapes were indeed closed. However, when John walked around back, he spotted a curtain that was torn in one corner and open at the opposite end about a foot. A Christmas tree rested on the porch, though, obscuring his view in.

Direct observation convinced John that he did not need to enter the apartment to get the evidence he needed. Immediately he left his recon position. Had he stayed more than a minute, he knew from past experience that most well-populated areas have unemployed/elderly nosey neighbors. Call it the Gladys Kravitz Principle.

So, John asked himself, what could he do to give himself and one more witness about ten uninterrupted moments to collect evidence from the outside?

Two days later a car and truck with ladders pulled up in front of the apartment. Out climbed four men in painters' hats. One man rang the front bell and said something loudly to the effect of promising to make the repairs quickly (actually, no one was home as an earlier phone call had confirmed). Another man, a lookout, immediately began to raise a ladder against the front of the building. The other three went around back. One of these started readying 35mm disposable cameras. The other took the cameras and placed the lenses against the rear glass (behind the tree and where the curtain was torn at a slight angle to prevent reflected flash light), then snapped away.

Twelve minutes after driving up, the two vehicles pulled away. They drove back to Richmond, where John bought his helpers lunch at the local McDonald's. From portal to portal, the entire operation had taken less than three hours. Total cost? The three men all owed John for previous work done. The truck and ladders belonged to one of the men. The painters' hats cost $4.22; the throw-away cameras, $54.60; gas, about $10. Total expenses under $75.

Was the ploy worth it? There were no Perry Mason courtroom theatrics when the clever attorney suddenly threw the pictures of the apartment's inside in front of the testifying ex-wife. A good P.I. knows that most cases are settled out of court; judges and juries are just too unpredictable. John did give the pictures to the father's attorney, who then informed the opposition that he had them plus the eyewitness testimony of three men. Because of technological advances that allow the nearly perfect altering of pictures, photos by themselves are not as effective as pictures with substantiation by professional parties—read John Landreth, P.I.

Given the psychiatrist's evaluation and the obtained evidence, the spouse decided not to contest the custodial transference. John received an unexpected cash bonus for his effective and quick action.

John would have been even quicker, but P.I.s don't have the luxury of taking just one case at a time. In the day between his being contacted by the lawyer and his photo opportunity, he was called by a wealthy widower in Lexington whose wife had just died in a car wreck in Indiana. The problem? She was supposed to be in Knoxville at the time. Could John look into matters soon?

Well, he had this horse theft in Texas, a wife who was cheating on her doctor husband with college students, a car that needed repo-ing, but sure . . .

## Real-Life Homicide Investigations
*by Russell Bintliff*

Some mystery writers have kept up with the growth and changes in police procedures, but many remain overly influenced by what they see on television, in movies and in books. We have all enjoyed *Columbo*, but the famous TV homicide detective has a habit of "pocketing" crucial evidence that links the murderer to the homicide and using it later to get arrest warrants. In law enforcement and legal jargon, that's called "tainting." An improper police procedure that would set a known killer free in a court of law—if the case ever reached that level of due process.

A homicide investigation is the greatest challenge faced by the law enforcement community. Unlike most portrayals in movies, television and books, the average police detective rarely has the advantage of a swarm of laboratory experts assisting him or her at the scene of the crime. They must know what to look for to piece together what happened, how it happened and when it happened. As a mystery writer, you need to know what your detective knows to piece together a realistic, authoritative story. To help you achieve that goal, I'll briefly outline the investigative techniques and procedures used by police detectives in homicide cases involving firearms.

## Post Mortem Conditions

Post mortem conditions are extremely important to the police detective's investigation. The presence of any of the following conditions should be recorded and brought to the attention of the pathologist performing the autopsy.

## Post Mortem Temperature Loss

After the vital functions of the body have ceased, body temperature drops due to heat loss. The rate and the total amount of heat loss depends on varying conditions that may impede or speed up the heat loss. At an environmental temperature of 70° Fahrenheit, the average body will lose 1.5° per hour for the first 12 hours after death. Variables include age, size and weight of the body, the kind of clothing worn and the environment. It may be possible to arrive at an approximate time of death based on the rate of the body's heat loss and the temperature of the environment. A frequently used formula to measure heat loss is: Post Mortem Internal = 98.6° F − Rectal Temperature ÷ 1.5.

## Livor Mortis

Livor mortis, or post mortem lividity, is the reddish-purple discoloration that occurs after death as the blood settles toward the lowest portion of the body. Livor mortis is usually noted within one-half to two hours after death, and the color of the livor mortis may provide some indication of the cause of death. For example, a bright cherry-red color suggests carbon monoxide poisoning.

If the distribution of livor mortis is inconsistent with the body position, the body may have been moved after death. When livor mortis begins, slight pressure against the skin will prevent blood from entering the blood vessels in a compressed area and will lead to blanching, which defines the body's after-death posture. After four to six hours, the livor mortis remains fixed in position, and movement of the body will not lead to a change in distribution of livor mortis. If livor mortis indicates the victim lay on his left side for several hours, but the detective finds him laying on his right, the victim may have been transported to the scene, and evidence may be sparse.

## Contusions

A contusion, or bruise, is a localized hemorrhage within the body or skin, generally caused by blunt impact. Bruises also can be caused by tissue spreading beneath the skin's surface caused by fractures or from torn soft tissue, such as ligaments and muscles. These injuries may be caused by indirect trauma, such as twisting or falls. A recent bruise is actually dark red, reddish-purple or blue, and is uniform in color. After a day or so, a yellowish margin appears. Later the bruise changes from green to brown to brownish-black. A detective should photograph the bruises with a color scale. Although it is very difficult even for experts to estimate the age of a contusion, a detective should seek a qualified pathologist's opinion.

## Bleeding

The presence and location of blood in relation to the body are significant. When injuries are noted, particularly about the head, and there is no evidence of blood or bleeding, it is possible that the injuries were inflicted after death or that the victim was killed at some other location.

At death, when the heart stops beating, blood pressure drops to zero, but gravity may still cause blood to drain from a wound. A detective should take a blood sample to determine type, which may be valuable in the investigation. He or she should note the amount, color, coagulation, location and the surface on which the blood rests.

## Rigor Mortis

Rigor mortis, or post mortem rigidity, is the stiffening of the body after death caused by the contraction of muscles as chemical changes take place within the muscle tissue. Rigor mortis begins in all muscles simultaneously, but first becomes apparent in the small muscles of the face, neck, lower jaw, hands and feet. Rigor mortis is usually complete within six to eighteen hours and diminishes in the same sequence it begins (visible reduction in the smaller muscles first). It usually disappears after twenty-four to forty-eight hours from the time of death. The chronology depends on environmental conditions and on the onset of decomposition.

Rigor mortis can be broken. For example, a leg can be straightened out, but it will require considerable effort. Once fully formed rigor mortis breaks, it will not return.

### Cadaveric Spasm

Sometimes called "death grip," a cadaveric spasm is rarely seen within the field of forensic pathology.

### Cutis Anserina

During cutis anserina, contraction of the erector muscles may create a "goose flesh" appearance on the skin. This appearance, however, has no value in determining the time of death.

### Putrefaction

The gradual disintegration of the body that commences upon death is called putrefaction, or decomposition. Once begun, it continues until the soft tissue of the entire body is consumed. It is a chemical and bacterial process. Temperature plays an important role in the speed with which putrefaction takes place — warmth fosters bacterial growth and action; cold retards it.

One of the first signs of putrefaction is greenish staining in the lower abdomen. The process gradually spreads and the tissue takes on a brownish appearance. The condition known as marbling stems from the bacterial action of blood in the veins, causing them to become dark red or purple and to stand out vividly in contrast to the skin.

Bacterial action on internal organs causes the formation of gases, which bloat the body enormously. Facial features become indistinguishable. Occasionally, the skin becomes so dark it may be difficult to determine the race of a body. As noted, the process continues until the body is consumed, unless the conditions of adipocere or mummification develop.

### Adipocere

This is a post mortem condition in which hydrolysis of the fatty parts of body, particularly the cheeks, abdomen wall and buttocks, turns these areas into fatty acids and soaps. Adipocere is yellowish-white in color, has a greasy feel, and has a strong, penetrating, musty odor. The chemical process is induced by enzymes and water in moist anaerobic climates (conditions in which bacteria do not need oxygen to survive).

Although adipocere fat may hide wounds, close examination of the body will reveal the wounds, even when the process is in an advanced stage.

## Mummification

Mummification is a process in which the tissues of the body become dehydrated. The process requires a hot, dry climate, devoid of the moisture required to support bacteria. In mummification, the skin has a leathery appearance.

Infants killed immediately after birth are sterile, so bacteria must enter from outside the body. Because of this sterility and the body size of infants, mummification happens more rapidly to dead infants than to adults.

## Insects and Animals

Insects and animals may begin to consume a body shortly after the victim's death. Flies, maggots and beetles attack exposed areas of the body, concentrating on soft tissue. Cats and dogs locked up in a room with a human body will eventually eat it. When a body is buried in a shallow grave, animals often burrow into the ground and eat the remains. When a body is found in a wooded area, police frequently find body parts spread over a considerable area because of animal activity.

Detectives sometimes (though infrequently) will contact an entomologist to aid in estimating time of death by observing insect larvae. This method may be helpful in some circumstances.

## Death Involving Firearms

Gunshot wounds account for the majority successful homicides, and guns are also the most prevalent weapons ed for suicide. Death due to accidental discharge of a weapon is also mmon. Unlike some other forms of violent or unnatural death, firea fatalities frequently offer the detective important trace evidence of t weapon left in or on the victim's body. This trace evidence lends itse scientific comparison with suspect weapons, and frequently indicate many of the circumstances surrounding the death.

In the medical/legal investigation of fatal injury by firearm, scientific evidence is particularly important. The solution of the crime or differentiation between homicide, suicide or accident often hinges on the gathering and evaluating of scientific evidence. This evidence is collected and evaluated by the detective's investigation, coupled with investigations conducted by the pathologist and laboratory technicians.

Other investigative objectives may be deduced or confirmed by attentive evaluation of the scientific evidence: identification and characteristics of the weapon and ammunition; relative position of the weapon and victim; and the cause and manner of death. Evidence in firearm death may include wounds, empty cartridge cases, spent bullets, and powder residues on the clothing and body of the victim. The basic items of evidence or information revealed from the above sources include the make, model and characteristics of the weapon and ammunition; the direction, angle and range of fire; the number of shots; and possibly the time of the shooting.

## Firearm Investigative Terms

Detectives, investigators and pathologists should use consistent, mutually defined terminology in describing gunshot wounds. Some common terms are defined below.

- *Contusing:* Causing a bruise.
- *Glancing:* Striking the body without making any visible injury.
- *Penetrating:* Entering the body or organ with no exit wound.
- *Perforating:* A shot passing completely through the body with both an entrance and exit wound.
- *Superficial perforating:* A lacerating wound that is often mistaken for a cutting wound made with a knife or similar instrument.
- *Pseudo perforating:* A wound that occurs when the bullet stays in the body while an apparent exit wound is caused by a bone fragment that has become a secondary missile.
- *Secondary missiles:* Environmental or body components that become missiles themselves when struck by a bullet. Equipment, wood from bunkers or trees, stones and bone fragments may become secondary missiles.

## Gunshot Wounds

Typical entrance wounds are round, regular holes producing minimal bleeding. Often, the skin, being resistant, is stretched by the impacting bullet, producing a hole characteristically smaller than the bullet. A narrow ring around the bullet hole may have grayish soiling left by carbon and lubricants on the bullet. A reddish-brown abrasion collar is created by the bullet's impact.

Bullet entry wounds will sometimes remain concealed or inconspicuous. Such wounds are normally small caliber and are hidden under clothing, in hair, in body folds, in orifices or behind closed eyelids. They are normally distinguishable from exit wounds, but sometimes this distinction is difficult to ascertain and should always be confirmed by medical exam determinations.

The bullet and other products of the weapon's discharge produce several other characteristic marks and effects on the skin and clothing of the victim. These marks and effects indicate the distance from the point of discharge and are discussed below.

## Contact Wounds

These are inflicted with the gun muzzle held directly in contact with the victim's body or less than two inches away. Contact wounds, particularly those overlying bony surfaces, normally produce large, ragged wounds called *stellate wounds* because of the explosive force of gases produced by the discharge. Skin and tissue surrounding the bullet hole often appear torn, producing ragged, everted lacerations radiating from the hole. The abrasion collar is present, but the laceration must be pulled back together before it is identifiable.

The edges of the contact-type hole and the bullet track are burned, and the flame and smoke may create a sooty, grimy ring or halo around the wound. Particles of unburned powder and debris from the bullet and weapon muzzle blow into the bullet track below the skin's surface. When a weapon is discharged through clothing, the surrounding fabric will be burned and scorched.

In contact wounds in which the gun's muzzle remained tightly against the skin, the bullet hole will *not* be "tattooed" with powder grains embedded in the surrounding skin. (Tattooing occurs with close-range wounds.) Small caliber pistols—such as .22 and .25 caliber—may produce smaller, more regular contact wounds because the smaller gaseous force may not be sufficient to disrupt the surrounding tissues. Contact wounds in which exploding gases dissipate in a large body cavity, such as the chest, may not produce a large irregular wound. But in the skull, such gases have no opportunity to expand and may cause massive bursting fractures, especially when the wound was caused by a high-powered rifle. A patterned bruise often occurs at the wound, caused by expanding gases blowing the skin back and against the muzzle. These bruises may resemble the muzzle end, sights or retractor spring rod.

Determining how the bullet entered and exited the body (and from what direction it was fired) is sometimes difficult. With wounds in bodies that have been subject to decomposition, the macerating action of water currents or other mangling injury, this is especially true. It is also difficult if wounds were produced by ricochet bullets whose irregular surfaces and tumbling action may create ragged perforations resembling contact wounds.

In these difficult cases, examination marks and the effects on the victim's clothing may be, as mentioned earlier, the best indicators of the direction of the bullet's flight. The detective also can evaluate pieces of cloth, metal and bone fragments carried onward by the bullet after exiting the body.

A couple of other hints detectives use:

• Metal residue, detectable by spectrograph and X ray, is heavier at entrance wounds than at exit wounds when the wound is in a flesh area.

• The physical damage to the bone will often show the direction the bullet traveled.

### Close-Range Wounds

These wounds are inflicted with the muzzle held two to twenty-four inches from the victim. These wounds are normally circular, but the edges may show minor splitting. Close-range wounds are most readily distinguished from contact or longer-range wounds by the presence of burns and powder tattooing in the skin surrounding the bullet hole. Burning is a strong indication of close-range wounds. Powder residues and other discharge products are projected onto the victim in large amounts when the gun is fired within about two feet of the target.

The zone of burning and powder tattooing is roughly circular and becomes larger and more diffused or scattered as the distance between weapon and victim is increased. Powder tattooing has three zones: (1) The flame zone of burned skin around and in the bullet hole; (2) the zone surrounding the flame zone and containing the most powder tattooing in the form of powder grains and combustion products burned and embedded in the skin; and (3) the zone created by powder grains embedded in the dermis under the skin, consisting of sparsely scattered powder grains and residues. Washing will not remove powder grains in the dermis.

If the marginal rings of burning, tattooing and abrasion are concentric and circular, the bullet probably struck the body perpendicularly. Wounds produced by bullets striking at an angle show marginal bruising and surface abrasions created when the skin was struck by the first bullet.

Gunshot wounds inflicted from an extreme angle may produce shallow, furrowed wounds, sometimes called grazed wounds or tangential wounds. These wounds may also include an entrance wound or close-spaced entrance and exit wounds, depending on the conformation of body surfaces in the path of the bullet.

A weapon discharged at close range and at an angle creates powder marks that appear to spread away from the bullet hole in an irregular "V" shape, with the point of the "V" pointing to the weapon. If the bullet was fired through the victim's clothing, much of the burning and the deposit of residues appear on the clothing instead of the body.

Powder residues and other discharge products are projected onto the victim in large amounts when the gun is fired within about two feet of the target.

The size of the ammunition and type of powder also have a bearing on the nature and extent of powder residue deposits. Beyond a distance of about two feet, powder marks are normally not made on a victim shot with a handgun. Types of powder residues can also be differentiated by chemical, photographic, radiographic and spectrographic laboratory tests.

Recognition of powder marks and residues is an important factor in early differentiation of entrance and exit wounds. The pattern and composition are useful in deducing the range of fire and the type of ammunition used.

## Longer-Range Wounds

These wounds are inflicted with the gun muzzle more than twenty-four inches from the victim. Such a wound usually appears as a rounded hole with a circular abrasion collar and no burns or powder tattooing. The detective must remember, however, that small caliber contact wounds and other wounds over soft tissue areas may have the appearance of long-range wounds. Differences are distinguished by the presence of powder residues deep in the tissues in the bullet track.

## Exit Wounds

Exit wounds are often larger than the bullet or the entrance wound, and are ragged and irregular in shape. Exit wounds normally produce more obvious damage than entrance wounds because tissues compressed in front of the bullet burst when the bullet breaks through to exit. Also, exiting bone fragments may greatly increase tissue damage. Exit wounds often bleed more than entrance wounds because of their ragged nature. Pieces of internal tissues often protrude from the wound.

Because momentum is lost when the bullet passes through the body and through the toughness and elasticity of the skin, a bullet often will use its last remaining energy at the point of exit. With that energy spent, the bullet may protrude from the skin, lodge just below the skin surface, or be lost in a victim's clothing. The bullet is often fragmented, deformed and tumbled by impact.

## Clothing

The victim's clothing should be removed at the scene and examined in a lab, especially if a bullet passed through the garments. Clothing may contain a variety of leads about the person. To avoid cross-contamination clothing must be placed in separate plastic bags and identified, whenever possible. If the garments are damp, they may be dried by hanging in a dry room to preserve the evidence.

In cases where necessary or feasible, clothing may be cut from the body; however, the detective must not cut through any holes and must cut so the clothing will remain intact for comparison to the body injuries. While examining the clothes, the detective also should look for powder residue or burns on the victim's hands. These may (or may not) help to determine if the death was a suicide or whether a struggle for the gun preceded the shooting.

## Shotgun Wounds

When a shotgun is discharged from about ten feet or less, the charge strides in a compact mass, which may carry away a large circular part of the victim's body. The large central hole has extremely ragged edges torn by the many separate and overlapping perforations of the shotgun pellets. This type of shotgun wound is often called a "cookie cutter" wound. Smaller holes, created by separate shot beginning to scatter in flight, surround the large central hole.

Wounds made from a distance of zero to three feet are grossly burned and tattooed. Wounds made from a distance of three to nine feet show less tattooing and no burning. In wounds beyond ten feet, the shot scatters in flight and penetrates the body in a more scattered grouping.

The dispersion of the shot and the scattered pattern of the wound is influenced by the length of the shotgun barrel. A sawed-off barrel allows more rapid dispersion. Dispersion of shot lessens if the shotgun is choke-bored, which means the muzzle is narrowed slightly to concentrate the shot to delay dispersion.

The force and destruction of a shotgun blast at close range is very great. For head wounds, the structure of the head may be altered and large sections of the head or face may be blown away. Close-range wounds of the trunk and abdomen often permit loops of intestine or other organs to protrude from the hole.

## Birdshot, Buckshot and Shotgun Pellets

Even when fired at close range, birdshot will normally not pass through the trunk or abdomen of an adult person. Large, lacerated exit wounds occur when the load of shot passes through a thinner part of the body such as the neck, a limb or the shoulder. Small, ragged exit wounds occur when only a part of the birdshot load exits the body.

At close range, buckshot, which is larger than birdshot, has greater weight and energy, and produces wounds comparable to large bullets.

Shotgun pellets are larger than birdshot or buckshot, but just like them it cannot be linked to a particular weapon by ballistics markings (as can rifled projectiles). However, the size of shot often shows on printed material on the top wad, by impressions left in the wadding, or by printed information in the shot column. The gauge of the weapon is often determined by comparing the diameter of the wad with other wads. If the gun is discharged within ten feet of the victim, the wadding often carries into the body with the load of shot. If the wadding doesn't strike an intervening surface, it's often found within 50 feet of the place where the weapon was discharged.

Many manufacturers of shotgun shells use mercury fulminate in the powder load. This chemical leaves a residue of mercury vapor inside the gun's barrel, but disappears after a few days. The residue can be detected by a laboratory test. When preparing a weapon for a mercury detection test, the breech and muzzle should be corked or sealed to prevent further dissipation of the residue before the laboratory test.

## Other Aspects of Gunshot Wounds

High-velocity projectiles (muzzle speed greater than 2,500 feet per second) such as bullets from higher energy rifle ammunition, may create tissue damage out of proportion to the size of the bullet, destroying tissue several inches from the bullet track. This phenomenon, called *transient cavitation*, stems from the bullet's energy and the shock waves of its impact, which dissipate in a radial fashion away from the bullet. This creates a track of permanently disrupted tissue far wider than the projectile.

Identification of entrance wounds does not invariably determine the number of shots fired into a body. One of the detective's objectives in cooperating with a pathologist is to trace the path of the bullet. This scientific method correlates multiple wounds from the same bullet. A single bullet *can* penetrate the body more than once, producing multiple entrance wounds. For example, a bullet may pass through a limb before entering the trunk. Or a bullet striking a bony surface at an angle may split into two or more projectiles, creating multiple exit and re-entry holes. Instances have happened where more than one bullet entered through the *same* entrance wound. In one unusual suicide case, a defective round did not exit the barrel, and a second round propelled the first in tandem through a single entrance hole.

The location and number of empty shell cases at the scene may provide information about the number of shots fired and the relative positions of the weapon and victim. Lining up such things as the final resting point of the bullet, position of the victim, and entry and exit holes on the victim can often help a detective deduce the position from which the weapon was fired.

All suspect weapons, cartridge shell casings, and expended bullets recovered at the scene or during autopsy must undergo various investigative laboratory tests. These tests establish connections between the physical evidence and the shooting. All susceptible surfaces of weapons, shells, magazines, etc., need examination for latent fingerprints. Powder residues on weapons, shells, the victim and suspects undergo comparative tests, chemically and microscopically. Bloodstains, hairs, fibers and similar trace evidences are identified and compared.

Sometimes, the weapon was rested on or fired in close proximity to some surface, and powder residues are deposited there, indicating the position from which the weapon was discharged.

Markings are made on the bullet by the weapon's bore, and various other identifiable marks may be placed on the cartridge case by the firing pin, breach block, chamber extractor and ejector. But these aren't the only marks that may help identify a bullet. A lead bullet impacting with cloth may receive a patterned impression of the fabric weave, sometimes confirming that a particular bullet did pass through the victim.

### Suicide, Homicide or Accident?

As in all medical/legal death investigations, for the detective investigating a shooting, the basic objective is to determine if the wounds to a victim's body indicate homicide, suicide or accident. First, the detective should consider, in cooperation with a pathologist, whether the victim could—considering the location and character of entrance wounds and bullet tracks—conceivably have inflicted the wounds on him or herself.

Unless the victim used a special contrivance, self-inflicted gunshot wounds require the gun be held within twenty-four inches of the body. Suicide wounds are characteristically single close-range or contact wounds involving a part of the body easily reached by the victim. Often, the suicide uncovers part of the body, such as drawing a shirt aside before placing the muzzle of a gun against the chest. The temple, mouth, and the chest over the heart are the most commonly selected sites for suicidal attacks with a firearm. Most firearm suicides result from a gun placed to the head slightly in front of and above the ear.

Occasionally, a suicide will shoot him or herself more than once before being incapacitated or killed. When using a rifle or shotgun for suicide, the person chooses the chest and abdomen as their target. Rifles and shotguns are normally discharged by pushing the trigger with a toe or by using a contrivance, such as a stick, or a string hooked around the trigger guard.

Below are a few more facts the detective must keep in mind when determining if a death was a suicide, homicide or accident.

## Suicides

- Evidence may indicate the person acquired the weapon for no other apparent reason than suicide.
- Even if a weapon isn't found beside the body, the death may still be a suicide. One way of making a weapon disappear after suicide is to rig a strong elastic band to pull the weapon into a concealed place.
- The presence of contrivances designed to pull the trigger, such as strings, or the removal of a shoe, are strong indications of suicide.
- Initially, evidence at the scene may not suggest suicide. Family or friends with an interest in life insurance claims or a fear of disgrace may tamper with evidence to conceal the suicidal intent and circumstances.

## Homicides

- A murderer may try to conceal homicide by manufacturing circumstances suggestive of suicide or accident. The absence of a weapon suggests that the shooting was homicidal. However, a suicide victim may live long enough to dispose of the weapon or may arrange contrivances to cause the weapon to disappear after being discharged.
- A weapon in excellent operating condition, needing normal force to pull the trigger and having effective safety devices, may cause an

investigator to disfavor the notion of accidental shooting in favor of homicide.

## Accidents

- Circumstances, such as the victim's being on a hunting trip or cleaning, loading or otherwise working on the weapon, may show a logical reason for the weapon's presence and the potential for an accident.
- Evidence the victim was handling the weapon unsafely, demonstrating how another person committed suicide, or playing "quickdraw," may indicate the accidental nature of the shooting.
- Evidence that a weapon is defective—that it had no safety or had a defective safety device, or that it could be discharged by dropping it— suggests accidental circumstances.
- Evidence may show the trigger caught in something, discharging the gun accidentally. These accidents happen less often than homicides and suicides and are often witnessed. Sometimes these accidents are reported by the person who discharged the weapon.
- Accidental gunshot victims usually are shot because of careless handling of a weapon or because of ignorance about the operation of the weapon. Sometimes accidental deaths occur when persons are "quickdrawing" with supposedly empty weapons or pointing weapons at others as a prank. Accidents may also happen while the victim is hunting, or cleaning, loading or unloading a weapon.
- In some instances, particularly with old or defective weapons, the gun may discharge accidentally when dropped on the floor. Children and young people often become involved in gunshot accidents while playing with firearms.
- An accidental gunshot fatality, when not witnessed, may closely resemble a suicide. However, the known attitude and lifestyle of the victim, plus the lack of apparent motive for suicide, present strong indications of the accidental nature of the incident.

### A Few More Bubbles Worth Bursting

Unlike fictional police detectives, real detectives rarely have the luxury of working one homicide case for as long as it takes to solve it. Even in rural areas where homicides rarely occur, other types of crimes do occur. The investigator has to merge the homicide case with these crimes and with the spectrum of other daily police duties and responsibilities.

However, unlike the fictional harried cop who works endlessly and relentlessly to bring a culprit to justice, rarely will a police officer or detective work more than a normal eight-hour shift five days a week. Few departments can afford to pay extensive overtime, and most officers six months out of the academy recognize that they alone cannot solve every case or thwart the commission of every crime. Police detectives work hard for their pay but leave work behind after their shifts. They rely on the detectives on the next shift to further the investigation. Despite the too-common fictional "lone wolf maverick" who breaks all the rules and works twenty-four hours a day, successful law enforcement always relies on proper procedures and team effort.

— To learn more about how real police detectives work, see my new book, *Police Procedural: A Writer's Guide to the Police and How They Work*, part of the Howdunit series from Writer's Digest Books. It will help you get the facts right, making your mystery or action film, TV show or book even better.

## Glossary of Mystery Terms

In the following glossary we've included general publishing terms as well as specific mystery terms. The mystery terms are set in boldface type.

Advance—Payment by a publisher to an author prior to the publication of a book, to be deducted from the author's future royalties.

All rights—The rights contracted to a publisher permitting a manuscript's use anywhere and in any form, including movie and book-club sales, without additional payment to the writer.

**Amateur sleuth**—The character in a mystery (usually the protagonist) who does the detection but who is not a professional private investigator or police detective. The amateur sleuth has another career or is independently wealthy and becomes involved in the murder by circumstance, chance or interest.

Auction—Publishers sometimes bid against each other for the acquisition of a manuscript that has excellent sales prospects.

**Bickering team or cohort mystery**—Usually a mystery series in which there are two detectives working together. This may be a married couple or friends, or the two may start out with nothing in common. Although the detection of the crime is still the primary focus, the relationship between the pair is developed throughout the series.

Book producer/packager—An organization that develops a book for a publisher based upon the publisher's idea, or that plans all elements of a book—from its initial concept to writing and marketing strategies—and then sells the package to a book publisher and/or movie producer.

**Caper**—A crime story, usually told from the viewpoint of the perpetrator. The tone is often lighthearted or even comical, and the crime is a theft rather than a murder. Favorite caper targets: art or jewelry.

Cliffhanger—Fictional event in which the reader is left in suspense at the end of a chapter or episode, so that interest in the story's outcome will be sustained.

Contributor's copy—Copy of a magazine or published book sent to an author whose work is included.

Copyright — The legal right to exclusive publication, sale or distribution of a literary work.

Cover letter — A brief letter sent with a complete manuscript submitted to an editor.

**Cozy or English cozy** — A murder mystery set in a small English or New England town and featuring an amateur sleuth who is often a genteel old lady or gentleman. The setting is refined and the violence subdued.

First North American serial rights — The right to publish material in a periodical before it appears in book form, for the first time, in the United States or Canada.

Galleys — The first typeset version of a book that has not yet been divided into pages.

**Gothic mystery** — A mystery with a decidedly dark, brooding tone, often set at an old estate. A gothic contains elements of romantic suspense and sometimes even supernatural overtones.

**Hard-boiled detective** — A detective character type popularized in the 1940s and 1950s, now a mainstay in mystery fiction. The hard-boiled detective is usually male, streetwise and hardened by life.

**Heist** — A mystery involving a theft, which is more serious than the caper. The focus is on solving the crime, but emphasis is placed on the planning and execution of the theft as well.

Imprint — Name applied to a publisher's specific line (e.g. Owl, an imprint of Henry Holt).

**Locked room puzzle** — A classic mystery format in which a murder takes place within a room locked from the inside, with no visible way the murderer could have entered or exited.

**Maguffin** — A sort of red herring, or a story element that distracts the reader from the real solution.

**Malice domestic** — A mystery featuring a murder among family members, such as the murder of a spouse or parent.

**Mass market paperback** — Softcover book on a popular subject, usually measuring around $4 \times 7$ inches, directed to a general audience, and sold in drugstores and groceries as well as in bookstores.

Ms(s) — Abbreviation for manuscript(s).

**Novella** (also **novelette**) — A short novel or long story, approximately 7,000-15,000 words.

**One-time rights** — Permission to publish a story in periodical or book form one time only.

**Outline** — A summary of a book's contents, often in the form of chapter headings with a few sentences under each one describing the action of the story; sometimes part of a book proposal.

**Over the transom** — Slang for the path of an unsolicited manuscript into the slush pile.

**Page rate** — A fixed rate paid to an author per published page of fiction.

**P.I.** — Private investigator, also known as a private eye, a gumshoe, and other slang terms.

**Playing fair with the reader** — Planting clues in such a way that the reader encounters everything needed to solve the crime, though the reader can (and should) be distracted from those clues.

**Police procedural** — A mystery featuring a police detective or officer who uses standard professional police practices to solve the crime.

**Private eye** — A professional independent investigator. Many mystery series feature private eyes.

**Proofs** — A typeset version of a manuscript used for correcting errors and making changes, often a photocopy of the galleys.

**Proposal** — An offer to write a specific work, usually consisting of an outline of the work and one or two completed chapters.

Query—A letter written to an editor to elicit interest in a story the writer wants to submit.

**Red herring**—False clues written into a mystery story with the intention of throwing the reader off track. The term comes from the practice of dragging a smoked red herring through the woods to disrupt a fox hunt by throwing the hounds off the fox scent.

Reporting time—The number of weeks or months it takes an editor to report to an author about a query or manuscript.

Reprint rights—Permission to print an already published work after one-time rights have been sold to another magazine or book publisher.

**Romantic suspense**—A mystery or suspense story with strong elements of romance, usually between the detective and the victim or the detective and the suspect.

Royalties—A percentage of the retail price paid to an author for each copy of the book that is sold.

SASE—Self-addressed stamped envelope.

Second serial rights—Permission for the reprinting of a work in another periodical after its first publication in book or magazine form.

Serial rights—The rights given by an author to a publisher to print a piece in one or more periodicals.

Serialized novel—A book-length work of fiction published in sequential issues of a periodical.

Series—Novels that feature a common detective—Agatha Christie's many novels starring Miss Marple, for instance. The novel series is more common in mystery fiction than in any other kind of fiction, with the possible exception of the Western.

**Shamus**—Sleuth or private eye.

Simultaneous submission — The practice of sending copies of the same manuscript to several editors or publishers at the same time. Some people refuse to consider such submissions.

Slush pile — A stack of unsolicited manuscripts in the editorial offices of a publisher.

Subsidiary — An incorporated branch of a company or conglomerate (e.g. Alfred Knopf, Inc., a subsidiary of Random House, Inc.).

Subsidiary rights — All rights, other than book publishing rights included in a book contract, such as paperback, book-club and movie rights.

**Suspense story** — Although in recent years mystery and suspense have been used interchangeably, a suspense story is one in which the main action (crime or murder) has not yet taken place and the culprit may be known or at least suspected. The emphasis is on the tension built by the anticipation of the outcome, such as stopping a murderer from striking again. A mystery, on the other hand, starts with a murder and emphasizes the solving of the crime.

Synopsis — A brief summary of a story, novel or play. As part of a book proposal, it is a comprehensive summary condensed in a page or page and a half.

Tearsheet — Page from a magazine containing a published story or article.

Trade paperback — A softbound volume, usually measuring 5 × 8 inches, published and designed for the general public, available mainly in bookstores.

**True crime** — Nonfiction about actual murders and serial killings, often told with "new journalism" fiction techniques made famous by Truman Capote's *In Cold Blood*.

Unsolicited manuscript — A story or novel manuscript that an editor did not specifically ask to see.

**Watson** — A detective's assistant or friend who narrates the story, named after Dr. Watson of the Sherlock Holmes novels.

**Whodunit** — Another name for the classic mystery in which the focus is on finding out the identity of the murderer.

**Work-for-hire** — Work that another party commissions you to do, generally for a flat fee. The creator does not own the copyright and therefore cannot sell any rights.

**Young adult** — The general classification of books written for readers ages 12 to 18.

# *About the Authors*

Stephanie Kay Bendel teaches and runs fiction writing workshops in Boulder, Colorado. She is the Author of *Making Crime Pay* and *A Scream Away*. Her short stories appear regularly in *Alfred Hitchcock's Mystery Magazine*. She is presently at work on a mainstream novel.

Russell Bintliff has been an investigations professional for more than twenty years, working with the Arkansas State Police, the Criminal Investigation Division of the army, and the CIA. He is the author of books for the profession: *Training Manual for Law Enforcement Officers*, *How to Write Effective Law Enforcement Reports*, *The Complete Manual for Corporate and Industrial Security*, and *The White Collar Crime Prevention Handbook*. His novel, *The Corsican*, published by Simon & Schuster, was based on parts of his life. Bintliff was technical advisor for the Sylvestor Stallone film *Nighthawks*.

Hal Blythe is a full professor at Eastern Kentucky University, where he specializes in creative writing. In addition to several hundred critical and pedagogical articles, he has coauthored numerous short stories with Charlie Sweet and is currently working on a novel and another book for Writer's Digest.

John Lutz is the author of twenty-five novels, including *SWF Seeks Same*, which was adapted for the film *Single White Female*. He has published over 175 short stories and articles and his work has appeared in foreign publications, textbooks, and foreign and domestic anthologies, as well as being adapted for radio and television. He has received many awards, including MWA Scroll, 1981; MWA Edgar Award, 1986; PWA Shamus nominations, 1983, 1984, 1987; PWA Shamus Awards, 1982, 1988; and Throphee 813 Award for best mystery short story collection translated to French language, 1989. His upcoming books include: *Spark*, a novel published in January 1993 by Henry Holt; *Thicker Than Blood*, a novel to be published in late 1993 by St. Martin's Press; and *Hot*, a paperback edition of a Henry Holt novel to be published in late 1993 by Avon. He is a reviewer for the *St. Louis Globe-Democrat* and other publications.

Gary Provost is the author of sixteen fiction and nonfiction books, including *Fatal Dosage: The True Story of a Nurse on Trial for Murder*, *Without Mercy: A True Story of Obsession and Murder Under the Influ-*

*ence*, and *Make Your Words Work*. He has written thousands of stories, articles and columns for national, regional and local publications; humorous columns for more than one hundred newspapers; and celebrity profiles for a dozen magazines. He is a popular speaker around the country and also conducts several writing seminars and workshops a year.

Michael Seidman, a *Writer's Digest* correspondent, is the mystery editor of Walker & Company. His most recent books are *Living the Dream: An Outline for a Life in Fiction* and *From Printout to Published: A Guide to the Publishing Process* (Carroll & Graf).

Charlie Sweet is a full professor at Eastern Kentucky University. His specialty is American literature. He has coauthored many articles and stories with Hal Blythe. Once a ghost writer for Brett Halliday's Mike Shayne series, he is currently collaborating on a novel, another Writer's Digest book, mystery weekends and several articles with Hal Blythe.

## Contributors

Anne Bowling, freelance writer and editor
Donna Collingwood, staff editor
Robin Gee, staff editor
Dorothy Maxwell Goepel, freelance writer
Jack Heffron, staff editor
Kathleen M. Heins, freelance writer
Carol Lloyd, freelance writer
Lauri Miller, freelance writer and editor
Michelle Moore, freelance writer and poet
Sheri Toomey, freelance writer

# GENERAL INDEX

# CATEGORY INDEX

## Dark Mystery

## Espionage

## Hard-Boiled Detective

## Light Horror

## Malice Domestic

## Romantic Suspense

## Surrealistic Mystery

## Suspense

## Thrillers